CARN

The New Historicism: Studies in Cultural Poetics
Stephen Greenblatt, General Editor

Number 25
Daniel Boyarin
Carnal Israel:
Reading Sex in Talmudic Culture

Of related interest in the series:

Nancy Armstrong and Leonard Tennenhouse
The Imaginary Puritan:
Literature, Intellectual Labor, and the Origins of Personal Life

Caroline Walker Bynum
Holy Feast and Holy Fast:
The Religious Significance of Food to Medieval Women

Stephen Greenblatt
Shakespearean Negotiations:
The Circulation of Social Energy in Renaissance England

François Hartog
The Mirror of Herodotus:
The Representation of the Other in the Writing of History
translated by Janet Lloyd

Debora Kuller Shuger
Habits of Thought in the English Renaissance:
Religion, Politics, and the Dominant Culture

Gabrielle M. Spiegel
Romancing the Past:
The Rise of Vernacular Prose Historiography in Thirteenth-Century France

CARNAL ISRAEL

READING SEX IN
TALMUDIC CULTURE

DANIEL BOYARIN

UNIVERSITY OF CALIFORNIA PRESS

Berkeley · Los Angeles · London

University of California Press
Berkeley and Los Angeles, California

University of California Press, Ltd.
London, England

© 1993 by
The Regents of the University of California

First Paperback Printing 1995

Library of Congress Cataloging-in-Publication Data

Boyarin, Daniel.
    Carnal Israel : reading sex in Talmudic culture / Daniel
Boyarin.
       p.   cm. — (The New historicism, 25)
    Includes bibliographical references and index.
    ISBN 978-0-520-20336-5
    1. Sex in rabbinical literature.   2. Body, Human, in rabbinical
literature.   3. Women in rabbinical literature.   4. Rabbinical literature—History and criticism.   5. Sex—Religious aspects—
Judaism.   6. Body, Human—Religious aspects—Judiasm.
7. Women in Judaism.   8. Judaism—History—Talmudic period,
10–425.   I. Title.
BM496.9.S48B69   1993
296.1'2—dc20   92-9507
                                                 CIP

Printed in the United States of America

11   10 09 08
12 11 10 9 8 7 6

The paper used in this publication meets the minimum
requirements of ANSI/NISO Z39.48-1992 (R 1997)
(*Permanence of Paper*). ∞

Dedicated to Chava,
with honor and gratitude
for twenty-five years of intimate friendship

The second implication which R. Hanina bar Papa found [in the verse, *Many . . . are Thy wonderful works . . . and Thy thoughts which are towards us* (Ps. 40:5)], was this: Many are all the wonderful works and thoughts which Thou, O God, dost employ to have a man feel desire for his wife. Of this feeling it is written *Adam knew his wife yet more* (Gen. 4:25). What is implied by Scripture's saying *yet more*? That his desire had been increased by so much more desire than formerly: formerly he had not felt desire when he did not see his wife, but now he felt desire for her whether he saw her or did not see her.

It is such strong desire which compels traveling merchants and seafarers—so said R. Abba bar Yudan in the name of R. Aḥa—to be reminded of their wives and return to them.

William G. Braude and Israel J. Kapstein, trans.,
Pĕsiḳta dĕ-Rab Kahăna: R. Kahana's Compilation of
Discourses for Sabbaths and Festal Days

Contents

Acknowledgments

This book began with a conversation between Chana Safrai and me about Beruria and the study of Torah for women in the talmudic period. The conversation grew into a paper (now Chapter 6 of this book) and then into a book. My goals for this work, which are set out more fully in the Introduction, have several aspects. I wish to continue my overall intellectual/cultural project of inserting rabbinic textuality into critical discourse and critical discourse into the scholarship of rabbinic literature. I also wish to correct prevailing misconceptions of the ideology of sex-uality, gender, and the body in rabbinic culture, which seriously distort our ability to make sense of this culture and to make use of it for the third project of this book, which is feminist restructuring of sex and gender in very late antiquity—that is, in our own time.

Earlier versions of several of the chapters have been published in the following journals or edited volumes: *Critical Inquiry*, *The Journal of the History of Sexuality*, *People of the Body* (edited by Howard Eilberg-Schwartz), *Poetics Today*, *Representations*, and the *Yale Journal of Criticism*. I thank the editors of all of those publications for permission to revise and reprint texts that they first published.

Grants from the following organizations helped in the research leading to this book: the Littauer Foundation, the faculty of Letters and Sciences at the University of California at Berkeley, and especially the National Endowment for the Humanities, which provided for a crucial period of leave during the final stages of writing the book. The Shalom Hartman Institute for Advanced Jewish Studies has provided a safe environment for receiving sharp critical input at several stages of this research, as well as important material aid.

I wish to acknowledge here the gift of new friends (especially, but not only, David Biale and Howard Eilberg-Schwartz, who work on the same problems and the same texts, without competition among us) and the wonderful intellectual life of my new home in Berkeley. I thank the

University and its donors for having the wisdom to found the Taubman Chair of Talmudic Culture. To Stephen Greenblatt who has encouraged my cultural studies from their very embryonic beginnings, I owe a special debt of gratitude, particularly now that he has taken this book into his series, "The New Historicism: Studies in Cultural Poetics," and to the editors of the Press: Stanley Holwitz, who charmed me, and Doris Kretschmer, who made it happen.

I firmly believe that scholarly production, like artistic work, is not the creation of an author but the production of a culture. I want to make explicit in this case my sense of dependence on a contemporary cultural discourse on the body that made this work possible, and particularly on the work of Peter Brown, which appeared six months after I began this project and had an enormous effect on it. The following friends and colleagues have read all or part of the manuscript. Their help has been enormous and in another discipline some of them would be signed on as coauthors: Robert Alter, Mieke Bal, Albert Baumgarten, David Biale, James Boon, Alice Boyarin, Jonathan Boyarin, Sidney Boyarin, Jeremy Cohen, Arnold Davidson, Carolyn Dinshaw, Howard Eilberg-Schwartz, Arnold Davidson, Arnold Eisen, Steven Fraade, John Gager, Alon Goshen-Gottstein, Stephen Greenblatt, Erich Gruen, David Halperin (MIT), Sarah Hammer, Verna Harrison, Galit Hasan-Rokem, Judith Hauptmann, Christine Hayes, Marc Hirshman, Elliot Horowitz, Moshe Idel, Karen King, Ross Kraemer, Chana Kronfeld, Joshua Levinson, John Miles, Haim Milikovsky, Shlomo Naeh, Ilana Pardes, David Resnick, Amy Richlin, Chana Safrai, Dov Samet, Elissa Sampson, David Satran, Ellen Spolsky, Dina Stein, Ruth Stein, David Stern, Brian Stock, Guy Stroumsa, Deborah Weissman, Shira Wolosky, Eli Yassif, and especially Regina Schwartz and Froma Zeitlin, who read and commented on most of the book in several versions. I also thank the editors of *Critical Inquiry*, the editorial board of *Representations*, an anonymous reader for the *Yale Journal of Criticism*, several anonymous readers for the University of California Press, and the Cultural Critique Collective of Jerusalem.

My son, Jesse Boyarin, and his friend Shoham Carmi "discovered" the painting that is reproduced on the dust jacket.

Finally, I thank my students at the University of California at Berkeley for intellectual stimulation and fellowship, "from them more than from anyone."

A Note on the Term *Rabbis*

In this book the word *Rabbis* will be capitalized when it refers to the particular group of Jewish religious leaders known technically as "the Rabbis." When it refers to Jewish religious functionaries in general, it will be put in lowercase. "The Rabbis" flourished from the second until approximately the end of the sixth centuries in Palestine and Babylonia. Growing out of a particular sect of first-century Judaism, their cultural hegemony over the masses of Jews steadily grew during this period, in which the major literary productions of rabbinic Judaism—the midrashim and Talmuds—were produced. Their closest historical cognates are, therefore, the Fathers of the Church.

All Hebrew and Aramaic texts cited in this book have been translated by me unless otherwise noted.

Introduction

CARNAL ISRAEL

In his *Tractatus adversus Judaeos*, Augustine lays the following charge against "the Jews":

> *Behold Israel according to the flesh* (i Cor. 10:18). This we know to be the carnal Israel; but the Jews do not grasp this meaning and as a result they prove themselves indisputably carnal.
>
> (vii, 9)

Augustine knew what he was talking about. There was a difference between Jews and Christians that had to do with the body. He begins by quoting a hermeneutic remark made by Paul in the Epistle to the Corinthians in reference to a verse of the Hebrew Bible that speaks of "Israel." Paul claims by this statement that the verse refers to Israel "according to the flesh," that is, "Israel" understood literally. Paul here is alluding to his platonizing doctrine that external realities—things in the flesh—all have spiritual signifieds. This is as true of the words of the text as it is of the things of the world. Just as there is an Israel in the flesh, there is also an "Israel according to the spirit," the Gentile (and Jewish) believers in Christ. Augustine here argues with fine paradox that Israel according to the flesh—i.e., the Jews—*by its very insistence that it is the true Israel* demonstrates that it does not understand that there is both a carnal and a spiritual sense to scripture, and by this demonstration, this people condemns itself to remain forever and indisputably carnal and not spiritual.[1] The carnality of Israel's understanding is what consigns it forever to the realm of the flesh. That is to say, the hermeneutic practices of the rabbinic Jews,[2] their corporeal existence as a people and their emphasis

---

1. For a brilliant interpretation of Augustine's hermeneutic of Judaism and Christianity, see Robbins (1991, 21–70). My reading of Robbins also supplied the title for this book.

2. Rabbinic Judaism is, by Augustine's time, virtually the only kind of Judaism extant, although, as Brian Stock reminds me, it is quite unlikely that Augustine refers

on sex and reproduction, are all stigmatized as "carnal" by the Father. This accusation against the Jews, that they are indisputably carnal, was a topos of much Christian writing in late antiquity.

I propose in this book to account for this practice of Augustine and the others who characterize the Jews as carnal, indeed to assert the essential descriptive accuracy of the recurring Patristic notion that what divides Christians from rabbinic Jews is the discourse of the body, and especially of sexuality, in the two cultural formations. I will also explore the consequences of that difference for the construction of gender and other aspects of social life in the Judaism of the Rabbis who produced the talmudic literature and their followers.[3]

Although in many modern accounts the difference between "Jewish" and "Christian" discourses of sexuality has been homogenized into a putative Judaeo-Christian tradition, Peter Brown, one of the leading modern interpreters of the Church Fathers, regards the fundamental difference between Christianity and "Judaism" as having to do with the body and sex in the two cultures:

> The division between Christianity and Judaism was sharpest in this. As the rabbis chose to present it, sexuality was an enduring adjunct of the personality. Though potentially unruly, it was amenable to restraint— much as women were both honored as necessary for the existence of Israel, and at the same time were kept from intruding on the serious business of male wisdom. It is a model based on the control and segregation of an irritating but necessary aspect of existence. Among the Christians the exact opposite occurred. Sexuality became a highly charged symbolic marker precisely because its disappearance in the committed individual was considered possible, and because this disappearance was thought to register, more significantly than any other human transformation, the qualities necessary for leadership in the

---

to living Jews at all. It is important to emphasize that the term *rabbinic Judaism* refers not to the Judaism practiced by Rabbis but to the Judaism practiced by Rabbis and by those who considered the Rabbis their spiritual authority.

3. I am well aware that this very formulation already raises serious theoretical and epistemological issues, not all of which I am able to control. Who were the followers of the Rabbis? What does it mean to speak of their social life? If we speak of the "culture" as misogynistic (or as not misogynistic), what does this mean, or rather, to whom are we referring? To the men, the women, the elites, hoi polloi? What would it mean, indeed, to call any culture misogynistic? Are we ignoring the existence of women as part of the culture, or assuming that they are victims of false consciousness and themselves have internalized misogyny? I shall try to avoid the most obvious traps of my discourse, without, however, any real confidence that this will always be possible.

religious community. The removal of sexuality—or, more humbly, removal from sexuality—stood for the state of unhesitating availability to God and one's fellows, associated with the ideal of the single-hearted person.

(Brown 1987, 266–67)

Although in this passage Brown sets up the opposition between a reified Judaism and Christianity, he himself has made us aware that this is not the relevant taxonomy, for the *gran rifuto* is just as Jewish in its social origins as the acceptance of sexuality (however ambivalent) by the Rabbis. Brown has made this point explicitly in a passage near the one cited:

> It is claimed that a disgust for the human body was already prevalent in the pagan world. It is then assumed that when the Christian church moved away from its Jewish roots, where optimistic attitudes toward sexuality and marriage as part of God's good creation had prevailed, Christians took on the bleaker colors of their pagan environment. Such a view is lopsided. The facile contrast between pagan pessimism and Jewish optimism overlooks the importance of sexual renunciation as a means to singleness of heart in the radical Judaism from which Christianity emerged.

(Brown 1987, 266)

In this book, I will focus more intensively on the Jewish side of this equation than Brown has done, sketching the culture of the body both in that "radical Judaism" and in the rabbinic reaction to it. I suggest, however, that Brown's "radical Judaism" was not so radical at all but, in fact, rather typical of the ideologies of various Jewish subcultures around the Mediterranean.[4] Further, in the first century these orientations to the body cannot yet be separated out as "Jewish" and "Christian"; Pauline religion should be understood as contiguous with other Hellenistic Judaisms, and a separation between Jewish and Christian religio-cultural formations

---

4. Brown may have been referring to apocalyptic sects, such as the one at the Dead Sea. The archaeological evidence suggests, however, that despite undergoing periods of withdrawal from sexual relations, they were *not* a celibate community. Whatever Paul's spiritual origins, the Christian community as it developed did not grow out of Palestinian Jewish apocalyptic. In support of my notion that the attitudes toward sexuality among the Fathers owe more to the Greek-speaking Judaism of Philo and his congeners than to Semitic-speaking apocalyptics stands the fact that both Philo and Josephus *describe* the Essenes as a celibate group. There may or may not have been such a group, but, in any case, these two Greek-speaking Jews have testified to their values by that declaration.

should properly be attributed only to a later period.[5] Among the major supports for such a construction are the similarities between Paul and Philo—similarities that cannot easily be accounted for by assuming influence, since both were active at the same time in quite widely separated places (Chadwick 1966 and Borgen 1980). The affinities between Philo and such texts as the fourth gospel and the Letter to the Hebrews are only slightly less compelling evidence, because of the possibility that the authors of these texts already know Philo (Borgen 1965; Williamson 1970). I take these affinities as prima facie evidence for a Hellenistic Jewish cultural *koine* throughout the eastern Mediterranean, undoubtedly varying from place to place in many respects but sharing some common elements throughout the region.

Moreover, as Wayne Meeks (1983, 33) and others have pointed out, it is impossible to draw hard and fast lines between Hellenistic and rabbinic Jews in the first century.[6] On the one hand, the rabbinic movement per se does not yet exist, and on the other hand, Greek-speaking Jews like Paul and Josephus refer to themselves as Pharisees, and Paul is allegedly a disciple of Rabban Gamaliel, the very leader of the putative proto-rabbinite party. Nonetheless, I am going to suggest that there were tendencies, which, while not sharply defined, already separated first-century Greek speakers, who were relatively acculturated to Hellenism, from Semitic speakers, who were less acculturated. These tendencies were, on my hypothesis, to become polarized as time went on, leading *in the end* to a sharp division between Hellenizers, who became absorbed into Christian groups, and anti-Hellenizers, who formed the nascent rabbinic movement.[7] The adoption of Philo exclusively in the Church and the fact that he was ignored by the Rabbis are symptomatic of this relationship,

5. I am aware that I am placing myself in the middle here of a great contest in the interpretation of Paul. Suffice it to say here that I am cognizant of the different ways to read the Pauline corpus, including in particular the stimulating (but ultimately unconvincing) revisionist reading of Gaston (1987). In my work in progress, *A Radical Jew: Paul and the Politics of Identity*, I will, Deo volente, detail my reasons for making these judgments.

6. Several of the essays edited by Neusner, Frerichs, and McCracken-Flesher (see Collins 1985) also deal with these issues, particularly those in the section entitled "Defining Difference: The First Century" (73–282).

7. We must not forget that there were anti-Hellenists in later Christianity as well. Tertullian is the most obvious example, and in some respects, his sensibility about the materiality or corporeity of human essence is similar to that of the Rabbis, although his ideology of sexuality is in total opposition to theirs.

through which the Christian movement became widely characterized by its connection with middle and neo-platonism. In fact, this connection (between philonic Judaism and Christianity) was recognized in antiquity as well, for popular Christian legend had Philo convert to Christianity. Even some fairly recent scholarship attributed some of his works to Christians (Bruns 1973; and see Winston 1981, xi–xii and 313–14).

The central thesis of this book is that rabbinic Judaism—the cultural formation of most of the Hebrew- and Aramaic-speaking Jews of Palestine and Babylonia—was substantially differentiated in its representations and discourses of the body and sexuality from Greek-speaking Jewish formations, including much of Christianity. My fundamental notion, which will be explored and defended throughout the book, is that rabbinic Judaism invested significance in the body which in the other formations was invested in the soul. That is, for rabbinic Jews, the human being was defined as a body—animated, to be sure, by a soul—while for Hellenistic Jews (such as Philo) and (at least many Greek-speaking) Christians (such as Paul), the essence of a human being is a soul housed in a body.[8] For most of the Greco-Roman world an ontological dualism became as natural

---

8. See Boyarin 1992 for evidence and qualification of this statement. To prevent misunderstanding at this point, let me state here that such dualism does not *necessarily* imply contempt for the body. It would be a mistake to characterize Paul (and many early Christians, even among the dualists) simply as misomatists. Where some dualists represent the body as a grave for the soul, Paul represents it as a garment and affords it a positive role even in the eschaton. It seems, nevertheless, that the essence of human-being is for him the soul, whereas I am arguing that for the Rabbis it was the body.

For an analogous case in which a platonistic view is identified as common in Hellenistic culture and absent in rabbinic Judaism compare the following statement of E. P. Sanders:

> I must now reaffirm, against Robinson, that I think there is some validity to discussing the general character of religion which obtained in a given geographical/cultural milieu. I think that there is some sense in speaking of "Platonism," for example, when referring to the widespread view in the Hellenistic world that the true is to be identified with the immutable. Robinson might object to this as too essentialist a category and as insufficiently dynamic, and it may be that one can give a history of the conception, but the category of Platonism as just defined does, in my view, point to something real in the ancient world. (It is, by the way, a view which is notable by its absence in most of Palestinian Judaism.)
>
> (Sanders 1977, 24)

I will be arguing in this book that an analogous patterning obtains with regard to the platonic (or rather platonistic) idea that the soul is the essence of the human being, and it is housed in a body.

a way of thinking as the conscious and unconscious is for us, but the proto-rabbinite Jews of Palestine seem to have strongly resisted such dualist notions. I will claim that this resistance was at least partly owing to cultural politics, for, as we have seen, one consequence of at least the post–Pauline Christian adoption of dualist notions was to allegorize the reality of Israel quite out of corporeal existence. The notion that the physical is just a sign or shadow of that which is really real allows for a disavowal of sexuality and procreation, of the importance of filiation and genealogy, and of the concrete, historical sense of scripture, of, indeed, historical memory itself. The emphasis, on the other hand, on the body as the very site of human significance allows for no such devaluations.[9] Sexuality is accordingly not just a subheading under ethics but situated at the core of alternate individual and collective self-understandings.[10] A self and a collective that conceive of their actuality as spiritual will behave very differently from a self and a collective that see the body as the privileged site of human essence. Rabbinic Judaism and early Christianities were very different from each other in their ideologies of sexuality and thus of the self and the collective and cannot be subsumed under a rubric of Judaeo-Christianity, a term which, if it means anything at all, only takes on that meaning in modernity.[11] Religious symbols such as the incarnation and the virgin birth are important signs of cultural difference that functioned at levels of social practice and not only theology (Gager 1982).[12] In late antiquity itself, both Jews and Christians realized and remarked (with mutual acrimony) this difference around the body as a key area of cultural contention between them. The counter-charge of

---

9. Verna Harrison has pointed out to me that this formulation too strongly equates body with sexuality and that there are Christian writers (in particular the Cappadocian Fathers) who positively mark the role of the body while still disavowing sexuality. They simply understand sexuality as a secondary and temporary entity within the body itself. I think the point is well taken and should be kept in mind. Caroline Bynum's work on resurrection in the Western tradition (1991) also points in this direction.

10. I owe this brilliant formulation to John Miles.

11. Below I will argue that in spite of the enormous variations within both Christianities and rabbinic Judaism, the near-universal privileging of virginity, even for Christian thinkers who valorize marriage, produces an irreducible difference between that formation and rabbinic Judaism, for which sexuality and procreation are understood as acts of ultimate religious significance and for which virginity is highly problematic, as Christian writers in antiquity correctly emphasized.

12. In Boyarin (1992, 497) I argue that the incarnation of God constitutes not an affirmation of corporeality but rather a hypostatization of dualism.

Jews against Christians, that they were deficient because they did not marry and have children, was not unknown. The Mesopotamian Father, Aphrahat, represents this topos precisely and accurately, citing a Jewish voice, as well as his disdain for that voice:

> I have written to you, my beloved, concerning virginity and holiness because I heard about a Jewish man who has reviled one of our brethren, the members of the church. He said to him, "You are impure for you don't take wives. But we are holy and more virtuous for we bear children and multiply seed in the world."
>
> (Wright 1869, 355)[13]

Some of these differences persist until this day. Witness the difference between the meanings of the declarations, "I am not a Christian," and "I am not a Jew." The former says something about beliefs and commitments, while the latter says something about genealogy. This book will explore the historical roots of this difference in the formative period of rabbinic Judaism (the ancestor of virtually all later Judaism) and Christianity.

The contestation around the body between rabbinic Judaism and its Hellenistic (that is, Greek-speaking) competitors (whether forebears or contemporaries), including Paul, manifested itself in several seemingly disparate areas of socio-cultural practice, indeed in arenas as seemingly unconnected as gender and marriage practices, methods of interpretation of scripture, and ideologies of ethnicity and history. The organization of this book itself reflects to a certain degree these different areas of culture and attempts to show how they work together in the discourse of rabbinic Judaism. To be sure, the lion's share of the book (all but the last chapter) deals directly with the discourse of sexuality per se, but the argument of the book is completed in the last chapter, where an attempt is made to show how precisely the same set of differences between rabbinic Judaism and its Greek-speaking contenders works itself out with respect to the question of the literal or figurative interpretations of Jewish ethnicity. For the Jews of late antiquity, I claim, the rite of circumcision became the most contested site of this contention, precisely because of the way that it concentrates in one moment representations of the significance of sexuality, genealogy, and ethnic specificity in bodily practice. The contest between the two broadly defined types of Jewish religiosity here shifts

---

13. For further discussion of this fascinating passage, see below Chapter 5, n. 10.

from the direct discourse about sex, gender, and marriage to an indirect contest over language and the interpretation of history, scripture, and ritual practices, but it is, nevertheless, the same contest. I claim not only that I see a nexus between the interpretations of sexuality and the interpretations of ethnicity but that this connection was perceived in late antiquity.[14]

Thus, when Augustine consigns the Jews to eternal carnality, he draws a direct connection between anthropology and hermeneutics. Because the Jews reject reading "in the spirit," therefore they are condemned to remain "Israel in the flesh." Allegory is thus, in his theory, a mode of relating to the body. In another part of the Christian world, Origen also described the failure of the Jews as owing to a literalist hermeneutic, one which is unwilling to go beyond or behind the material language and discover its immaterial spirit (Crouzel 1989, 107–12). This way of thinking about language had been initially stimulated in the Fathers by Paul's usage of "in the flesh" and "in the spirit" to mean, respectively, literal and figurative. Romans 7:5–6 is a powerful example of this hermeneutic structure: "For when we were still in the flesh, our sinful passions, stirred up by the law, were at work on our members to bear fruit for death. But now we are fully freed from the law, dead to that in which we lay captive. We can thus serve in the new being of the Spirit and not the old one of the letter." In fact, exactly the same metaphor is used independently of Paul by Philo, albeit to make exactly the opposite point:

> It is true that receiving circumcision does indeed portray the excision of pleasure and all passions, and the putting away of the impious conceit, under which the mind supposed that it was capable of begetting by its own power: but let us not on this account repeal the law laid down for circumcising. Why, we shall be ignoring the sanctity of the Temple and a thousand other things, if we are going to pay heed to nothing except what is shewn us by the inner meaning of things. Nay, we should look on all these outward observances as resembling the body,

14. Note that we find exactly the same nexus in the conflict of the Shakers, Koreshantists, and Sanctificationists with "mainstream" Christianity in nineteenth-century America. For these groups as well, as Kitch (1989, 67) points out, celibacy was conjoined with "the Bible as a symbolic rather than a literal history. They objected to baptism by water and to the use of bread and wine in the sacrament on the same grounds; they regarded such things as symbolic, not literal or substantive." All of these groups also believed in an androgynous God, whose image was restored in celibate, spiritual communion between men and women. The parallel is, thus, exact.

and their inner meanings as resembling the soul. It follows that, exactly as we have to take thought for the body, because it is the abode of the soul, so we must pay heed to the letter of the laws.

(Philo 1932, 185)[15]

For both Paul and Philo, hermeneutics becomes anthropology.

This congruence of Paul and Philo is one of the features of their thought that suggests they share a common background in the thought-world of the eclectic middle-platonism of first-century Greek-speaking Judaism (Chadwick 1966).[16] Their allegorical reading practice and that of their intellectual descendants is founded on a binary opposition in which meaning exists as a disembodied substance prior to its incarnation in language, that is, in a dualistic system in which spirit precedes and is primary over body.[17] Midrash, the hermeneutic system of rabbinic Judaism, seems precisely to refuse that dualism, eschewing the inner-outer, visible-invisible, body-soul dichotomies of allegorical reading. Midrash and platonic allegory are alternate techniques of the body.

15. For a good, concise description of Philo's hermeneutics, see Fraade (1991, 11–14). Philo rather compromises his argument by admitting, "If we keep and observe these, we shall gain a clearer conception of those things of which these are the symbols; and besides that we shall not incur the censure of the many and the charges they are sure to bring against us." Like Paul, it seems, he at least sometimes maintained observance of the literal commandments, in the flesh, to escape the censure of fellow Jews. It is important to note that Philo himself is just the most visible representative of an entire school that understood the Bible and indeed the philosophy of language as he did—as is suggested by his very censure of those who pay attention only to the allegorical meaning and ignore the physical observances. See Winston (1988, 211).

16. The notion that Paul has a background in Hellenistic Judaism has been advanced fairly often. It has generally had a pejorative tinge to it, as if only Palestinian Judaism was "authentic," and such terms as *lax*, and, surprisingly enough, *coldly legal*, are used to describe Paul's alleged Hellenistic environment. Recently, this idea has been rightly discarded on the grounds that there is no sharp dividing line between Hellenistic and Palestinian Judaism. If we abandon the ex post facto judgments of history, moreover, there is no reason to accept the previous notions of *margin* and *center* in the description of late-antique Jewish groups, and no reason why Philo should be considered less authentic than Rabban Gamaliel. The question of cultural differences between Greek- and Hebrew-speaking Jews can be reapproached on different, non-judgmental territory. In that light, I find the similarities between Paul and Philo, who could have had no contact with each other whatsoever, very exciting evidence for first-century Greek-speaking Jews.

17. I have limited the scope of this claim to allow for other types of allegory, including such phenomena as Joseph's interpretations of Pharaoh's dreams, as well as for an untheorized allegorical tradition in reading Homer. When I use the term *allegory*, therefore, this is to be understood as shorthand for allegories of the type we know from Philo and onward.

My claim must not be misunderstood as a sort of standard modern apologetic interpretation of rabbinic Judaism (often reified into "Judaism") as unproblematically "accepting" or "affirming" of This World, the flesh and no devil. I argue that a culture adopting the ideological position that sexuality is a benefit given by God to humans, both for procreation and for other positive ends, acquired problems as well as solutions. Indeed, I am arguing that there was much social conflict within the societies which rabbinic Judaism helped form, precisely owing to the strength of this position, for the insistence on embodiment and sexuality as the foundational primitives of human essence almost ineluctably produces gender and sex-role differentiation as dominant characteristics of the social formation. Some Christians (whether Jewish or Gentile) could declare that there is no Greek or Jew, no male or female. No rabbinic Jew could do so, because people are bodies, not spirits, and precisely bodies are marked as male or female, and also marked, through bodily practices and techniques such as circumcision and food taboos, as Jew or Greek as well.

READING SEX

Since the major form of discourse in this book will be close readings of literary texts of various types, the question arises: In what sense can I be said to be reading "sex" here? In what sense can I be said to be reading anything other than some literary texts? The question of the relation of the literary text to the rest of culture has always been a live one in the modern interpretation of rabbinic texts. In traditional positivistic historiographical approaches to the study of rabbinic literature, the biographical narratives of the Rabbis were considered to be legendary elaborations of "true" stories, that is, stories that contained a kernel of biographical-historical truth, which could be discovered by careful literary archaeology.[18] The biographical stories about the Rabbis were treated as the "historical background" for the study of both their halakhic (ritual law) views and midrashic interpretations of the Bible. In my work, in direct contrast to that approach, these will be treated as the least transparent of texts, as fictions requiring foregrounding to explain *them*. Many critics have realized

18. One still finds such methods being employed occasionally, as in, e.g., McArthur (1987).

that these texts are essentially literary, that is, fictional, accounts about men and (occasionally) women who probably lived but functioned primarily as signifiers of values within the culture, as exempla (Fränkel 1981). But once we read the individual narratives as "fictions," it becomes increasingly difficult not only to imagine any outside to the text but even to connect the different moments of the Talmud itself one to another, that is, to read the biographical legends and the legal-ritual discourse together. Since we no longer imagine that the stories reflect the "real" events of "real" lives of the "authors" of the legal discourse, the latter seems to come from no-one and nowhere.[19] Once the biographical narratives are bereft of referentiality, the legal texts have no authors and are disconnected from the stories.[20]

The notion, however, that rabbinic literature of any genre is autonomous (in the New Critical sense) seems counter-intuitive in the extreme. If ever there was a literature whose very form declares its embeddedment in social practice and historical reality, it is these texts. How may we, then, historicize our readings of these stories, given the historical skepticism I have outlined above? I propose that the older insight that there is connection between the genres of rabbinic textuality and also between them and a society can be preserved when we understand literature as discourse—as discourse in the Foucauldian sense, best defined by Hodge:

> When literature is seen as a contingent phenomenon produced in and by discourse, then a whole set of new objects and connections becomes immediately and directly available for study: social processes that flow through and irresistibly connect "literary" texts with many other kinds of texts, and social meanings that are produced in different ways from many social sites. This concept, following Foucault's influential usage, emphasizes literature as a process rather than simply a set of products; a process which is intrinsically social, connected at every point with mechanisms and institutions that mediate and control the flow of knowledge and power in a community.
>
> (Hodge 1990, viii)

19. Jacob Neusner's solution of regarding all texts as the products of their final redactors (1990) does not solve this problem either, simply because we know as little about the redactors as we do about the Rabbis quoted.

20. Thus even Weller (1989), who attempts to read the whole series of stories in Ketubbot as an ideological production (and does so with a fair degree of success), effectively ignores the halakhic context, seeing the stories as placed here only by "association" and not as an effort to work out the same cultural dynamic and problem encoded in the halakhic text.

This notion of literature as a process integrally connected with other social processes is a very powerful one for the study of talmudic texts. It enables us to consider how the social meanings produced in the halakhic discussions and innovations that the documents preserve are reproduced in the stories about the Rabbis that the same documents tell. If we can no longer write biographies of Rabbis, which can then be used to explain (even partially) their halakhic interventions (as, for example, the classic biography of Rabbi Akiva by Louis Finkelstein [1964]), we can, it seems, use both halakha and aggada together to write a history of discursive processes and social sites, of communal mechanisms and institutions.

How do we translate this idea into interpretation of texts? Having abandoned the notion that texts simply *reflect* the intentions of their authors or the extra-textual reality of their referents, what alternative to a purely intra-textual reading remains? The answer lies in an appropriate apprehension of the concept of intertextuality, and particularly the special form of intertextual reading pursued by a group of scholars called the "new historicists."[21]

The research paradigm loosely known as the new historicism is more a sensibility than a theory. Indeed, certain of its practitioners have defined themselves explicitly (if somewhat ironically) as being "against theory."[22] Nevertheless, I believe that we can discover one overriding principle that both constitutes the paradigm as a significant theoretical intervention and explains the convergence of sensibility between critics of otherwise very diverse interests and methods. This principle is rejection of the view that literature and art form an autonomous, time-less realm of transcendent value and significance, and concomitantly, promulgation of the conviction that this view is itself the historical, ideological construction of a particular time and place in cultural history. Stated more positively, literature and art are one practice among many by which a culture organizes its production of meaning and values and structures itself. There follow from this hypothesis several postulates:

1. The study of a literary work cannot be pursued in isolation from other concurrent socio-cultural practices.

---

21. Below, however, I will propose that this appellation be abandoned.

22. Specifically, of course, I am referring to Walter Benn Michaels, one of the authors of the original "Against Theory" essay. See Thomas (1991).

2. So-called high culture has no essential privilege over "popular" and "mass" culture, nor do the latter more truly reflect society than the former. These very distinctions are a cultural practice and an ideological intervention that must be examined.

3. Some kind of materialism must be assumed (not necessarily Marxian).

4. Much of the rigid barrier between the current humanities and social sciences must be dismantled.

This axiom and its postulates involve a radical restructuring of our understanding of critical practice and indeed of human culture altogether. Posing them as such and basing one's work upon them is an already transgressive practice vis-à-vis the ideology underlying the current division of scholarship into "humanities" and "social sciences."

A founding assumption of the practice of new historicism, rendered heavily problematic in theory, is nevertheless that the document, proclamation, deed, diary, or private letter provides access in some sense to a less processed, more transparent version of the discursive practices of the period and can thus serve as explanatory context for the "text."[23] In an essay written in the new-historicist mode, my text would open with a historical anecdote drawn from some kind of palpably documentary source— a letter, memoir, or memorandum to the king—and then proceed to reading it together with a literary text par excellence, deconstructing, as it were, the very dichotomy between the literary and the documentary, showing not that the documentary is literary but that the literary is no less documentary than the document.[24] But when we study the Talmud, this sense of the documentary must be abandoned once and for all. All of the texts available are of the same epistemological status. They are all literature or all documents in precisely the same degree; indeed, they all occur within the same texts, between the same covers. There is literally (virtually) nothing outside of the text.

Stephen Greenblatt often prefers a different terminology and definition instead of *new historicism*, namely, *cultural poetics*, that is, simply a

23. In that sense, "new historicism" has sometimes appeared to be only a much more sophisticated version of the old historical type of literary criticism, which reduced the text to an expression of the "reality" in which it was produced.

24. Fineman (1989) offers an important and serious investigation of the status of the anecdote in new-historicist writing.

criticism, which can be based on different underlying theories of culture and which seeks to understand literature as social practice (Greenblatt 1990).[25] Under the rubric of cultural poetics, the problem disappears entirely. Unlike an older historicistic criticism (including that of Marx) and formalist criticism of the new-critical mode, both of which assumed an essential difference between literary and other practices, such that literature either "reflected" practice in the one or was autonomous of it in the other, here the opposition between literature and other practices is simply dissolved. Literature is one practice among many, but for this as for many past cultures it is virtually the only practice to which we have access. Since no assumption is made of an essential difference between literature and other texts or between textual and other practice, we read what we have as a textual practice, co-reading many different sub-texts in search of access to the discourse of the society in which they were produced. The specific research and critical strategy deployed here is thus cultural poetics, a practice that respects the literariness of literary texts (that is, as texts that are marked by rhetorical complexity and for which that surface formal feature is significant for their interpretation), while attempting at the same time to understand how they function within a larger socio-cultural system of practices.

Because, as I have said, the culture of the Talmud is a formation for which we have virtually no evidence "outside the texts," we must substitute some other kinds of correlations for the powerful and exciting ones of document to literary text. There would seem to be no point of entry from

---

25. The major implication of this shift is that it no longer implies that a *particular theory* (beyond the axioms and postulates I have outlined above) is at stake here, but rather proposes a new disciplinary formation that grows out of those axioms and postulates. Practitioners of cultural poetics are not thereby committed to the philosophical doctrines of historicism, implying radical irreducible difference between historical periods. Some practitioners of cultural poetics may be historicists, while others may wish to question historicism as a doctrine. As a more generic name, as well, it separates the research paradigm from the specific work of the Berkeley school (whatever that means—Greenblatt's work is, after all, thoroughly different in style and theme from that of the late Joel Fineman, for example). This work has been largely concerned with the early modern period, where projects of domination and colonialization, as well as power-relations between genders, were particularly live issues. "New historicism" has also been characterized by a particular Foucauldian theoretical base, in which power is read as the dominating feature of nearly all cultural work. Broadening the paradigm to "cultural poetics" thus allows for that school to be conceived of as one tributary to a river of research in which theoretical issues are at question, debatable and debated.

which we can read against the grain of the texts and learn anything about
ideological conflict and power relations within this culture, and indeed,
most scholarship on such a culture is non-critical, at best reproducing the
ideology of the dominant voices structuring the texts of the culture. My
practice here will be to look at texts as (necessarily failed) attempts to
propose utopian solutions to cultural tensions. The tensions are what interest me, so using the sensibilities and even techniques of the various
hermeneutics of suspicion, I hope that by observing the effects of the
energy expended by the culture in attempting to suppress or (put more
positively) deal with the tensions, the underlying strains and pressures
can be brought to light. Like astronomers who discover heavenly bodies
too small for their eyes to see by observing the distorting effects of such
bodies on other entities, the equivocations in the texts will be taken as
evidence for tensions in the society. As a stand-in for the documentary
richness that historicists of more fortunate climes have at their disposal, I
will substitute a method of arguing that texts from the talmudic literature
(including midrash) of very different genres share the same cultural prob-
lematics as their underlying (sometimes implicit) themes. I will refer to a
complex of such texts that deal with a given cultural problematic as a *discursive formation.*[26]

Cultural poetics thus provides tools for a unitary explanation of
halakha (religious law) and aggada (narrative), especially biographical
legends about the Rabbis, as participating in the same discursive formations. Where previous generations of researchers in Jewish history have
seen the biographical legends as preserving a "kernel" of historical truth,
which may be used as explanatory "background" to explain legal opinions
and innovations, and a later generation of scholars insisted on the "autonomy" of the aggada qua literature (Fränkel 1981), the method of cultural
poetics recombines aggada and halakha, but in a new fashion. I assume
that both the halakha and the aggada represent attempts to work out the
same cultural, political, social, ideological, and religious problems. They
are, therefore, connected, but not in the way that the older historicism
wished to connect them. We cannot read the aggada as background for
the halakha, but if anything, the opposite: the halakha can be read as
background and explanation for the way that the rabbinic biographies are

---

26. It should be obvious from this statement why form-critical methods are foreign
to this particular research project. I do not, of course, discount them in general.

constructed—not, I hasten to add, because the halakha represents "reality" which the aggada "reflects," but only because the halakha as a stipulated normative practice is, almost by definition, ideologically more explicit. The assumption that I make is that the very assignment of a story or a halakhic view to a named Rabbi, *whether or not this assignment is "historically" true,* is of semiotic significance and can be interpreted as part of the history of rabbinic discourse.[27] This is not to contest the possibility that there is a kernel of "historical truth" in some or even all of the stories, only to argue that this kernel is insignificant compared to the amount of history of discursive practice that can be written using these materials. Thus, for instance, in Chapter 5, I shall be studying in detail a romantic and clearly fictional story of the marriage of Rabbi Akiva. The story will be interpreted here as having very little to do with the life and times of Rabbi Akiva himself in second-century Palestine and a great deal with Babylonian Jewish marriage and sexual practices in the fourth and fifth centuries. Nevertheless, the question of why the story is told about Rabbi Akiva is highly significant and is interpreted here.[28] Similarly, the complex of texts that represent Rabbi Eliezer as variously ascetic and "misogynist" are also significant in the production of a type of rabbinic religiosity, whether or not the attributions are "authentic."[29]

Rabbinic Culture as Colonized Culture

Jewish culture in Roman Palestine was a colonized culture. The dominant political force was, of course, pagan (and then Christian) Rome. The dominant cultural influences were those of Hellenism in late antiquity (Bowersock 1990). The literature of the Rabbis is formed within this cultural-political matrix, and though I believe it is very difficult to discuss specific historical events to which a given rabbinic text responds (Boyarin 1989), there can be no doubt that this general historical context is of great interpretative significance. James Dunn has eloquently described the general politico-cultural situation of threatened first-century Jewry:

27. On the question of rabbinic biography, see Green (1978).

28. I have discussed a similar example at length in a paper specifically on the martyrdom stories about Rabbi Akiva (Boyarin 1989).

29. Hoshen (1990), an excellent example of this method applied to Rabbi Eliezer, is, however, a work that seriously contests the usual understanding of this character as misogynist.

Whatever the precise details of these various incidents the overall picture is clear enough. During the period in which the Antioch incident took place Jews had to be on their guard against what were or were seen to be repeated threats to their national and religious rights. Whenever such a threat was perceived their reaction was immediate and vigorous. In Palestine itself more and more were resorting to open violence and guerrilla warfare. The infant Christian sect was not exempt from this unrest. Indeed we generalize a fairly firm conclusion from the above review of evidence: wherever this new Jewish sect's belief or practice was perceived to be a threat to Jewish institutions and traditions its members would almost certainly come under pressure from their fellow Jews to remain loyal to their unique Jewish heritage.

(Dunn 1990, 135)

Although Dunn is accounting here for the background of controversies *within* the nascent Christian movement and in the first century, I believe that the same pressures also explain, *mutatis mutandis,* much of the development in the literature of the Rabbis in the second and following centuries, when Christianity becomes more and more the source of the threat to "Jewish institutions and traditions." While this general socio-cultural situation is assumed here, this book will *not* be a historical account proper, but rather an analysis of texts conducted under the sign of cultural poetics.

Among the tools that cultural poetics has at hand is the description of cultural or literary practices as forms of resistance or accommodation or accommodating resistance and resistant accommodation to the dominant practices of a colonizing culture. At several points in my discussion, I will argue that a given rabbinic textual or cultural moment represents precisely such resistance. Thus, for instance, in Chapter 1, "Behold Israel According to the Flesh: On Anthropology and Sexuality in Late-Antique Judaisms," I analyze the hermeneutic strategies of Hellenistic and rabbinic Judaism vis-à-vis the first human. Within both formations we find interpretations that solved the problem of the dual creation stories of Genesis 1 and 2 by assuming that the first-created human, the male and female of Genesis 1, was an androgyne. But the Hellenistic formations, Philo, some of the Orthodox Fathers, and many gnostics understood that this primal androgyne was without a body, and that the human with a body described in Genesis 2 represents a separate act of creation.[30] Many of the Rabbis

---

30. See Chapter 1 below for discussion of the relationship of this myth to the famous Aristophanes passage in Plato.

understood the Genesis 1 creation to be an actual corporeal androgynous human being, which was then split in two in the second chapter to form the two sexes. My claim is that these two versions of creation are not only literary but have an analogue or homologue in social practice, for while the first group regard the highest form of human life as a de-gendered, uncorporeal spirituality, as practiced in celibate communities, the Rabbis regard marriage and sexual intercourse as the return to the originary and ideal state of the human being. Cultural poetics allows us then to interpret the connection between the "literary" practice of biblical interpretation and the social institution of marriage, without resort either to a reductionism by which the biblical interpretation is the product of ideology or to an idealism according to which the biblical interpretation produces the ideology. Both the interpretation and the ideology are co-existing practices within a single socio-cultural field. Thus, when the Rabbis cite the myth of the primal androgyne but reverse its meaning, they are enacting a classic move by which the colonized culture undermines the hegemony of the colonizer.

Beyond "Rabbinic Thought"

Precisely this method of going beyond the reading of texts to the reading of the larger text of a culture which is made up of many texts gives me the possibility of claiming that I am indeed "reading sex"—reading, that is, the discourse of sex in talmudic culture and not merely some literary documents. My ambition is to escape the paradigm of "rabbinic thought," as if rabbinic literature were a sort of philosophy manqué, and instead study culture, as a set of complexly related practices both textual and embodied.[31] We can see then that halakhic discussions and decisions as well as stories about the Rabbis, and even the reading of the Bible, are all ways in which this culture expresses its concerns and unresolved tensions and attempts to work them out. We can accordingly learn quite a bit about the culture and its problems, and even about the differences between different branches of it, from studying these discursive practices together.

IN

The "in" of "Reading Sex in Talmudic Culture," the subtitle of this book, also needs to be interpreted. I am reading sex "in" talmudic culture here,

---

31. For a similar point made in another context, see Bynum (1991, 245).

and the "in" functions in two senses, accenting both the partiality and partialness of the interpretative construct of this book. These are readings that claim only to be part of the story, and they are, moreover, readings that are situated by the reader's (my) status as a self-defined inheritor of the tradition which the texts constitute. There is no pretense at objectivity and disinterest in this text. I am both a "rabbinic Jew" and a "feminist,"[32] and these dual (some would claim oxymoronic) commitments motivate both my very enterprise of writing a book like this and the specific constructions and readings that I make of the texts and their interconnections. Because this may sound to some like an abandonment of any claim to historical meaningfulness for my discourse, I shall take a few lines to elaborate on this point.

Reading any cultural production, even one as relatively simple as a single lyric, involves the mobilization of large sets of assumptions *before reading,* including, often enough, the very assumption that the given text is autonomous and can be read in isolation from other texts. This truism is only multiplied manifold when the attempt is made, as here, to read much more complex and large-scale cultural practices, such as the discourse of sexuality. What texts to choose, which to see as context for which, how to read the individual text and how to co-read it with others, these are all choices made by the reader—some conscious and others that are not even conscious but are produced for the reader by her or his ideological window on the world. Nevertheless, reading is reading—looking through a window, not just peering into a mirror—or at any rate, it can be such. Given the concerns that I have, the background that I have, and even my unexamined notions of what is natural and possible, it is inevitable that my interpretation, particularly in its larger-scale moments, will be in part a product of all of these factors. At the same time it is, for all that, an interpretation of the text, a reading for which philological and historical knowledge have been mobilized to the best of my ability to interpret the text. I am, myself, "in" talmudic culture, at least in part, and my readings will undoubtedly reflect that identity. However, I would wish to insist that the book is not, therefore, apologetic or defensive, for it is not my intention to construct arguments that would cover over or explain away those aspects of rabbinic Judaism that I find ethically problematic or to defend it against the depredations of a rival religion, but rather, I would say, to construct from it a

---

32. For the difficulties in the notion "male feminist," see Jardine and Smith (1987) and especially Heath (1987).

"usable past," discovering and marking out those areas within the culture that can serve us today and finding ways to contextualize and historicize recalcitrant and unpalatable aspects of the culture such that we can move beyond them. For that past to be usable, it must carry conviction (at least for me) that it is a plausible reconstruction based on the data before us, and to do that I have utilized the best of whatever abilities and knowledge I have of the languages and textual and cultural history of the texts I read.

Franz Rosenzweig wrote:

> Why has the word *apologetics* acquired such a bad reputation? The same seems to be true of the apologetic profession par excellence, that of the lawyer. A general bias against him sees his legitimate task, as it were, as lying. Perhaps a certain professional routine appears to justify this prejudice. Nevertheless, defense can be one of the noblest of human occupations—to wit, when it goes to the very bottom of issues and souls, and ignoring the petty device of lies, ex-culpates itself with the truth, the whole truth. In this broad sense, literary apologetics can also defend. In so doing it would not embellish anything, much less evade a vulnerable point. Instead, it would make the basis of defense the points of greatest jeopardy. In a word: it would defend the whole, not this or that particular. It would not be a defense in the usual sense, but an open presentation—not of some random thing, but of one's own province.
>
> (1923, 272)

What Rosenzweig calls "apologetic," I shall call cultural critique. My work begins with the assumption that the task of criticism is "to change the world," the task that Marx assigned to philosophy. I accept the challenge of Justin Martyr, who asked an ancient interlocutor, "Are you, then, a philologian, but no lover of deeds or truth? and do you not aim at being a practical man so much as being a sophist?" I wish to contribute to the healthy transformation not of "some random thing, but one's own province." My province is rabbinic Judaism, both because I practice that religion and consider myself an heir to its traditions and memories and also because I have chosen it as my province of intellectual discourse. That is to say, I have developed a certain facility for reading its texts and a certain familiarity with their style and contents.

Both of these declarations of intent and identity obligate me, I think, to engage in a critical practice of reading these texts. The question at hand for me then is how do I pursue a critique of a past culture and especially of one that I feel identified with? Or, to put it another way, how do

I protect my culture without playing false either to the historical "truth" or to my ethical commitment to changing the present gender practices of that culture? As in so many areas of thought, Franz Rosenzweig here also suggests a way, a way that he chooses to call apologetic, which is an open and frank presentation of the culture that contextualizes its practices both structurally and historically. This will have to be a presentation that refuses the arrogance of cultural Darwinism, the idea that culture evolves from less advanced to more advanced forms. It will have to be an account that is not judgmental but critical. Rather than apologetic, I shall call this mode of cultural critique (which I attempt to put into practice in this book) *generous critique*, a practice that seeks to criticize practice of the Other from the perspective of the desires and needs of here and now, without reifying that Other or placing myself in judgment over him or her in his or her there and then. I will suggest that such a practice is appropriate for any presentation of a past culture, but most imperative when the past is my own. Precisely the critique of Orientalism (Said 1979) as a practice that stands in judgment of other cultures and homogenizes them can be in turn applied to much critical, historical practice vis-à-vis our own ancestors.

As I have already said, cultural phenomena can be read in several different ways; the more complex the phenomenon, the more numerous the possibilities for reading. The texts of rabbinic Judaism and the construction that we put on the whole are therefore ambiguous, necessarily so. Later stages of Judaism have chosen to read the rabbinic texts in certain fashions and have closed off other options for reading. This does not mean that their readings were wrong or inauthentic, or that I think that I have discovered the true meaning of rabbinic Judaism, but it does leave open the possibility for other understandings of the same texts. Since our cultural situation is different from that of the medieval Rabbis, it is incumbent on us, as scholars and as cultural critics, to discover other faces in the same texts—faces that can be more useful for us in re-constructing our own versions of culture and gender practices. Such discovery would constitute an apologetic, in the degraded sense, only if it insisted on having discovered an authentic truthful interpretation that was distorted, if it hid that which is inimical to the new reading, or if it did not allow other traditions the same opportunity to be reread and reconstructed.

Let me elaborate on this last point. It has become a fairly common strategy of feminist historians of religions to ascribe true feminist impulses to their own tradition and to relegate the unfortunate sexism of the actually existing socio-cultural practices to the deleterious influence of "others." Concurrent with this practice goes a mode of writing whereby one's own tradition is described as heterogeneous, while those of others are rendered monoliths. This has often happened in Christian feminist accounts of the feminism of Jesus and even Paul, whose unfortunate lapses are laid at the door of a "Jewish" or "rabbinic" residue or even backsliding. I will not mention simple vulgar examples of such writing, but even as careful a scholar as Elizabeth Schüssler Fiorenza does not escape it entirely when she reproduces approvingly a student's paper that attributes Paul's backsliding between Galatians and Corinthians as "reverting to his rabbinic prejudices"! (Fiorenza 1983, 63–64). I mention this point not so much to protest, which others have done already and I believe to good effect (at least with Fiorenza), but to emphasize how great the temptation has been *for me* to do the same sort of thing: to paint the rabbinic tradition as non-misogynistic in essence and marginalize the evidence for woman-despising to a popular, Hellenistic residue, which moreover characterizes Christianity. I have tried assiduously to avoid this temptation, perhaps not always and entirely successfully. I am more and more convinced that reception history closes off options of reading virtually any tradition, and that an important task of criticism is to re-open the options that have been suppressed.

On the other hand, I do not wish to undermine my very project by describing each cultural formation as so heterogeneous that there are no important differences between cultures. This reading of talmudic culture does insist that rabbinic Judaism as a whole was different from the Others of this culture, Hellenistic Judaism and Pauline (and post-Pauline) Christianity, in spite of the internal heterogeneities of each formation. A major danger haunting the work from the beginning, then, has been a tendency, connected with the danger described in the last paragraph, toward a triumphalist comparison of Judaism with Christianity in which Judaism emerges as pro-body or pro-sex, and thus healthier. Indeed, such comparisons are a commonplace of recent American Jewish apologetics (David Biale 1992). Since this is not my intent, I have spent considerable time developing a method of presentation that I call *cultural dialectics*. By cultural dialectics, I intend a mode of analysis that compares related cultural formations by showing that they represent complementary "solutions" to given cultural "problems." Among other things, this method of presentation allows for cultural comparison without triumphalism, for each formation provides critique of its Other.

I hope that my discourse has managed to avoid all of these ethical and intellectual pitfalls. Well aware of the ways in which expectations shape results even in the hard sciences, and even more so in the hermeneutical ones, I invite readers to recast their expectations of gender and sexual representations in one ancient tradition. The proof of the pudding being in the eating, only the plausibility of these readings to other readers (and particularly those who do not share my peculiar investments) will demonstrate the success or failure of this project.

TALMUDIC CULTURE

Since a major ambition of this entire project is to make talmudic culture accessible to students of culture who are not Hebrew scholars, I want to pause here to introduce the literature with which I will be dealing.

The Documents of Rabbinic Literature

The following are brief introductions to the actual documents of rabbinic literature:

The Mishna   The Mishna is certainly the earliest rabbinic document that has been preserved. It is a highly edited compendium of opinions on halakha from the Rabbis of the two centuries preceding its publication. Its redaction was early in the third century.

The Tosefta   The Tosefta is the earliest commentary to the Mishna. It parallels the Mishna text closely, offering other or expanded versions of the utterances contained in the earlier text. Its traditions are often antithetical to the Mishna.

The "Halakhic" Midrashim   There is a body of texts that are conventionally referred to as "halakhic" or "tannaitic" midrashim—rabbinic works of commentary on the Torah whose main interest is the discovery of or proof of the legal-ritual practices of the Rabbis in the Written Torah. Their nature and origin is much contested in recent scholarship. I belong to the school of thought that regards these texts as no less (or more) authentic than any other rabbinic texts—that is, as highly redacted anthologies composed of earlier materials and not as pseudepigraphs. In their present form, these texts were probably redacted in the third or fourth century.[33]

The Aggadic Midrashim   Another type of rabbinic literature that will be important for our study is rabbinic commentaries on the Bible (not only the Torah!) that are primarily interested in elucidating the narrative of the Bible and not the halakhic implications of its legal texts. These aggadic midrashim often preserve earlier materials, though they are several centuries later than the works in the previous category, achieving their present literary state in the fifth and sixth centuries.[34]

The Talmuds   There are two Talmuds, one produced in Babylonia and one in Palestine, both roughly (very roughly) contemporaneous with the aggadic midrashim. These constitute far-ranging literary discussions, loosely growing out of commentary on the Mishna. They are practically encyclopedias of rabbinic culture in late antiquity. The Babylonian Talmud became definitively authoritative for all medieval rabbinic Jewish cultures.

Between Babylonian and Palestinian:
Early and Late

By speaking of talmudic culture, I am emphatically not suggesting that there was one homogeneous form of this culture for the nearly six hundred years and two major geographical centers which attest to it. Beyond a shadow of a doubt, there were consistent differences between the earlier and later forms of the culture and between its western version in Palestine under Hellenistic cultural domination and its eastern version in Babylonia, where Persian culture reigned supreme. At several junctures in this

33. For a counterview see Neusner (1990) and my review of this work to appear in the *Journal of the American Oriental Society*.

34. Lest I be misunderstood, I am *not* suggesting for a moment that we have unmediated access to earlier traditions through the attributions in these, or any other, rabbinic works.

book I will point to tentative handholds on some of those differences. But the texts, particularly the later ones, such as the Talmuds, are encyclopedic anthologies of quotations, comprising all of the places and times of rabbinic culture production. We can assume with confidence neither that a given passage quoted from a particular authority represents an expression of that authority's time and place, nor that it doesn't and that it only belongs to the culture in which the text was put together (contra Neusner 1990). Indeed, even the redaction of the midrashic and talmudic texts cannot be assigned with any certainty to a particular time, place, or set of persons. Even within the individual texts, there is evidence that different sections received their final forms in very different historical moments. For these reasons, even were I capable of doing it, I think that producing a book like Peter Brown's elegant and magisterial *The Body and Society* is quite impossible for the rabbinic culture of the talmudic period (though it could be done for later periods); Brown's work is dependent on analyzing bodies of doctrine produced by given individuals whose biographies, life situations, social and political context, philosophical backgrounds, etc., are to some extent known to us, and we have almost no such information regarding late-antique rabbinic Jewish literature.[35] By default, then, I am generally constrained to write of rabbinic culture as a whole, even knowing that such discussion represents only a gap in our knowledge. Where I believe that I have found converging evidence for difference between the subcultures I have attempted to represent that difference. Examples of such attempts may be found in Chapters 5 and 6, where I argue for different ideologies in Palestine and Babylonia with respect to certain issues of gender and sex.

Dialectic and the Description of Rabbinic Culture

There are important ways in which rabbinic culture structures its main literary expression differently from the cultural-literary patterns we are

---

35. This was recently brought home to me once more upon reading Ford (1989), who is able to make precise differentiations in Chrysostom's thinking based on different periods of his life and activity as, respectively, anchorite and bishop. Such analysis is impossible for any pre-Islamic rabbinic figures. We often do not know whether they "really" said what they are quoted as saying, and if so, when, in what circumstances, and in what literary context.

used to. These differences of form are the signs and producers of major differences in cultural meaning as well. The first is that the texts are openly intertextual (dialogical) in their structure, perhaps more so than any others in literary history. As opposed to literary systems that imply or construct authors for texts, all of the texts of the rabbinic period are authorless (see Fraade 1991, 17). They present themselves as anthologies of quotations and discussions, *as if* we had access to the actual raw material of rabbinic oral interactions. The second formal feature (closely related to the first) is that the texts are primarily structured as dialectic, even as arguments between rabbis, and that most often and typically the dialectic is open-ended. The text does not finally resolve the issue in one direction or the other.

While other literary cultures obviously register dissent and controversy as well, the social semiotics of controversy are different when dissent appears between single-authored tracts or as dialectic within the same text. Let us compare the situation of early Christian textuality. There is, of course, not the slightest doubt that the earliest church was full of sharp dissent on almost every issue, from Christology to the Commandments of the Torah and circumcision to the status of marriage. But the different options were not incorporated into books in which they are set into dialectical relations with each other, with the different ideologues on equal footing in terms of authority. They are rather presented to us in a series of tracts, some of which are Pauline and others of which are anti-Pauline, and ultimately it was the Pauline version that won, and the others disappeared.[36] This is not the case for the talmudic culture. All of the opinions are of the same literary origin. Formally, they have the same authority. They come from the same source. There is no possibility whatsoever of rejecting or definitively accepting one. In practice, of course, later decisions were made as to halakha in order to prevent chaos, but at the same time the epistemological privilege of the established view was generally denied. It would simply be incoherent for Jews to declare themselves

---

36. For Christianity, this should be qualified in one important way. There is a sense in which the deutero-Pauline letters provide precisely the heterogeneity that talmudic dialectic provides, although not, I think, to the same degree. Since these letters are often highly revisionistic with respect to Paul's doctrines, they provided the developing Pauline church with various cultural options. I am thinking, for example, of the way that the *Haustfafeln* of the later letters revise the doctrine of marriage presented in Corinthians.

Akivans or Meirites, for authority resides not in the individual Rabbi but in the entire community of the Rabbis. Speaking in Bakhtinian terms, the texts are not monological but dialogical, presenting different views on most issues dialectically at nearly every turn.

This is by now familiar ground. This feature of rabbinic textuality has often been characterized as its undecidability. David Stern has made a salutary move beyond the "theory" approaches to understanding this phenomenon and begun historicizing it in terms of the social structure of the rabbinic community (Stern 1988). Stern noticed that in contrast to commonplace descriptions of rabbinic interpretation as characterized by radical doubt or indeterminacy (Handelman 1982, 75), in point of fact the Rabbis of the Talmud and midrash are very vigorous (even aggressive) in support of their particular views. They are given, indeed, to the usage of such expressions as, "How long will you pile up nonsense?" or "What do you know about aggada? Go study the minutiae of obscure halakha!" Expressions such as these and others seem hardly compatible with a notion that these were people who did not hold that their own interpretations were correct. Moreover, the Talmud tells us of several instances in which schools of Rabbis came to blows and worse over their differences of opinion on interpretation and practice. The "indeterminacy," therefore, is not to be located at the level of epistemology or theology but at the level of a social practice that does not wish to decide between competing views of a dialogical authority. Each one of the Rabbis may indeed be sure that he is correct in his views, but our finally redacted and authoritative texts encode an inability or unwillingness to decide between competing views, and it is this which becomes the dominant in this cultural moment. Indeed, matters go so far that in the course of a talmudic discussion, an argument that threatens to resolve a controversy is considered a difficulty [*kushia*], while one that restores the controversy itself is called a solution [*terutz*]! One elegant way of describing this formation has been provided by Gerald Bruns: "From a transcendental standpoint, this theory of authority is paradoxical because it is seen to hang on the heteroglossia of dialogue, on speaking with many voices, rather than on the logical principle of univocity, or speaking with one mind. Instead, the idea of speaking with one mind . . . is explicitly rejected; single-mindedness produces factionalism" (1990, 199). The implication of this statement is, of course, that "speaking with many voices" is an alternative to factionalism, which it is, precisely in the sense in which I have discussed it above.

There is no faction within rabbinic Judaism with which to attach oneself, because the opposing views are all incorporated into the same canonical texts. Declaring oneself, then, an adherent of either Rabbi Meir or Rabbi Akiva would involve precisely the denial of some part of the canonical text. Indeed, given the notorious difficulties of relying on the attributions of utterances to named authorities in the Talmud and midrash, we cannot even describe what it would be to be an Akivan or a Meirite, and this, itself, can be understood as a cultural practice. Ideologies are always, then, in dialogue with their others within the culture.

To take a salient example from a case which has already been mentioned above: the fundamental question about whether the first Adam was androgynous or male, with its attendant corollary of the ontological status of sex and woman, is debated within the talmudic and midrashic texts and not resolved. To be sure, the majority opinion seems to have been that when the Torah says, "male and female created He them," it means that God created an androgyne, but there is simply no mechanism within the texts for finally suppressing or dismissing the other view. Both views come from the same source and have the same authority, in a way that the same controversy debated, for hypothetical example, between Origen and Augustine would not. This latter practice bids us to try to decide which view is correct, while the rabbinic textual practice labels as almost heretical any attempt to so decide.

There is a fundamental semiotic difference between two interpretations that are presented in two separate works by named authors and the canonized dissensus of midrash and Talmud (Boyarin 1990c, 78–79). Any view or interpretation that is undercut by another in the same canonical work unsettles, almost by definition, its own use as a foundation for cultural and social practice. Accordingly, in the research on this culture it is vital always to pay very close attention to the structures built into the very texts, to the interplay of view and counter-view. I think that it is this last point that is most often ignored when history is written by non-talmudists using talmudic texts. Thus, a view will often enough be quoted as if typical of rabbinic Judaism when in fact it has been cited in the talmudic text only to be discredited or at any rate undermined by a counter-text. An example of this can be found in Chapter 4 below, where a text that has often been cited as evidence for a rabbinically repressive attitude toward sexual practice is interpreted as in fact cited in the Talmud only in order to reject it.[37] Note that the point is not that there was more or less dissent and controversy within the rabbinic culture than in the cultures of other forms of Judaism or Christianity but that in this culture, as in none of the others, it is precisely dissent that was canonized. The cultural model is one in which "these and these are the words of the Living God," in which even God is not allowed to decide whose interpretation is correct (Boyarin 1990c, 34–37). This particular structure must be taken very seriously in any attempt to describe rabbinic culture or any sub-system of it. We must be able to recognize not only that there were different views at any given time but also that the very fact of the existence of contradictory views all being asserted at the authoritative level would have had fundamental effects on the nature of social practice and ideology within the formation.

The argument of this book is, then, that while in most matters of detail precisely what marks the rabbinic culture is its heterogeneity, this very heterogeneity is founded on an underlying unity, the interpretation of human being as fundamentally, essentially corporeal. This idea, which itself grows out of its own material causes, becomes the spring that drives multifarious aspects of socio-cultural practice within the formations of rabbinic Jews in Palestine and Babylonia from the second century until the Arab conquest, when rabbinic culture is entirely transformed by a new and massive contact with Greek philosophy in Arabic translation.

Given the inextricability of ontological and hermeneutic theory from the discourse of gender, one of the major tasks of this book is going to be the examination of the discourse of gender in a culture that by and large does *not* operate with the system of dualistic oppositions outlined above. The point is not, of course, to argue or suggest that rabbinic social practice was more "egalitarian" than that of Hellenistic Jewish or Christian society but rather to ask what difference the different cultural configuration of its gender asymmetry made. How does a culture that does not identify man with mind and woman with body, or man with culture and woman with nature (because it does not operate with those ontological categories), nevertheless maintain a hierarchy in which men are socially dominant over women? How is this hierarchical structure different in

---

37. To be sure, once cited it is put into cultural play as well, but certainly in a much more nuanced and complex fashion than most accounts would have us believe.

theory and in practice from the hierarchical structures that determine platonized cultures (whether Jewish or Christian)? Can any useful cultural criticism be achieved by historically specifying the ways in which the rabbinic Judaism of late antiquity is different in its discourse of the body and with it of gender from the cultural formation in which we have all participated since the early Middle Ages? Specifically, can the dialectical description of these cultures as alternate solutions and failures to solve socio-cultural problems provide us with tools for a synthesis that will enable both the valorization of sexuality and the liberation of women (see also Kraemer [1992, 199–200])? Let us begin, then, to read some of the texts produced in this culture in the light of these questions.

"Behold Israel According to the Flesh"
On Anthropology and Sexuality
in Late-Antique Judaisms

DEFINING THE HUMAN BEING:
PHILO, PAUL, AND THE RABBIS

One of the tendencies of Greek-speaking Judaism—including Paul's—that divided it from rabbinic Judaism seems to have been the acceptance of what might be broadly called a platonic conception of the human being, for which the soul is the self, and the body only its dwelling place or worse. "In this life itself, what constitutes our self in each of us is nothing other than the soul" (Laws 12:959a7–8; Vernant 1991, 190). For Philo, "the soul may be seen as entombed in the body" (Winston 1988, 212). This was a commonly held conception through much of the Hellenistic cultural world.[1] Philo speaks of the body as "wicked and a plotter against the soul," as "a cadaver and always dead," and claims that

---

1. Brian Stock has reminded me that not all platonists would have defined the human being as a soul trapped in a body either, that "Some platonist thinkers, notably Philo, Plotinus, and Porphyry, thought that the soul was trapped in the body; others, those, for instance, interested in medicine, astrology, or other sciences, combined their otherworldliness with a model of macrocosm/microcosm, which placed greater weight on the body, sexuality, and one's activity in the world." Dillon has discussed this issue with regard to the middle platonists, e.g., Antiochus of Ascalon, and concludes that for him, "We *are* our minds not our bodies," but remarks that that same "second-rate philosopher"—one of the founding figures of middle platonism—in a treatise on ethics could maintain that we are both mind and body (Dillon 1977, 98). Dillon comments that these writers would somewhat modify their doctrine depending on the rhetorical needs of a particular genre. Nevertheless, it seems at any rate that most thinkers, Jewish and Christian, who adopted the platonistic dualisms as their philosophical base were led to a severe downgrading (at best) of the role of the body in the constitution of the human being. See also Spidlík (1986, 108), who writes, "No matter what school they belonged to, the philosophers arrived at the same conclusion: the body was despised as the 'enemy' of the soul, or it became a thing that was useful, like a 'slave'; one either used it at one's good pleasure or got rid of it. In the Platonic tradition the union of the body with the soul was viewed as a fall."

the chief cause of ignorance is the flesh and our affinity for it. Moses himself affirms this when he says "because they are flesh" the divine spirit cannot abide. Marriage, indeed, and the rearing of children, the provision of necessities, the ill repute that comes in the wake of poverty, business both private and public, and a host of other things wilt the flower of wisdom before it blooms. Nothing, however, so thwarts its growth as our fleshly nature.

(Philo 1981, 65)

Paul also uses similar platonizing imagery, but significantly, without such negative attributes. The clearest example appears in 2 Corinthians 5:1–4:

For we know that if the earthly tent we live in is destroyed, we have a building from God, a house not made with hands, eternal in the heavens. Here indeed we groan, and long to put on our heavenly dwelling, so that by putting it on we may not be found naked. For while we are still in this tent, we sigh with anxiety; not that we would be unclothed, but that we would be further clothed, so that what is mortal may be swallowed up by life.

Beyond any doubt, Paul refers here to a resurrection in the body, though the resurrected body is not the same kind of body as the one "that we dwell in" now. Paul considers some kind of a body necessary, in order that the human being not be naked, and he polemicizes here against those who deny resurrection in the flesh.[2] It is out of the question, therefore, to regard Paul as a radically anti-body dualist on the model of Plotinus, for example. But crucially, Paul maintains an image of the human being as a soul dwelling in or clothed by a body. In the very text in which Paul is valorizing body, arguing against those who deny body, he nevertheless refers to "we who are in this tent."[3] The coincidence between Philo and

2. See also 1 Corinthians 15:35–49, a notoriously difficult passage, and discussion in Conzelmann (1976, 280–88). According to Robinson (1952, 77), Paul does not refer here to the body of resurrection as in standard commentaries but to the Body of Christ. See also Meeks (1972, 55).

3. The reason for my qualified language is simply because it is clear here, as well as in 1 Corinthians 15, that the resurrected body is of an entirely transformed nature, apparently a body without "flesh." In general, the solution to some conundra of apparent discontinuities in early Christian discourse, which seems at one and the same time to affirm bodiliness and disavow sexuality, is to emphasize the distinction for some of these writers between "body" and "flesh." The first is a term that often has positive valence, while it is the latter which is usually of nearly exclusively negative connotation. Robinson (1952) has well drawn this distinction for Paul himself. It is, in this sense, of a body without flesh—that is, a body without sexuality among other matters—that various early Christian thinkers can assert the positive status of "the body." Thus Verna Harrison informs me that the Cappadocian Fathers held that the creation

Paul in their anthropologies, in spite of many significant differences between them, leads me to think that such platonizing notions of the human being were commonplace—although not necessarily universal— among Greek-speaking Jews. Certainly, such concepts of the human being became common among the Fathers of the church, who promulgated such metaphors for the body as "prison, tomb, fetters, vestment, ugly mask, garment of skin, dwelling place" of the soul (Spidlík 1986, 111; Dodds 1965, 30).

Rabbinic Judaism, in contrast, defined the human being as an animated body and not as a soul trapped or even housed or clothed in a body.[4] Alon Goshen-Gottstein has brilliantly articulated this difference:

> Rabbinic anthropology differs in this respect from Hellenistic [including Hellenistic Jewish], and later—Christian—anthropology. The distinction between soul and body may be seen as a soft distinction rather than a hard one.[5] There is much talk of soul and body in the rabbinic sources. There is also a recognition of their different qualities. However, there is not a fundamental metaphysical opposition between these two aspects. There may be an existential confrontation, but metaphysically soul and body form a whole, rather than a polarity. Crudely put— the soul is like a battery that operates an electronic gadget. It may be

---

of humanity was for the purpose of bringing God into the material world, thus uniting the world with God, but they, nevertheless, considered sexuality as temporary and a sign of "man's" fallenness. Bynum (1991) is a very important discussion of these questions from a different point of view. Although her focus is on the medieval period, her discussion raises the question of whether the "platonic" ideology of the person as soul was ever fully accepted in Christian culture.

4. See Robinson (1952, 14) for very similar formulations regarding biblical Judaism. Rubin (1989) is a very useful collection of "anthropological" rabbinic texts from various periods. Although Rubin describes a shift from a fully monistic conception of the person to a "moderate dualism," there is still nearly nothing that bespeaks an understanding of the human being as a soul trapped or imprisoned in a body or of the task of the soul to liberate itself from the body, as we see in Philo and Origen, as well as several of the Church Fathers.

In any case, Rabbi Meir's famous dictum in the Babylonian Talmud, Sanhedrin 90b, "If a grain of wheat, which is buried naked, sprouteth forth in many robes, how much more so the righteous, who are buried in their raiment," is totally irrelevant. Rabbi Meir is arguing that the righteous will be resurrected with clothes on—literally, not figuratively! Indeed, if R. Meir is using a traditional figure of speech, the very reversal of its meaning from a dualistic, philosophical to a concrete mythological valence is a further demonstration of my point in this chapter and the entire work.

It should be pointed out here that Urbach (1975, 248) argued for a historical shift from the period of the tannaim to that of the amoraim, with the latter more dualist in its understanding of soul and body. See also Stiegman (1977, 510–12).

5. For "soft" dualism in modern thought, see Swinburne (1986, 298–312).

different and originally external to the gadget. However, the difference is not one of essence. Nowhere in rabbinic literature is the soul regarded as Divine. It may be of heavenly origin, but is not Divine. More significantly, the gadget and its power source ultimately belong together, rather than separately. Thus the soul is the vitalizing agent, whose proper place is in the body, not out of it.

(Goshen-Gottstein 1991)

The Rabbis are thus only one ideological group within late-antique Judaism, and their anthropology is one of their main distinguishing marks. The soul is frequently likened in their writings to salt which preserves meat (Theodor and Albeck 1965, 320–21; see also Urbach 1975, 220–21 and Stiegman 1977, 508–16). Perhaps the most elegant demonstration of the essentially monistic anthropology of rabbinic Judaism is from its daily prayer service; after urinating or defecating, the Jew is enjoined to pronounce the following blessing:

Blessed art Thou O Lord, King of the Universe, Who has made the human with wisdom, and created in it orifices and hollows. Revealed and known it is before Your Throne of Glory, that should any of these be opened or shut up, it would be impossible to live before You. Blessed Art Thou, the Healer of all flesh Who does wondrous things.

This text shows clearly two things: first, the acceptance of fleshliness in its most material and lower-body forms as the embodiment of God's wisdom, and second, the definition of the human as his or her body.[6] No wonder that Augustine regarded the Jews as indisputably carnal.

Nonetheless, the body was hardly unproblematic or uncontested in the rabbinic culture, nor was asceticism unknown. In a recent essay, Steven Fraade has formulated the question which must be addressed in a study of this discourse:

[A] broader understanding of asceticism sees it as responding, in a variety of ways, to a *tension* inherent in all religious systems: humans (whether individually or collectively) aspire to advance ever closer to an ideal of spiritual fulfillment and perfection, while confronting a self and a world that continually set obstacles in that path, whatever its particular course. How can one proceed along that path with a whole,

---

6. I am going to use this form for ethical reasons rooted in present practice. It does not constitute a declaration that sex is a "natural" category, which will be precisely raised as an issue in the concluding section of this book. For the nonce, see Butler (1990, 152 n. 15). In any case, both men and women say this blessing.

undivided, undistracted "heart" (all one's energies and intentions)
while living among the distractions of the present world?

(Fraade 1986, 255)

Although "confronting a self" and "spiritual fulfillment" seem to beg some
questions they ought rather to be asking, Fraade's definition is useful.
Asceticism is not, on his account, a product of dualistic contempt for the
body; indeed, that dualistic contempt, which we find in several forms of
ancient Judaism, is one response to the ascetic tension. *Askesis* itself is
religious athleticism, "the willful and arduous training and testing, often
through abstention from what was generally permitted, of one's creaturely
faculties in the *positive* pursuit of moral and spiritual perfection" (Fraade
1986, 257; see also Dodds 1965, 24).

Unlike other forms of asceticism, sexual renunciation was excluded for
the Rabbis. Everyone was expected to marry, have sex, and have children,
and people who refused to do so were hyperbolically stigmatized as mur-
derers and blasphemers (Tosefta Yevamot 8:7 and Babylonian Talmud
Yevamot 63b). The necessity for such hyperbole attests to the attractions
of celibacy for Semitic-speaking Jews.[7] The Rabbis were part of the Hellenistic world, even though their conception of the body departed significantly from (or even resisted) prevailing Hellenistic anthropological
notions that other Jews had assimilated. Because the Rabbis understood
the human being as a body, sexuality was an essential component of being
human, while in platonized formations, one could imagine an escape from
sexuality into a purely spiritual and thus truly "human" state.[8] The rabbinic insistence on the essentiality of the corporeal and thus the sexual in
the constitution of human being represents then a point of resistance to
the dominant discursive practices of both Jewish and non-Jewish cultures
of late antiquity.

INCORPORATING
THE PRIMAL ANDROGYNE

One of the clearest arguments for rabbinic resistance to the surrounding discourse of the body is the Rabbis' citation of that discourse while

7. For discussion of this matter, see Chapter 5 below.
8. See Mopsik (1989, 50). See, however, n. 3 above, concerning the important
qualification of this point by Verna Harrison.

significantly modifying its meaning. The myth of a primal androgyne was widespread in late antiquity, particularly among platonists in the Jewish (and eventually, Christian) traditions (Meeks 1973; Crouzel 1989, 94).[9] This myth is cited in Genesis Rabba, the earliest midrash on the first book of the bible.[10] The midrashic version is, however, significantly different from preceding and surrounding versions of the narrative. One of the motivations of this myth in the midrash is to harmonize the two different accounts of the creation of humanity contained in the first and second chapters of Genesis:

Genesis 1:27–28
[27] And God created the earth-creature[11] in His image; in the image of God, He created him; male and female He created them. [28] And God blessed them, and God said to them: Reproduce and fill the earth. . . .

Genesis 5:1–2
[1] This is the book of the Generations of Adam, on the day

Genesis 2:7 ff.
[7] And God formed the earth-creature of dust from the earth and breathed in its nostrils the breath of life, and the earth-creature became a living being. . . . [20] And the earth-creature gave names to all of the animals and the fowls of the air and all of the animals of the fields, but the earth-creature could not find any helper equal to it. [21] And God

9. See also Daube (1973, 71–89). I would like, however, to note that I think Daube errs in associating the rabbinic citation of the Septuagint as evidence for an early date for this myth in Jewish circles, an error repeated in Tov (1984) as well. Bereshit Rabba cites the Septuagint as reading the verse, "A male with orifices created He him," involving what is in the Hebrew a very slight emendation of "female" to "orifices." Daube (72–73) sees here a version of the primal androgyne myth, because he understands "orifices" here to refer to female genitals. The word, *nequvaw*, however, means no such thing. It is well attested in rabbinic Hebrew with the meaning of all of the bodily orifices, including specifically male ones, so that when the Mishna in Berakhot says that one who needs to attend to his orifices should not pray, it means simply a man or woman who needs to urinate! The Septuagint emendation, if it is authentic, would indicate a Hebrew text which tendentiously changed the verse from indicating simultaneous creation of male and female, whether as androgyne or not, to the single creation of a wholly male human. It may, nevertheless, perhaps be taken as evidence for the early date of the androgyne myth in that it seemingly seeks to refute it.

10. Genesis Rabba, from which this quotation comes, is the classic and most important midrash on Genesis. This interpretation appears in several parallel versions, for which see Theodor and Albeck (1965). As are all midrashic texts, Genesis Rabba is a collection of many different sayings from different Rabbis and different periods, edited however into a single, multi-vocal text in Palestine some time in the fifth century or so. Its closest cultural congeners are, accordingly, the Greek Fathers.

11. Following Trible (1978) and Bal (1987), I do not translate "adam" as man, but as earth-creature (at this stage) both to reproduce the pun of its name: adam/adama (earth) and to avoid prejudging the question of its gender.

that God created Adam in the image of God He made him. [2] Male and female He created them, and He blessed them, and called their name Adam, on the day He created them.

caused a deep sleep to fall on the earth-creature, and it slept, and He took one of its ribs and closed the flesh beneath it. [22] And the Lord God constructed the rib which He had taken from the earth-creature into a woman and brought her to the earth-man.[12] [23] And the earth-man said, this time this one is bone of my bone and flesh of my flesh. She shall be called wo-man, for from man was she taken.

In the first story it seems clear that the original creation of the human species included both sexes, while the second suggests an original male creature for whom a female was created out of his flesh. The contradiction presents a classic hermeneutic problem.

The Spiritual Androgyne: Philo

In the interpretation of Philo, the first Adam is an entirely spiritual being, whose non-corporeal existence can be defined as both male and female. The second chapter introduces a carnal Adam, who is at first ungendered or male and then from whom the female is constructed.[13] Bodily gender is thus twice displaced from the origins of "man." Further, in this reading, the creation of Eve, and thus sexuality itself, rehearses the Fall (Bloch 1987, 10):

> "It is not good that any man should be alone," For there are two races
> of men, the one made after the (Divine) Image, and the one molded out
> of the earth. . . . With the second man a helper is associated. To begin
> with, the helper is a created one, for it says "Let us make a helper for
> him": and in the next place, is subsequent to him who is to be helped,
> for He had formed the mind before and is about to form its helper.
>
> (Bloch 1929b, 227)

---

12. Again, I am following Bal (1987) on this. If the earth-creature is sexually undifferentiated (in one way or another), only the production of a woman turns it into a man.

13. The ambiguity, indeed the contradiction, in my own discourse between referring to the first Adam as "male" and as "ungendered" is no accident. If there is no other sex, then there is no gender, so Adam is ungendered. On the other hand, when Adam refers to "his" situation before the creation of Eve, he remembers himself as male. See Bal (1987) and Boyarin (1990d).

Philo is resolving the hermeneutical contradiction. He here[14] regards the two stories as referring to two entirely different creative acts of God and accordingly to the production of two different races of "man."[15] Because the texts, Genesis 1 and Genesis 2, refer to two entirely different species, he can claim that only the first species is identified as "in the image of God"—that is, only the singular, unbodied Adam-creature is in God's likeness, in which context its male-and-femaleness must be understood spiritually. In other words, the designation of *this* creature as male-and-female means really neither male nor female. The verse "It is not good that a man be alone" is understood in accordance with both species of man, the purely spiritual, androgynous one and the embodied, male one. For the first, the verse has the allegorical significance of the necessity of the soul for God; with reference to the second, the text says that a helper is necessary. Another passage of Philo is explicit on this point:

> After this he says that "God formed man by taking clay from the earth, and breathed into his face the breath of life" (Gen. ii. 7). By this also he shows very clearly that there is a vast difference between the man thus formed and the man that came into existence earlier after the image of God: for the man so formed is an object of sense-perception, partaking already of such or such quality, consisting of body and soul, man or woman, by nature mortal; while he that was after the Image was an idea or type or seal, an object of thought, incorporeal, neither male nor female, by nature incorruptible.
>
> (Philo 1929, 107)

The second story refers, then, to humanity as we know it, and "woman" is explicitly marked as supplement. This double creation provides Philo with one of his sources for platonic "ideas" in the work of Moses, who according to Philo anticipated Plato's philosophy (Tobin 1983, 132).[16]

Philo's interpretation is not an idiosyncrasy. As Thomas Tobin has shown, Philo refers to a tradition he already knows (1983, 32; see also Mack 1984, 243). The fundamental point is that for the Hellenistic Jews, the oneness of pure spirit is ontologically privileged in the constitution of

14. Philo contradicts himself on this point in several places. I am not interested here in sorting out Philo's different interpretations and their sources. Moreover, this has been very well done already in Tobin (1983). My interest here is in how the reading given here enters into a certain tradition of discourse on the body.

15. For further discussion of this passage in the writings of Philo and his followers, see Tobin (1983, 108–19) and Jeremy Cohen (1989, 74–76 and 228).

16. My friend and colleague Albert Baumgarten reminded me of this point.

humanity. Fraade elegantly summarizes this platonic Jewish anthropology in its relation to Philo: "Philo inherits from Plato a radically dualistic conception of the universe. In this view, the material world of sense perception is an imperfect reflection of the intelligible order which emanates from God. The human soul finds its fulfillment through separation from the world of material desires, a world that lacks true reality, and through participation in the life of the spirit and divine intellect; the soul finally reunites *the true self* with its divine source and thereby achieves immortality" (Fraade 1986, 263–64; emphasis added). If the primal state is one of spiritual androgyny, in which male-and-female means neither male nor female, this fulfillment entails the return to a state of non-corporeal androgyny—a notion with social consequences for Philo, which he presents in an image of perfected human life.

In his *On the Contemplative Life*, Philo describes a Jewish sect called the Therapeutae that lived in his time on the shores of Lake Mareotis near Alexandria. The tone of his depiction of this sect and its practice makes clear that he considers it an ideal religious community. The fellowship consisted of celibate men and women who lived in individual cells and spent their lives in prayer and contemplative study of allegorical interpretations of scripture (like the ones that Philo produced). Once a year, the community came together for a remarkable ritual celebration. Following a simple meal and a discourse, all of the celebrants began to sing hymns together. Initially, the men and the women remained separate from each other in two choruses, but as the celebration became more ecstatic, the men and the women joined to form one chorus, "the treble of the women blending with the bass of the men."[17] The model of an ecstatic joining of the male and the female in a mystical ritual re-creates in social practice the image of the purely spiritual masculo-feminine first human of which Philo speaks in his commentary; indeed, this ritual of the Therapeutae is a return to the originary Adam (Meeks 1973, 179).[18]

17. An article by Ross Kraemer (1989) is the most recent and fullest description of the Therapeutae.

18. This hypothesis explains the otherwise seemingly unmotivated reference in Philo's text to the *Symposium* of Plato and especially to Aristophanes's story of double-creatures (not necessarily androgynes by any means) at the origins of humanity. Philo is counterposing to this "abhorrent" image of physically double bodies an ideal one of spiritually dual humans. Philo's reversal will be double-reversed in part by the Rabbis, as I argue below.

Regardless of whether or not the community of Therapeutae ever re-ally existed, the description is testimony to Philo's translation of anthro-pology into social practice. If the community did exist, we have further evidence that Philo is representative of larger religious traditions and groups. But whether Philo's Therapeutae were actual or only ideal, there certainly were many other groups throughout the early Christian world that believed that the first human being was a non-corporeal androgyne, and that "male and female" of Genesis 1:27 meant really "neither male nor female." Not surprisingly, such groups, whether gnostic, Encratite, or "Orthodox" Syrian Christians, all held to a rigid celibate ideal. Dennis Macdonald has documented how widespread among them was an (apoc-ryphal?) Dominical saying to the effect that salvation in Christ consisted of putting off the garments of shame (the body and sexuality), "making the two one," and erasing the distinction between male and female (Mac-donald 1987 and 1988). The loss of virginity parallels the Fall, represent-ing a descent from or disturbance to the oneness of perfection. As Meeks puts it, "Baptism restores the initiate to the virginal innocence of Adam, who had 'no understanding of the begetting of children'" (1973, 194).[19] Such notions, widespread in early Christianity, underlie the near-universal privileging of celibacy and virginity in all branches of the early church, however much they differed in that privilege's extent.

There was, to be sure, extraordinary variety in the views on sexuality and marriage among the ancient Christians—ranging from extreme con-demnation to warm appreciation (Jeremy Cohen 1989, 221–70). The most extreme Montanists and others like them denied the lawfulness of sex and marriage entirely. For them, the "male and female" of Genesis 1:27 could only be understood allegorically or as referring to the androg-yny of the disembodied spirit. Less extreme ancient Christian authors also interpreted it in this fashion. Thus, Origen held a view of the dual crea-tion quite similar to that of Philo. The anthropos of Genesis 1 consisted of pure soul created after the image of God (Crouzel 1989, 94), but *"differ-entiation within the human species subverted that primal perfection"* (Jeremy Cohen 1989, 236). Origen permitted marriage, "yet a whole series of texts

19. Meeks has discussed Gnostic rituals which consist of a reconstitution of the androgyny of the first human and moreover considered the interpretation of various Pauline passages in their light in his excellent paper (Meeks 1973, 188–96). I have purposely omitted any discussion of Paul in this section, because the interpretation of his doctrine is so contested.

sees an impurity in sexual relations even when they are legitimated by marriage" (Crouzel 1989, 138).[20] On the other hand, Clement and others who supported marriage against the Encratites cited the verse "Male and female created He them" as prefiguring the creation of woman and therefore as endorsing marriage (Alexandre 1988, 198). Similarly, somewhat later, John Chrysostom wrote with great enthusiasm of the creation of humanity in two sexes and of sexual desire and intercourse as restoration of the "male and female" of Genesis and even of the "neither male nor female" of Galatians 3:28 (1986, 43). Many of the formulations of Chrysostom's later writings on sexual desire and marriage are nearly indistinguishable from those of the Rabbis: "From the beginning God has been revealed as the fashioner, by His providence, of this union of man and woman, and He has spoken of the two as one: 'male and female He created them' and 'there is neither male nor female.' There is never such intimacy between a man and a man as there is between husband and wife, if they are united as they ought to be." And perhaps even more movingly, "But suppose there is no child; do they then remain two and not one? No; their intercourse effects the joining of their bodies, and they are made one, just as when perfume is mixed with ointment" (1986, 76).[21]

But even those Fathers who were in this latter category privileged virginity over marriage as the higher state (Jeremy Cohen 1989, 231–35, 237–38, 243–44). Clement was the most friendly of the Fathers toward marriage, but "when he set out his own matrimonial ideal, it amounted to sexless marriage, lived as if between a brother and a sister" (Fox 1987, 359; but see Ford 1989, 21). Also Gregory Nazianzen, in the midst of precisely an encomium to marriage, says "I will join you in wedlock. I will dress the bride. We do not dishonour marriage, because we give a higher honour to virginity" (quoted in Ford 1989, 25). The same John Chrysostom who so warmly and movingly praised desire and the intimacy of husband and wife remained a virgin and highly valued the virgin life over the married state, while the Rabbis disallowed virginity in principle.[22] As

---

20. See also Peter Brown's magnificent chapter on Origen (Brown 1988, 160–78).

21. See also Ford (1989, 43–49). See, however, next note.

22. I am quite convinced by Ford's description of the later John Chrysostom's ideology of sexuality that his mature view was not very different from that of the Rabbis (Ford 1989, 49 and passim), but, once again it is important to note that despite all that, Chrysostom himself was celibate, and as Ford notes, "he continued all his life to consider a life of virginity in dedication to God as an even higher calling" (73).

close as some of these Fathers come to the Rabbis in their appreciation, then, of human sexuality, there remains an irreducible kernel of difference in the anthropologies. The difference is not so much, sometimes, in the ethics as in the fundamental understanding of human essence.

The Corporeal Androgyne: Palestinian Midrash

Palestinian midrash also knows and cites the myth of a primeval androgyne as a solution to the contradiction of the two creation stories in Genesis, but it metamorphoses the meaning and virtually reverses the understanding of the myth. According to these midrashic texts, the primordial Adam was a dual-sexed creature in one body.[23] The story in the second chapter is the story of the splitting off of the two equal halves of an originary body:

> And God said let us make a human etc. . . . . R. Yermia the son of
> El'azar interpreted: When the Holiness (Be it Blessed) created the
> first human, He created him androgynous, for it says, "Male and female
> created He them."[24] R. Samuel the son of Nahman said: When the
> Holiness (Be it Blessed) created the first human, He made it two-faced,
> then He sawed it and made a back for this one and a back for that one.
> They objected to him: but it says, "He took one of his ribs (*tsela'*)." He

---

23. Neither Daube (1973), Meeks (1973, 185), Stiegman (1977, 517), nor Macdonald (1987, 38) seems to have sensed how different the rabbinic androgyne myth is from that of Philo and the Gnostics. On the other hand, Daube (1973, 71–73) makes a very convincing case for reading Mark 19:3 ff. as based on the androgynous interpretation of this verse, arguing that Jesus's "What God has put together, let no man put asunder" is only intelligible on that reading. If his proposal be accepted then Jesus certainly understood the primal androgyne as a physical one, as did the Rabbis somewhat later. On the other hand, while Idel (1989, 211–12) well understands the implications of the spiritual androgyny of Gnosticism and some "Orthodox" Christian imagery, he does not see that Philo is very close to this view as well. Moreover, again, while he clearly understands how different rabbinic sex ideology was from that which longed for a restoration of an asexual androgyny, he does not cite the midrash from which this point can be most clearly supported, namely the one treated here.

24. The inconsistencies in the pronouns in the translation of this sentence reflect ambiguities that I perceive in the text (and the culture). On the one hand, there is virtually no question that the appellation of God usually translated as "The Holy One, Blessed be He" is so mistranslated, for the term translated "Holy One" means literally "Holiness," as proven by Ancient Aramaic renditions of this formula. On the other hand, it is very difficult to use the pronoun "it" with reference to God, as I think the culture did imagine "Him" as male (with female attributes).

answered [that it means], "one of his sides," similarly to that which is written, "And the side (*tsela͑*) of the tabernacle" [Exod. 26:20].

(Theodor and Albeck 1965,
54–55)

In this text, we have two accounts of the origin of the sexes of humanity. The first interpretation is that the first human, the one called "the adam," was androgynous. It had genitals of both sexes, and the act of creation described in Genesis 2 merely separated out the two sexes from each other and reconstructed them into two human bodies. The second statement (that of Rabbi Samuel) seems best understood as a specification and interpretation of the first, namely that the first human was like a pair of Siamese twins who were then separated by a surgical procedure. Both of these interpretations use Greek terminology (*androgynos, dyprosōpos*) to describe the original two-sexed (or two-faced) Adam, and, as usual, the use of the "alien" word is not culturally innocent.

The myth of the first human as androgyne, which is mocked in Plato's *Symposium,* is of course well known from Greek literature as old as the pre-Socratic Empedocles (Macdonald 1987, 25). The Rabbis, however, were much more likely to have encountered the myth in the form in which it became widely known among both Jews and Gentiles in late antiquity: the myth of the spiritual, primal androgyne. For Philo and his congeners, as we have seen, the return to the original state of humankind involves a putting off of the body and sexuality and returning to a purely spiritual androgyny (Macdonald 1988, 282–85, and King 1988, 165). Those Rabbis for whom the original state of physical androgyny was divided to create the two separate sexes believed that the physical union of man and wife restores the image of the original whole human.[25] What my reading proposes is the rabbinic usage of a topos of Hellenistic Jewish culture to reverse its meaning. The very allusion to the surrounding culture signals resistance to it.

The interpretation that the first human was an androgyne later split into two bodies is explicitly motivated by the same hermeneutic issue that led to Philo's interpretation: the desire to render the two accounts

25. Compare Augustine who "grants woman humanity as long as she is joined by a man, 'so the whole substance may be one image.' Marriage becomes a prerequisite for women's humanity. A single woman remains essentially incomplete. The male, on the other hand, represents the divine by himself" (von Kellenbach 1990, 207). I am *not* suggesting that Augustine's position represents all of Christianity.

coherent and produce them as a single narrative. But in addition to the widespread midrashic view that Primal Adam was a physical androgyne, we also find readings that take him to be a male, from whom the female was created, as in our Western culture's more familiar interpretations of the story:

> *And He took one of his ribs/sides (tsela*ᶜ*)*: Rabbi Samuel the son of Nahman says, "one of his sides, as you say *and the side (tsela*ᶜ*) of the Tabernacle on the North"* [Exod. 26:20]. And Shmuel said, "He took a rib from between two of his ribs."
>
> (Theodor and Albeck 1965, 157)

First, the reading of Rabbi Samuel the son of Nahman is recapitulated in brief, namely that the first human was androgynous and the so-called rib was really a side. But then this view is challenged by Shmuel, who understands the rib as a rib and therefore holds that the first human was male and the woman was a secondary creation. All of the Rabbis assume that the two accounts describe the creation of one kind of humanity, not two kinds. According to the Talmud, Shmuel, who holds that woman was not created at the beginning, understands the verse "Male and female created He them" to indicate that it was God's *intention* to create both male and female at the beginning. Indeed, because the Rabbis' non-dualist anthropology precludes a theory of dual creation such as Philo's, there is no other way to read the verse. Thus even Shmuel, who does interpret the woman as a secondary construction, understands sexuality and difference to be essential rather than supplemental to the constitution of the human. The traditional rabbinic marriage ceremony, in which the following blessings are chanted, also follows the "rib" version of the story and understands sexuality as essential:

> [Blessed art thou, O Lord King of the Universe,] who created the Adam in his image, in the image of the likeness of his form, and constructed for him, from him, an eternal construction. Blessed art thou, O Lord, the creator of humanity.
>
> The Barren Woman will be exceedingly joyful and glad when she gathers her children into her with happiness. Blessed art thou, O Lord, who makes Zion happy in her children.
>
> Make happy the loving friends, as you made your creature happy in the Garden of Eden in the beginning. Blessed art thou, O Lord, who makes the groom and bride happy.
>
> Blessed art thou, O Lord King of the Universe, who has created joy and happiness, groom and bride, bliss, rejoicing, elation and cheer, love, brotherhood, peace and friendship. Quickly, O Lord, our God,

> may there be heard in the hills of Judea the voice of joy and voice of
> happiness, the voice of the singing of bridegrooms from their bridal
> chambers and youths from their marriage celebrations. Blessed art thou,
> O Lord, who makes the groom rejoice with his bride.

This ritual text is a reading of the creation of gender and sex that is narrated in Genesis. Like Philo's ritual of the Therapeutae, it is a translation
into explicit social practice of the interpretative moment encompassed by
midrash. In the first of the blessings, God is thanked for making Adam
and then, from him, Eve. In the second blessing, abandoned Zion is figured as a barren woman. In the third, a prayer is said for the newly married couple, that they should be as happy together as Adam was at the
creation of Eve. The final moment of the ritual is the declaration that
God makes the groom rejoice with his bride. This "rejoicing," which certainly refers to the sexual act (Anderson 1989, 133–36), is that for which
God is being praised and thanked in the entire ceremony. It is in the joyful union of husband and wife that the happiness that God vouchsafed his
creature in the Garden of Eden is to be restored, for a moment in the
present and forever at the eschaton. And at the eschaton, as well, this
union will be the site and marker of the greatest redemption. If such a
celebratory attitude toward married sex is maintained even by a text that
adheres to the view that Eve was created second, how much more so do
we expect it according to the more common rabbinic view that Eve and
Adam (or at any rate, their genitals) were both contained physically in
the first human being.

In the rabbinic culture, the human race is thus marked from the very
beginning by corporeality, difference, and heterogeneity. For the Rabbis,
sexuality belongs to the original created (and not fallen) state of humanity. Humanity did not fall from a metaphysical condition, nor is there any
Fall into sexuality in rabbinic Judaism (Pardes 1989). The midrashic reading of the text cited above presents the originary human person as dual-
sexed, as two sexes joined in one body. The splitting of the androgynous
body ordains sexuality:

> Therefore a man leaves his father and his mother
> and cleaves to his woman
> and they become one flesh

There is nothing in the biblical text or in our midrashic reading of it that
indicates that marriage is either a Fall or a concession. The definitive rabbinic statement on marriage is from Genesis Rabba:

And God said, it is not good for the man to be alone: it has been taught:
one who has no wife remains without good, without help, without joy,
without blessing, and without atonement. . . . *R. Hiyya the son of Gu-
madi said, also he is not a complete human, for it says, "And He blessed
them and called their name, Adam"*[26] [Gen. 5:2]. And there are those
who say that he even decreases the likeness [of God], for it says, "In the
image of God, He made the Adam" [Gen. 9:6], and what does it say
after this? "And as for you, be fruitful and multiply" [Gen. 9:7].

(Theodor and Albeck 1965, 152)

This midrashic text explicitly grounds the Rabbis' ideology of marriage in
their interpretation of the creation stories of Genesis. The telos of marriage is a return to the condition of completeness or even of *imago dei* in
the act of marriage that reconstructs the Divine Image in which the original androgyne was created.[27] No wonder, then, that Augustine and other
Christian writers would make reference to this difference between Judaism and Christianity and consider the Jews "indisputably carnal."

THE RABBIS ON SEX:
PALESTINE AND BABYLONIA

The Jews disdained the beauty of virginity, which is not surprising,
since they heaped ignominy upon Christ himself, who was born of a
virgin. The Greeks admired and revered the virgin, but only the
Church of God adored her with zeal.

(John Chrysostom,
On Virginity 1,1)

In this passage the fourth-century Father represents the basic difference
between rabbinic Judaism and Christianity, as well as the Greek origins of
the valorization of virginity. Once again, I would claim, this sensibility is
grounded in cultural reality. Marriage is the positively marked term in
rabbinic culture, while virginity is marked as negative. Within this frame-

---

26. Emphasis mine. Here we have the most clear antithesis to the view held by
some Christian thinkers that only the virgin is a complete human. Whatever can be
said about the "status" of women in rabbinic Judaism, "woman" is not essentialized as
lack (as in Freud, e.g.), but as the fulfillment of lack. I will come back to this in
Chapter 3 and again in the conclusion, but meanwhile see duBois (1988).

27. Another take on this would be that procreation is the *imago dei*. Other rabbinic texts would certainly interpret that way.

work, however, there is a range of ideologies toward sexuality among the talmudic Rabbis. At one extreme is Rabbi Eliezer, who is said to have made love to his wife "as if being forced to by a demon, uncovering an inch (of her body) and immediately covering it again." He held that sex was only for procreation. His view on sexuality is closest to that of Clement, the most positive of the Fathers on sexuality (Clement 1989a, 259–63; Brown 1988, 133). Each of the cultures should be seen not as a monologic language but as a heteroglossic collection of dialects. However, the range of possibility within the two formations is different. Sexual renunciation is simply not an option in the rabbinic cultural formation and ideology. But for some early Rabbis in Palestine, a kind of ascetic sexual practice was possible. Their practice represents the rabbinic Judaism closest in appearance to the Hellenistic Judaisms of Philo and Paul. In fact, a fair amount of evidence suggests that the Palestinian Judaism of the Rabbis of the second and third centuries most closely approaches (but does not merge with) the ideology of sexuality of the Hellenized Jews, while as we move further in time and space from that moment, we also move further from that ideology.

Historical Variation in the Rabbinic Discourse of Sexuality

As I have mentioned, the rabbinic figure who seemed most negative on sex was Rabbi Eliezer (that is, the figure of Rabbi Eliezer as portrayed in much rabbinic writing, which may or may not be historically accurate). The story of how he had intercourse with his wife is a locus classicus for ascetic sexual practice:

> They asked Imma Shalom [Mother Peace], the wife of Rabbi Eliezer, "Why do you have such beautiful children?" She said to them, "He does not have intercourse with me at the beginning of the night, nor at the end of the night, but at midnight, and when he has intercourse with me, he unveils an inch and veils it again, and appears as if he was driven by a demon."
>
> (Babylonian Talmud Nedarim 20a)

The story represents a highly negative attitude toward sexual pleasure. Rabbi Eliezer's behavior as if driven by a demon apparently represents his conviction that he is fulfilling an obligation that should not be enjoyed but should be performed as quickly as possible. The text presents a point of view (similar to that of the Stoics, Philo, and Clement, among others) that sex is legitimate, but only for procreation, and when procreation is the sole rationale for sex, then the reward is beautiful children.[28] Rabbi Eliezer is strongly attracted to asceticism as a religious model—the same asceticism that characterized the life of the Hellenistic philosophical schools—but as a Rabbi he could not choose celibacy. The fact that he was married, despite such an ascetic personality, only strengthens this argument.

Rabbi Eliezer's point of view, however, is only one pole of the dialectic of the discourse of sexuality in marriage in rabbinic literature. If it is possible to interpret the represented views of this Rabbi as David Biale has done—"The goal . . . was a marriage in which a man could fulfill his procreative duties while remaining loyal to an ascetic sexual ideal" (Biale 1989, 26)—it is certainly not possible to follow Biale and regard this asceticism in general as the "goal of the Rabbis," for even in Palestinian stories Rabbi Eliezer is presented as an extreme figure, and in Babylonian talmudic texts his practice is sharply rejected. As Biale himself points out, the story's implied prescription to wear clothes while having intercourse is vigorously contested by a Babylonian talmudic statement:

> Rav Yosef cited a tannaitic tradition, "*Flesh:* This means the intimacy of the flesh, namely that he should not behave with her in the manner of the Persians, who make love while dressed." This supports the view of Rav Huna, for Rav Huna said, "One who says, I do not desire it unless she is in her clothing and I in mine, must divorce his wife and pay her the marriage settlement."
>
> (Ketubbot 48a)[29]

28. The continuation of the story, however, renders this interpretation problematic:

I asked him, "What is the reason [for this strange behavior]?" And he said to me, "In order that I not imagine another woman, and the children will come to be bastards."

Reading this text carefully, we see that it is not at all an unambiguous representation of a negative attitude toward sexuality. While Rabbi Eliezer's behavior certainly would have had the effect of reducing dramatically the pleasure of sex, it is not presented as having that intention, but rather as being the expression in practice of a severe rabbinic prohibition on having sex with a woman that one does not fully desire or of fantasizing about another partner during sex. My student, Dr. Dalia Hoshen, first made me aware of this dimension of interpretation of this story in her doctoral dissertation on the religious personality of Rabbi Eliezer. For a fuller exposition of this reading of the text, see Chapter 4 below.

29. It is relevant to note that the Babylonian Talmud Berakhot 8b has Rabban Gamaliel, the first-century Palestinian Pharisee, citing the Persians as appropriate models for sexual behavior. If that tradition be authentically Palestinian in origin

Among the three debts that a man owes his wife are "her flesh, her cover-ing, and her seasons" (Exod. 21:10). While the last is normally under-stood to mean sexual relations and the first to mean food, Rav Yosef the Babylonian knows of a tannaitic tradition (*perhaps* of Palestinian origin but not cited in Palestinian texts) that interprets the first term to mean bodily intimacy, the touching of skin during sexual intercourse, and he interprets this to mean nudity during sex. Further evidence for this differ-ence between Palestine and Babylonia can be adduced from the fact that in a Palestinian text, Rabbi Shim'on the son of Yohai is reported to have said that God hates one who has intercourse naked (Wayyiqra Rabba 21:8), while in the Babylonian version of precisely the same statement, this has been changed to one who has intercourse in front of any creature (Babylonian Talmud Nidda 17a; see below Chapter 4, discussion of this passage). Whatever the views of some of the Palestinian tannaim, such views were certainly not characteristic of the ethos of all of rabbinic Judaism. The pattern of an earlier asceticism replaced later (and espe-cially in Babylonia) by an anti-ascetic discourse of sexuality can be found in several other passages of the talmudic literature. One of the clearest signs of early Palestinian ambivalence about the body and sexuality is the talmudic discussion of requisite immersion in a ritual bath before resum-ing the study of Torah after sex:[30]

> Rabbi Yehoshua the son of Levi said: How do we know that those who have had a seminal emission may not study Torah, for it says *And you shall make them known to your children* [Deut. 4:9], and He appended to it: *The day on which you stood before the Lord, your God at Horev:* Just as there, those who had had seminal emissions were forbidden, so here, those who have had seminal emissions are forbidden.
>
> (Berakhot 21b)

Rabbi Yehoshua the son of Levi draws an analogy between the receiving of the Torah on Mt. Sinai and the study of Torah for all of the genera-tions. Just as the Jews were commanded not to have sexual intercourse for three days before receiving of Torah, so one who has had sex or another seminal emission is forbidden to study Torah until purifying himself by immersion in a ritual bath.

(even if not belonging to Rabban Gamaliel), it is fascinating to see that the Sassanian Rabbis resisted and opposed a practice of their surroundings, while precisely the dis-tant Palestinians approved of it.

30. For an alternative reading of this material see Eilberg-Schwartz (1989).

The Talmud, however (after some further discussion of this point irrelevant to our purposes), indicates unambiguously that the requirement of
immersion in a ritual bath after sex was later abrogated. The anxiety
about sexuality that was manifested by such an idea of impurity was incompatible with later rabbinic sensibilities around the body:

> It is taught: Rabbi Yehuda the son of Betayra used to say: "The words
> of Torah are not susceptible to impurity." There was a case of a student
> who was hesitating to speak in the presence of Rabbi Yehuda the son
> of Betayra. He said to him: "My son, open your mouth and let your
> words be radiant, for the words of Torah are not susceptible to impu-
> rity, for it says *Behold my words are like fire; a speech of the Lord* [Jer.
> 23:29]. Just as fire is unsusceptible to impurity, so the words of Torah
> are unsusceptible to impurity." . . . Rav Nahman the son of Yitzhaq
> says: "The community is accustomed to follow the view of that vener-
> able sage Rabbi Yehuda the son of Betayra with regard to the words of
> Torah, in accordance with what Rabbi Yehuda the son of Betayra has
> said, 'The words of Torah are not susceptible to impurity.'" When Zeiri
> came, he said: "They have rescinded immersion, in accordance with
> the view of Rabbi Yehuda the son of Betayra."

The early Palestinian authority Rabbi Yehuda ben Betayra is represented
as having opposed the entire principle of immersion after sex and before
the study of Torah. He gives a technical midrashic reading in support of
his position, arguing that since the words of Torah are like fire, they cannot be made impure by contact with an impure person, and that there is
no reason for one made impure by seminal emission to refrain from the
study of Torah. Passing through fire is one of the ways that objects become pure in rabbinic law, so the Torah would purify the one who studies
it. The prohibition against the study of Torah in this state of impurity,
however, did not have a technical basis in the laws of purity. Rather, it
was based on a moral/psychological foundation: as the Torah had been
received in a state of full concentration on spirituality, so also should it be
studied. Otherwise, it would be impossible to understand why menstruating women whose state of technical impurity is identical to that of men
who have had a seminal emission (or, if anything, more severe) would be
permitted to study Torah without immersion, a point made at several
junctures in the Palestinian literature (see below, p. 180). Furthermore,
by the talmudic period, cultic impurity had been abrogated because of the
destruction of the Temple. Clearly, then, the belief that a man must
immerse after sex was not held on the basis of technical, cultic impurity
but because of a sense that sex was somehow incompatible with holy

activity. It follows, therefore, that Rabbi Yehuda ben Betayra's objection to the requirement of immersion before Torah-study constitutes a rejection of the moral notion that the earlier Palestinian text represented. Strong support was later given to his view by the Babylonian authority Rabbi Nahman the son of Yitzhaq and the Palestinian tradition of Rabbi Zeiri. These later traditions indicate the shift in sensibility that took place diachronically—a shift that the text renders explicit by saying that the earlier practice had been abrogated. To have had sex was no longer held an obstacle to fully serious Torah-study, any more than menstruating had been such an obstacle earlier in Palestine. I suggest that it is much more plausible to interpret this change as evidence for differing discourses of sexuality than for a shift in the status of Torah.

Further evidence of the incompatibility between enthusiastic acceptance of sexuality and the requirement of immersion after any seminal emission can be seen in a very curious report of earlier attempts to ameliorate (perhaps) the effects of the requirement of immersion after sex on the love-lives of Torah-scholars. The Talmud continues with the following account:

> The Rabbis have taught: One who has had an emission upon whom nine pecks of water is poured is pure. Nahum the man of Gamzu whispered it to Rabbi Akiva who whispered it to Ben-Azzai who went out and taught it in the marketplace.
>
> Two amoraim [the later authorities] disagreed about it in the West [Palestine], namely Rabbi Yose the son of Avin and Rabbi Yose the son of Zevida. One teaches it "taught it" and one "whispered it." The one who says "taught it," says [that he did so to prevent] the neglect of Torah-study and the neglect of procreation, while the one who says "whispered it," so that the Torah-scholars will not be at their wives like roosters.

It is hard to imagine a more perfect representation of ambivalence. Either Ben-Azzai went out into the marketplace and declared that one need only take a shower after sex in order to study Torah, or he did the opposite, and whispered it as his teachers had done. Either he was trying to prevent scholars from neglecting either the Torah or their sexual obligations, or he was trying to prevent them from having sex too often. In any case, this text renders explicit the tension between seminal pollution, on the one hand, and affirmation of sexuality on the other.[31] The Talmud

---

31. In Chapter 4 below, I will make explicit my reasons for glossing "procreation" as "sexuality" in describing this culture.

leaves this question open, but the later halakha is codified in accord with the view of Rabbi Yehuda ben Betayra, supported by Rav Nahman the son of Yitzhaq, that the whole matter of seminal impurity is irrelevant for the study of Torah. We have seen evidence for a highly ambivalent set of notions about sex on the part of early Palestinian authorities and the reduction of that ambivalence in the later rabbinic (especially Babylonian) period. We will find this pattern repeated in other texts as well.

Some early Palestinian authorities seem to hold a highly ironic, ambivalent stance toward sexuality. One of the most colorful expressions of this stance is the utterance of the Palestinian Resh Lakish cited (and contested) in the Babylonian Talmud: "Said Resh Lakish, 'Come let us be grateful to our ancestors, for had they not sinned we would not have come into the world, for it says *I said, you are all angels and heavenly creatures, but you have spoiled your behavior; therefore like Adam you will die* [Ps. 82:6]'" (Babylonian Talmud Avoda Zara 5a). Resh Lakish's gnomon is subtle and complex. At first glance it seems to encode a highly negative marking for sexuality, allowing it place only insofar as it leads to procreation; it is similar, then, to the ideologies of Philo and Clement. But careful reading reveals a more complicated and sophisticated meaning. First, it is vital to realize that Resh Lakish's statement says nothing direct about sexuality at all. The psalm that he cites refers only to social evils, such as mistreatment of the poor in courts that favor the wicked rich. Resh Lakish can be understood to mean only that we should be grateful to our ancestors who sinned (not through sexuality) and, by sinning, brought death into the world, for without death there would be no generation, and we would not exist. Read this way, Resh Lakish does not explicitly call sexual intercourse sin. By seemingly understanding, however, that before the sin the ancestors were like angels, did not die, and *therefore* did not procreate, his apothegm nevertheless strongly encodes the association of sexuality with sin and death that lies at the bottom of Christian notions about the Fall and Original Sin. Even given this, however, Resh Lakish's utterance is hardly Christian in spirit, in its affirmation of having come into the world. It is hard to imagine an early Christian writer arguing that we should be grateful to Adam and Eve for having sinned. The Babylonian Talmud did not accept, however, even these tenuous or ironic associations, for it continues:

> Shall we say that had they not sinned, they would not have procreated? But it says, *And as for you, be fruitful and multiply*. Until Sinai. But

[that cannot be correct, because] at Sinai it also says, *Return to your tents*, [which means] for the joy of intercourse. . . . Do not say, We would not have come into the world, but it would be as if we had not come into the world,

which the eleventh-century commentator Rashi glosses, "For they would have lived forever, and as long as they live, we would not have been significant at all." The Babylonian Talmud could tolerate neither the ironic, ascetic implication of Resh Lakish's original statement, nor the possible associations it had with Christian doctrine. To escape such implications, the Talmud distorted his obvious meaning and provided us with some precious evidence for an alternative view of sexuality in the phrase "the joy of intercourse." In opposition to one rabbinic view (which held that sex was only for procreation), there was another view that strongly encoded a value for sexual pleasure in its own right. This hardly fits Brown's characterization of sexuality for "the Rabbis" as "an irritating but necessary aspect of existence."

Certain rabbinic texts, moreover, recognize the emotional value of married sex. Thus, when a decision must be made about whether consummation is necessary for the contraction of a valid marriage, it is made in the following terms: "Ravin asked, if she entered the marriage canopy but has not had intercourse, what is the law? Does the fondness of the marriage canopy effect the marriage or the fondness of intercourse?" (Babylonian Talmud Ketubbot 56a). Two things can be learned from this text. First, the validity of the speech-act of marrying is conditional upon a feeling of intimacy, and second, this feeling of intimacy is produced by—is one of the aims of—sexual intercourse.[32]

The strongest arguments that procreation was by no means the sole purpose of sex in rabbinic Judaism come from texts and situations in which the sex and procreation are differentiated or even in conflict with each

32. See Brown on Plutarch's notion of *charis*, "the 'graciousness' created by intercourse—that indefinable quality of mutual trust and affection gained through the pleasure of the bed itself," a notion as foreign, it would seem, to Philo as it was to Clement (Brown 1988, 133). Indeed, I would claim that the later rabbinic ethos of married love is very similar to the doctrine of Plutarch as described by Foucault (1986a, 207–08) even to the approving references to Solonic laws regarding the frequency of intercourse owed by a husband to a chaste wife as a "mark of esteem and affection," for which compare the Talmud Yevamot 62b, "Anyone who knows that his wife is God-fearing and does not sleep with her is called a sinner." See, however, Fox (1987, 349) for a somewhat different account of Plutarch's position.

other, as in the situation of the barren wife. In the following story, procreation and erotic companionship come into conflict, and love prevails:

> *We will rejoice and be happy with you* [Song of Songs 1:4]. There we
> have taught: If a man married a woman and remained with her for ten
> years and had no children, he is not permitted to refrain from procre-
> ation [i.e., he must divorce her and marry another].
>
> Said Rabbi Idi: There was a case of a woman in Sidon, who remained
> ten years with her husband and did not give birth. They came before
> Rabbi Shimon the son of Yohai; they wanted to get divorced one from
> the other. He said to them, "On your lives—just as you got married
> with feasting and drinking, so shall you separate in feasting and drink-
> ing." They followed his suggestion, and they made for themselves a fes-
> tival and a banquet, and she got him too drunk. When his sensibility
> returned to him, he said, "My daughter, choose any precious object of
> mine that is in the house, and take it with you when you go to your
> father's house." What did she do? When he was asleep, she told her
> manservants and maidservants and said to them, "Pick him up in the
> bed, and take him to Father's house." At midnight he woke up. When
> his wine had worn off, he said to her, "My daughter, where am I?" She
> said, "in Father's house." He said, "What am I doing in your father's
> house?" She said to him, "Did you not say to me this very evening,
> 'Any precious object which you have in your house, take and go to
> your father's house'? There is no object in the world which is more
> precious to me than you!" They went to Rabbi Shimon the son of
> Yohai. He stood and prayed for them, and they were remembered [she
> became pregnant].
>
> (Shir Hashirim Rabba 1:31)

There is one startling moment of narrative illogic in this otherwise perfectly constructed little tale. Why are we told that "she got him too
drunk," and then, "when his sensibility returned to him, he said . . ."?
What function did his drunkenness play, if all that we know about it is
that his sensibility returned to him afterwards, and why was it important
that he was *too* drunk? Note that it is impossible to understand this drunkenness as that which resulted in his being so sleepy that he didn't detect
that he was being first carried off, because that sleep takes place *after* he
has recovered from his drunkenness. I think that the most plausible way
to fill this gap is that the story delicately hints that they made love while
he was drunk, and that during intercourse they realized that they loved
each other too much to allow the halakha to separate them. This seems
to have been her plan, for after all, "she made him *too* drunk," too drunk

to resist. Moreover, this seems to have been the Rabbi's plan. Otherwise, what was his intention in suggesting that they make a marriage feast to celebrate their divorce? Indeed, the very language he uses is suggestive, for he says literally, "Just as you coupled with feasting, so shall you sepa-rate with feasting," the word "coupled" (*nizdavagtem*) having direct con-notations of sexual intercourse. To be sure, he may not have predicted how clever the wife would be in achieving the goal, or what the means would be, but the story only makes sense if the Rabbi was trying by gentle means and indirection to deflect them from their pious path of divorce. But whether or not this reading is accepted, the text is opposing "love" to procreation as the telos of marriage, and it is love that prevails. It goes without saying that the story, considering the context, must recuper-ate the halakha by the deus ex machina of the miraculous pregnancy at the end, but by returning to each other for however long it took for the Rabbi's prayers to work, the husband and wife had already violated the halakha, and the teller of the tale clearly approves. This legend may encode a moment of tension between a voice for which procreation was perceived as the sole or the overridingly important telos of marriage and one for which companionship was becoming increasingly important. This tension would bear some typological similarity to the development in the Roman world documented by Paul Veyne: "In the old civic code, the wife was nothing but an accessory to the work of the citizen and paterfamilias. She produced children and added to the family patrimony. In the new code, the wife was a friend, a 'life's companion'" (1987, 37).[33] In point of historical fact, the Jewish practice did change, and the halakha that a man must divorce his barren wife came to be honored more in the breach than in the observance (Biale 1984).[34] Sexual companionship had come

33. "Two things united them, he [Ovid] said: the 'marital pact,' but also 'the love that makes us partners.' It was possible for conflict to arise between duty and these extraneous tender feelings. What to do, for instance, if one's wife turned out to be ster-ile? 'The first man who repudiated his wife on grounds of sterility had an acceptable motive but did not escape censure [*reprehensio*], because even the desire to have chil-dren should not have outweighed lasting devotion to his wife,' according to the moral-ist Valerius Maximus" (Veyne 1987, 42). I am suggesting that the story here represents at least a partial accommodation here to these Roman mores, but one which "indige-nous" ideas of the role of sexuality and intimacy had prepared for.

34. See the remarkable text quoted by Winston (1981, 369) from a nineteenth-century Orthodox Rabbi: "The Sages of previous generations could not find it in their hearts to permit in actual practice divorce against her will or the taking of a second wife because of childlessness."

to be valued for its own sake, even when procreation was impossible or contraindicated medically. Further support for this point can be drawn from the following facts: In rabbinic practice sex is recommended during pregnancy and following menopause; widowers are enjoined to remarry (by the Babylonian Shmuel Yevamot 61b) even when they have fulfilled the obligation of procreation; and widowers may even marry a woman proven to be infertile. To this should be compared, once more, Philo and Clement, for whom only procreation legitimated sexual intercourse (Clement 1989b, 391–92, 394; Clement 1989a, 261;[35] Brown 1988, 133; Winston 1981, 368).

The overall picture that I can draw, albeit guardedly, is of an earlier Palestinian discourse on sexuality that seems closest in spirit to that of the Stoics, who indeed considered sex to be an irritating and necessary part of human existence but also an "enduring aspect of the personality." Rabbi Eliezer personifies, perhaps, an extreme representation of this discourse. The view encoded in the later tradition and especially its Babylonian variant, however, strongly opposed even this ambivalence. Both the earlier and the later views assert the value of procreation, but only the later and Babylonian variants seem to regard sexuality as a beneficence of God for the pleasure and well-being of humans.

I wish to propose a historical hypothesis to account for the relation between these two discourses of sexuality. As I claim above, in the first century there was no sharp distinction between Hellenistic and Pharisaic Judaism. Philo, Paul, and Josephus all attest to this; though all of them were highly acculturated Greek-speaking urban Jews, they manifest considerable Jewish (if not Hebrew) learning and apparently cannot be distinguished from other Jews in Palestine in terms of religious practice.[36] There appears to have been a fair degree of Greek culture among Semitic-speaking Palestinian urban Jews. Paul, however, created Gentile Christianity, which, aside from its Christology, seems largely to have been contiguous with certain extreme allegorizing and spiritualizing tendencies within Hellenistic, platonized Judaism, at least in Egypt and likely in

35. Thus Clement explicitly forbids intercourse with a pregnant or lactating woman, precisely the opposite of the Rabbis' view. Philo also prohibited intercourse with an infertile woman (Philo 1937, 497). The prudery of the Victorian editors of the ante-Nicene Fathers who thought it necessary to bowdlerize Clement by translating his Greek into Latin and not English is simply stunning. What made them think that they had to be more pious than a holy Father of the Church?

36. Until Paul's "conversion," of course.

Palestine. Philo, after all, rails against those who maintained that the allegorical meaning had replaced the physical practice of the commandments, thus suggesting the existence of such groups, not altogether different from Pauline Christianity.[37] With the increasing threat to the corporeal integrity of the Jewish people from these platonizing tendencies within Judaism, which culminated in post-Pauline Christianity, the Rabbis more and more rejected dualistic understandings of the relation of body to soul. Such rejection—which the Fathers characterized as carnality— became the very marker of the rabbinic formation. Increasing distance from both platonic dualism and Stoicism carried with it a logic that affirmed sexuality per se. That affirmation has been documented here. There was to be, however, a reversal of this historical tendency when Greek thought re-entered the center of Jewish cultural practice in the Middle Ages.

THE RETURN OF THE DUAL:
MAIMONIDES'S INTERPRETATION
OF EVE

The religion and culture of the medieval Jewish scholastics, with Maimonides at their head, is quite distinct from that of the Rabbis.[38] Maimonides's reading of the story of the creation of Adam and Eve introduces into the later rabbinic culture the very dualisms from which the midrashic Rabbis escaped in theirs. Maimonides *accepts and interprets* the common rabbinic understanding of the Creation of Eve narrative as the splitting off of two halves of an originally androgynous being. However, this story is no longer read literally as the creation of an androgynous *body* which is split off *physically* into two bodies, one male and one female; rather, it is thoroughly allegorized. Again, the content of this privileged founding allegory thematizes and justifies the very form of allegory.[39]

37. This represents only one possibility of understanding Paul's position. It is, however, the interpretation that I find most compelling, as I shall argue in a forthcoming work.

38. I emphasize, "scholastics," because there were other opposing tendencies in medieval Judaism as well. In fact, in his day, Maimonides's philosophy was considered by many—if not most—Jewish authorities as heretical. His allegorization of rabbinic myth and biblical anthropomorphisms of God were particularly opposed. Moreover, texts directly opposing his negative view of the body and sexuality were also produced at this time.

39. For much of what follows I am dependent on Klein-Braslavy (1986, 193 ff.).

Maimonides justifies his move toward allegorical interpretation by citing an explicit example from Plato: "For they concealed what they said
about the first principles and presented it in enigmas. Thus Plato . . . des-
ignated Matter as the female and Form as the male" (Maimonides 1963,
43; see Klein-Braslavy 1986, 198). This example, presented as if random
and innocent, becomes in fact the *master* allegory of Maimonides's writing. The connection between matter and the female, according to Maimonides, lies in the fact that "woman" is a name for that which needs
to be joined to something else, and matter, of course, in Platonic-
Aristotelian physics, desires to be joined with a form. What is astounding
here is how quickly Maimonides's ontology and its connected hermeneutic practice bring him to expressions of virulent misogyny, much more
virulent, indeed, than any known in the older formation of midrashic
Judaism:

> How extraordinary is what *Solomon* said in his wisdom when likening
> matter *to a married harlot*, for matter is in no way found without form
> and is consequently always like a *married woman* who is never separated
> from a man and is never *free*. However, notwithstanding her being *a
> married woman*, she never ceases to seek for another man to substitute
> for her husband, and she deceives and draws him on in every way until
> he obtains from her what her husband used to obtain.
>
> (Maimonides 1963, 431)

Maimonides's allegorization of "woman" and "man" as matter and form,
and his physical philosophy of matter as always in need of form and always exchanging forms, essentializes woman (as the allegorized term) into
an ontological whoredom. We typically refer to such allegory as *personifi-
cation allegory* and forget that it is also a reification of persons. When
those persons are not individual fictional characters but categories of real
human beings, the social results can be dramatic—indeed devastating.
Maimonides continues his exposition of the relation of matter to form:

> For example, man's apprehension of his Creator, his mental representa-
> tion of every intelligible, his control of his desire and his anger . . . are
> all of them consequent upon his form. On the other hand, his eating
> and drinking and copulation and his passionate desire for these things,
> as well as his anger and all bad habits found in him, are all of them con-
> sequent on his matter. Inasmuch as it is clear that this is so, and as ac-
> cording to what has been laid down by divine wisdom it is impossible
> for matter to exist without form and for any of the forms in question to
> exist without matter, and as consequently it was necessary that man's

very noble form, which, as we have explained, is the *image of God and His likeness*, should be bound to earthy, turbid, and dark matter, which calls upon man every imperfection and corruption.

(1963, 431)

Maimonides rivals nearly any neo-platonist here in his horror of matter and his revulsion from bodily life. And as we might expect, Maimonides's doctrine regarding sexuality differs sharply from that of the talmudic Rabbis: "With regard to copulation, I need not add anything to what I have said in my Commentary on Aboth about the aversion in which it is held by what occurs in our wise and pure Law, and about the prohibition against mentioning it or against making it in any way or for any reason a subject of conversation" (1963, 434). This characterization of sex and the body in general as being held in "aversion" by the Torah needs only to be confronted by the talmudic story of the disciple who hid under his teacher's bed to observe him making love to his wife, "because it is Torah and I must learn,"[40] to show how far the medieval rabbi has moved from the Rabbis of the Talmud and midrash. Where the Rabbis had showed an easy acceptance of contained, married sex and the body and indeed had conversed about these subjects freely, for Maimonides they become subjects of shame and repression.[41]

Maimonides accepts and transmits the midrashic interpretation of the narrative describing the creation of woman at the same time as man. However, by introducing a Platonic conception of language and an Aristotelian physical theory, he effectively undermines the cultural import of that very midrash. Yes, Adam and Eve were created as one, but only because matter and form never exist without each other. And as for the second part of the story, the separation narrated in the second chapter of Genesis according to the midrash, Maimonides responds that it simply describes the *conflict* between form and matter. Even if, for Maimonides, matter was in harmony with form before the separation of the woman,

---

40. Babylonian Talmud, Berakhot 62a. In another section of the present project, I shall undertake a fuller reading of that story and its congeners.

41. It is true that an anthology of rabbinic sayings could be produced in support of Maimonides's disposition. Nevertheless, the statement that copulation is held in aversion by the Law is one that is impossible to support from talmudic sources, and indeed, the more traditional (i.e., non-Aristotelian) opponents of Maimonides roundly attacked him on this point, as well as on others closely related to it, viz. the corporeality of God and corporeal resurrection.

this is no longer the case afterward. Hence matter—the body—will be referred to as a "helper which is *over-against* him," and with this moment, rabbinic Judaism had come full circle. Maimonides reads, in this respect, like nothing so much as a recapitulation of Philo.

In the next chapter, we will see how much cultural struggle and tension was involved in the effort to produce sexual desire as "good" in a cultural environment in which it was heavily problematized.

2

Dialectics of Desire
"The Evil Instinct Is Very Good"

Far from being a simple legacy of its cultural heritage, the rabbinic insistence on the positive valence of sexuality seems to have been hard won and contested. The Talmud relates the following strange history of the returnees from the exile in Babylonia:

[1] "And they cried out unto God in a loud voice" [Nehemiah 9:4]. What did they say? Rav (and some say Rabbi Yohanan) says: "Woe, Woe: This is the one who destroyed the temple, and burned the Holy Place, and killed all of the righteous ones, and exiled Israel from their land, and still he dances among us. What is the reason You gave him to us? Is it not to receive reward [for resisting him]? We don't want him or his reward!" A sherd fell from heaven with the word "truth" written on it. *Said Rav Hanina: Learn from this that the seal of the Holy Blessed One is truth!* They sat in fast for three days and three nights, and he was given over to them. A figure like a lion of fire went out from the Holy of Holies. A prophet said unto Israel: "That was the Desire for worship of strange gods, as it is said, *This is the evil*" [Zach. 5:7]. While they were capturing him, a hair was pulled from his head. He cried out, and his voice carried four hundred parasangs [The entire distance from heaven to earth is five hundred!]. They said: "What shall we do? Perhaps, God forbid, they will have pity on him in heaven." A prophet said to them: "Throw him into a leaden pot and stop up his mouth with lead, for lead absorbs sound, for it says, *This is the evil, and he threw the leaden stone into its mouth*" [loc. cit.].

[2] They said, "Since this is a time of [God's] favor, let us pray regarding Desire for sexual sin." They prayed and he was committed into their hands. He said to them, "Be careful, for if you kill that one, the world will end." They imprisoned him for three days, and then they looked for a fresh egg in all of the Land of Israel, and they did not find one. They said, "What shall we do? If we kill him, the world will end. If we pray for half [i.e., that people will only desire licit sex; Rashi], in heaven they do not answer halfway prayers. Blind him and let him go." At least, a man does not become aroused by his female relatives.
(Babylonian Talmud Yoma 69b)

Here is perhaps the best example in all of the Talmud of the essentially mythical mode of thinking and expression of this culture. I am inclined to think that the narrative is a true myth—a story, neither fiction nor historiography (Boyarin 1993a), which articulates the most profound meanings and understandings of the world of the collective; for the present purposes, however, even if it be read as allegory, the same results will ensue.

This dark and strange tale is the way that the Rabbis of the Talmud communicate their deepest thoughts on human psychology and especially the complex notion of the *Yetser Hara*ᶜ, with which this chapter will be concerned. The concept of the *Yetser Hara*ᶜ, usually translated as the "Evil Inclination," is one of the most intriguing formations in talmudic culture and one, I think, that is easily misunderstood.

The first half of the story is an etiological myth, which explains why the Jews of rabbinic times are no longer attracted to the worship of idols. Upon returning from the Babylonian exile, the Jews prayed to God to have the desire for such worship removed from them, and their prayers were answered favorably. They were able to capture the Desire for idolatry and to execute him. In the second half of the story, the Jews attempt to rid themselves similarly of desire for sexual transgression, i.e., adultery and incest. They capture the personified Desire, but Desire himself warns them that he is necessary to the continuation of the world. Prudently, instead of executing him they imprison him for three days, only to discover that there are no eggs in the world. Eggs are, of course, the ultimate symbol of generation and regeneration. Realizing that nothing can be done about the situation, for halfway prayers are not answered, they blind him and let him go. The blinding avails to reduce the desire for incest with one's closest relatives—but no more.[1]

The crucial sentence in the story is that halfway prayers are not answered. It is this which gives us the central clue to the rabbinic psychology and their concept of Evil Desire. In order for there to be desire and thus sexuality at all, they are saying, there must also be the possibility of illicit desire. Desire is one, and killing off desire for illicit sex will also kill off the desire for licit sex, which is necessary for the continuation of life. Unlike the desire for idolatry, which serves no useful purpose other than testing resistance, the desire for sex is itself productive and vital— but it has destructive and negative concomitants. These concomitants

---

1. My brother the anthropologist reminds me that for Lévi-Strauss (as for Freud) this "blinding" is absolutely foundational.

need to be controlled, and can be, but only with difficulty. Desire itself is referred to as the "Evil Desire" because of this admixture of destructiveness and lawlessness that it necessarily carries, not because licit sexual desire and expression are evil in any way according to the Rabbis. This interpretation gives us important clues for the understanding of several seemingly mysterious rabbinic dicta.

Several rabbinic sayings seem paradoxically to identify the "Evil Desire" with good. The most explicit is perhaps the following:

> Nahman in the name of Shmuel [said]: *Behold it was good* [Gen. 1:31]. This is the Good Desire. *Behold it was very good* [ibid.]. This is the Evil Desire!
>
> Is the Evil Desire indeed good? Incredible!
>
> Rather, without the Evil Desire a man would not build a house or marry a woman or beget children.
>
> (Theodor and Albeck 1965, 73)

This is an unambiguous rejection of ethical dualism, that is, of the doctrine that two forces contend within a human being, one for evil and one for good. In contrast to other religious formations around and among the Rabbis (including Jewish ones), which held that there were opposing forces of good and evil in the world, the Rabbis insisted that everything came from God, and since everything came from God, then everything was good. This interpretation of the passage is supported from parallel texts in its context, in which suffering, punishment, and even hell are identified as "very good." We must then interpret the Evil Desire in these Rabbis dialectically, as itself composed of constructive and destructive forces within its own singular existence and essence. My hypothesis is that the Rabbis inherited the *term* "Evil Instinct" from a first-century Judaism much more averse to sexuality than they were, and unable to dispense with it, they ironized the term—"The Evil Instinct is very good"—and rendered the concept itself dialectical—blind in one eye, as it were. Sexuality, according to them, neither is itself evil (as apparently many first-century Jews held), nor is it an uncomplicated good, despite the fact that it leads to building houses, marrying, procreation, and eggs! It is called the Evil Desire solely because of its destructive side, *from which it cannot escape*, but at the same time there is full recognition not only of the necessity for desire but of its very positive overtones.

This interpretation is supported from the following text: "Rabbi Meir said: *You shall worship God with all of your heart* [Deut. 11:13]—The word 'heart' is written with an extra letter, to teach that one should worship God with both of his Desires, with the Good Desire and the Evil Desire" (Mishna Berakhot 9:5). Both of these midrashim have about them a touch of the provocative and the paradoxical. In both of them, the term "evil" in "evil desire" is turned on its head, from that which is condemned to that which is praised above all. These paradoxical texts can only be understood on the basis of the interpretation that I have given above, namely, that the Evil Desire is called thus because desire itself has within itself the necessary potential for evil, not because desire is essentially evil, for it would be impossible to worship God with that which is essentially evil or for God to have referred to it as "very good." In other words, just as the term "Evil Desire" is turned on its head by midrashic manipulations, so can its very evil be turned to good by psychological-spiritual manipulations. One text resists the unambiguous evil of the Evil Desire because God is its source, and the other insists that this very force can be turned for worship.

Questions remain, however. If the role and the possibility of the Evil Desire can be good, then what is the Good Desire? And more: since the Rabbis obviously consider Desire itself to be positive and important, why do they continue to refer to it as the Evil Desire and not as something neutral which can be turned to good or to evil?

Two Views of the Evil Desire

I wish to suggest that there were two partially conflicting psychologies within rabbinic culture. One was more straightforwardly dualistic,[2] considering the human will to be composed of good and evil instincts at war with each other; the other psychology, the one to which I have been relating up until now, regarded the human being as having a singly monistic nature, which is, however, dialectical in structure.[3] The force within the human being that causes him or her to create is precisely the same force that causes human beings to do evil and destroy. Good is

---

2. Porter (1901, 115 and especially 120) already perceived that there were two different ideologies on the *yeçer*.

3. Note that by "dualist" here I do *not* mean the dualism of body and soul or matter and spirit. Porter (1901, 98–105 and especially 133) already demonstrated very elegantly that the good and evil desires are not to be located in the soul and body respectively, against earlier interpretations which had held that they are. Gammie (1974) is especially useful in distinguishing different modes of dualism, a multi-variate phenomenon, which I am using here for taxonomic convenience.

inseparable from evil, because they are one and the same force. When one is strengthened, the other is necessarily strengthened as well:

> *And the Northern [or "hidden"] one, I will remove from among you:* [Joel 2:21]: This is the Evil Desire which is hidden and present in the heart of man. . . . *For it has performed mightily* [ibid.]: Said Abbaye: "Among the Torah-scholars more than anyone." As in the story of Abbaye who heard a certain man saying to a woman, "Let us get up early and go together on the way." He [Abbaye] said: "I will go and separate them from doing that which is forbidden." He went behind them for three parasangs in a meadow. When they separated from each other, he heard them, saying "Our way is long, and our company is sweet." Said Abbaye, "If that had been me, I would not have been able to control myself." He went and swung on the door-hinge [a sign of depression] and was miserable. A certain old man came by and taught him, "Everyone who is greater than his fellow, his Desire is greater also."
> (Babylonian Talmud Sukkah 52a)

Abbaye hears that an unmarried man and woman are to travel together, which he is certain will lead to illicit sex. How surprised and depressed he is when he discovers that they travel easily in each other's company, enjoy it, and then part when they arrive at the crossroads that leads to their respective villages. Abbaye's depression is generated by his self-understanding that he would not have been able to part from her without having sex (or at least trying to)—and he a great Rabbi, while *they* are only simple villagers. The tension is resolved (and the depression lifted) by the explanation presented in the story in the guise of an anonymous old man—the sort of character who frequently serves, along with children, to purvey truths in talmudic texts. The very passion that drives Abbaye to study Torah and become a "great man," which for the Rabbis always means one learned in and devoted to Torah, is the same passion that would have prevented him from simply saying good-bye to the woman and parting from her without sex. The desire is one, and the only way for the man of great desire to keep himself out of sin is simply to stay out of its way. The same drive that in the study-house will lead a man to study Torah will in bed lead him to have intercourse with his wife, and this is the very same drive that will lead him into sin when he is alone with a woman to whom he is not married. The passion is one.[4]

---

4. Another reading of this story, complementary with the first, would have it fit the Foucauldian paradigm perfectly. What Abbaye is saying is that the "naive," who

But other sayings on the same page of the Talmud (and in many other places [Porter 1901, 128]) indicate that Torah is the cure for the Evil Desire, suggesting a dualistic notion in which Desire is not the driving force of Torah but its enemy. My hypothesis is that the anthropology more generally held among Jews of this period was the dualist one, and that the dialectical one is an antithesis to that widespread construction (Porter 1901, 125). The use of the term Evil Desire, then, to refer to this dialectically composed force of Good and Evil would be partly a relic of the other structure and partly a purposefully paradoxical way of undermining that structure.[5] What could be more dramatic than the declaration that the Evil Desire was declared by God to be "very good"? Indeed, there are many rabbinic texts that reflect the dualist psychology, whereby the human being possesses two opposed inclinations, one good and one evil, which are at war in his or her breast. Typical of such a psychology is the quotation, "Let a man always incite his Good Desire against his Evil Desire" (Berakhot 5a). And it is on this version of rabbinic psychology that the Talmud could declare: "There are four things that God is sorry that he created: exile, Chaldeans, Ishmaelim, and the Evil Desire" (Babylonian Talmud Sukkah 52b; also Palestinian Talmud Ta'anith 66a, but

---

have not studied Torah and therefore do not know of the terrible power of Desire, are also not so plagued by precisely that power. The study of Torah, with its system of controls on sexuality, arouses and strengthens desire as effectively as (or even more effectively than) it restrains and constrains it. Therefore, one who is greater in Torah than his fellow has greater sexual desire as well. This is a perfect example of Foucault's "effects that may be those of refusal, blockage, and invalidation, but also incitement and intensification: in short, the 'polymorphous techniques of power'" (Foucault 1980, 11).

5. I do not attempt to place the two concepts in a chronological order. On the one hand, the monistic, dialectical view may be a survival of an earlier biblical conception. On the other hand, it may be a reaction against Hellenistic or Persian dualist anthropologies—or it may be both at one and the same time! Compare the view of Porter:

> The good impulse is rarely spoken of, and probably cannot be traced so far
> back, and *yeçer* frequently stands unmodified and always in the evil sense. This
> in itself suggests the error of connecting the evil *yeçer* with the body, the good
> with the soul, making them expressions of the character of two equally essential
> parts of man. Rather it is the nature of man as a whole that is in mind, and in it
> the evil tendency, or disposition, dominates.
>
> (1901, 109)

I am inclined to think that a good monographic study would be able to introduce more precise chronology, but that lies beyond the scope of the present work. My only dissent from Porter here would be in his assumption that for the "dialectical" or monistic position it is clear that the evil tendency dominates. Porter's work remains excellent and ought to be referred to more often.

without "exile" and attributed to the very early R. Pinhas ben Yair). According to the tradition that I have explored above, such a statement would be impossible (Porter 1901, 120–21), for it holds not only that God certainly does *not* regret having created this Desire, but that the world cannot exist without it.

Once again, my hypothesis here is that those rabbinic texts which speak of the Evil Desire as being necessary and even good represent a dialectical anthropological tradition that stands in opposition to an alternative dualist one, and that this oppositional dialectical tradition holds that good and evil are inextricably bound up in the human being and especially in sexuality. There is a strong tendency in the dialectical tradition to dispense with the term "Evil Desire" entirely and refer to that entity simply as "Desire," as in the legend from the Babylonian Talmud with which this section was begun. Because that legend is perhaps the most openly thematized representation of the impossibility of separating the evil from the good in sexuality, its language provides confirmation of my suggestion that texts which refer only to Desire hold to the dialectical and not the dualistic ideology.

The "Evil Desire" in Non-rabbinic Texts

Both psychological traditions appear in Jewish texts of the pre-rabbinic period. Perhaps the earliest text of post-biblical Hebrew literature, *The Wisdom of Ben Sira*, does not seem to know of a dualist anthropology at all. In the famous passage in which the metaphor of the two ways is developed, this book explicitly denies that human nature is anything but free and neutral in its valence:

> It was he, from the first, when he created humankind,
> who made them subject to their own nature.
> If you choose, you can keep his commandment;
>   (Skehan 1987, 267; translation slightly modified)

The word translated here as "nature," *yetser*, is actually the same word used later by the Rabbis to mean "desire," and in the dualist form with the appellations "good" and "evil."[6] Other texts, however, only slightly

---

6. Skehan translates this word as "free choice," which seems to me to be philologically unwarranted, although obviously Ben Sira is insisting here on human free will. On this passage see also Porter (1901, 136–46)

later than *Ben Sira*, already show fully developed notions of warring elements within the human breast. One of the most striking examples is the
Testaments of the Twelve Patriarchs, a Hellenistic Jewish text dated approximately to sometime in the late second century B.C.E. (Kee 1983,
778), where we find the following passage:

> God has granted two ways to the sons of men, two mind-sets, two lines
> of action, two models, and two goals. Accordingly, everything is in
> pairs, the one over against the other. *The two ways are good and evil;*
> *concerning them are two dispositions within our breasts that choose be-*
> *tween them.* If the soul wants to follow the good way, all of its deeds are
> done in righteousness and every sin is immediately repented. Contem-
> plating just deeds and rejecting wickedness, the soul overcomes evil
> and uproots sin. But if the mind is disposed toward evil, all of its deeds
> are wicked; driving out the good, it accepts the evil and is overmastered
> by Beliar, who, even when good is undertaken, presses the struggle so as
> to make the aim of his action into evil, since the devil's storehouse is
> filled with the venom of the evil spirit.
>
> (Kee 1983, 817)

There is nothing particularly remarkable about the suggestion that God
has granted two lines of actions to human beings; this is, after all, no
more than a paraphrase of the Torah itself, where God sets before humans
life and death and commands them to "choose life" (Deut. 30:15; and see
Josh. 24:15 and Jer. 21:8–14), and indeed, this notion is common to our
text and to the *Ben Sira* passage quoted above. But here, this biblical idea
is expanded by the notion that the choice between life and death is carried out in the struggle between "two dispositions within our breasts."[7]
We see here an entirely different moral psychology from that found in
Ben Sira, which emphasized a single *yetser* that has the power to choose
good or ill (Gammie 1974, 380). This passage is not unique or even unusual in the *Testaments*; there are at least twelve other chapters of
this relatively short text in which such a dualist notion of human moral
psychology is advanced—sometimes quite explicitly, as in the following:
"So understand, my children, that two spirits await an opportunity with
humanity: the spirit of truth and the spirit of error. In between is the con-

7. Accordingly, the references to *The Didache* and *The Epistle of Barnabas* made
by Kee (1983, 816) and Leaney (1966, 48) are entirely irrelevant, for while those documents speak of "Two Ways," they do not speak of "Two Spirits." To be sure, the latter does refer to the Two Ways as being presided over by two angels, but they do not
seem at all to be warring for hegemony within the spirit of the individual.

science of the mind which inclines as it will. . . . And the spirit of truth testifies to all things and brings all accusations" (Kee 1983, 800). In some of these passages, moreover, the "evil spirit" is explicitly defined as sexuality and opposed by a "good spirit" that is anti-sexual: "And the spirits of error have no power over him [the genuine man], since he does not include feminine beauty in the scope of his vision" (Kee 1983, 803). "For the person with a mind that is pure with love does not look on a woman for the purpose of having sexual relations" (Kee 1983, 827).

Other passages in this same text, however, seem to prefigure the later rabbinic dialectical understanding of sexuality. The following extract comes closer to the later doctrine, though it still maintains the separation between the good and evil sides and does not yet understand them as inextricably identified:

> And now give heed to me, my children, concerning the things which I saw during my time of penitence, concerning the seven spirits of deceit. For seven spirits are established against mankind, and they are the sources of the deeds of youth. And seven other spirits are given to man at creation so that by them every human deed (is done). First is the spirit of life, with which man is created as a composite being. The second is the spirit of seeing, with which comes desire. The third is the spirit of hearing, with which comes instruction. The fourth is the spirit of smell, with which is given taste for drawing air and breath. The fifth is the spirit of speech, with which comes knowledge. The sixth is the spirit of taste for consuming food and drink; by it comes strength, because in food is the substance of strength. The seventh is the spirit of procreation and intercourse, with which come sins through fondness for pleasure. For this reason, it was the last in the creation and the first in youth, because it is filled with ignorance; it leads the young person like a blind man into a ditch and like an animal over a cliff.
>
> In addition to all is an eighth spirit: sleep, with which is created the ecstasy of nature and the image of death. *With these are commingled the spirits of error.* First the spirit of promiscuity resides in the nature and the senses. A second spirit of insatiability, in the stomach.
>
> (Kee 1983, 782–83)

Although, to be sure, this text maintains a structure of opposing sets of spirits, nevertheless, it emphasizes that the two sets are commingled and indeed recognizes sexual desire as problematic but nonetheless belonging per se in the first set, among the "seven other spirits [which] are given to man at creation so that by them every human deed [is done]." The power of sexual desire, however, is such that it can lead the unsuspecting young over cliffs and into ditches, a formulation that prefigures the eventual rabbinic notion of a single spirit composed of both potentialities at one and the same time.

On the other hand, the competing notion of the human being as being composed of two spirits, one for good and one for ill, is also found in a very famous passage of the Dead Sea *Manual of Discipline:*

> He created man for dominion over the earth; and he set in him two spirits for him to set his course by them until the set time of his visitation. They are the spirits of truth and of perversity. . . . It was he who created the spirits of light and darkness and upon them founded every work and upon their ways established every deed. One God loves for all eternity and in all its deeds he will rejoice forever; the other—he loathes its assembly and all its ways he hates everlastingly. . . . But to the spirit of perversity belong a greedy mind and slackness of hands in serving righteousness, evil and lying, pride and a haughty heart, deceit and cruel treachery; hypocrisy in plenty, shortness of temper but full measure of folly and zeal in insolence; deeds abominable in a spirit of lust and ways of uncleanness in the service of impurity.
>
> (3:13–4:10; Leaney 1966, 144)

Here we have perhaps the most fully realized dualistic conception of human moral psychology anywhere in ancient Jewish literature.[8] Again, what is significant about this text, what divides it from the much earlier and more common doctrine of the Two Ways, is that "two spirits" are set into the human breast. We find, therefore, that the tension within rabbinic literature between competing notions of desire existed earlier in Palestinian Judaism and was continued by the Rabbis. In the next section I take up another aspect of the rabbinic figuration of the nexus between sexual desire and the body.

Sex as Food: The Body of Desire
Is the Body of Procreation

Modern societies tend more and more to separate the body that reproduces, a link in an immemorial genealogical adventure, from the body that desires, a lonely object, a consumer of briefly gratifying encounters. Thus, modern man [*sic*] has two distinct bodies, using one or the other as he pleases. This caesura is perhaps merely the persistence of a

8. For a summary of discussion of this passage and its relation to "ethical dualism," see Gammie (1974, 381).

split opened two millennia ago by the ideological victory over one part
of the inhabited world of the Christian conception of carnal relation—
and of carnal filiation—as separate from spiritual life and devalued in
relation to it.

(Mopsik 1989, 49)

Perhaps the most arresting fact about the discourse of sexuality throughout the talmudic literature is that desire is nearly always concatenated
with having children. We will see this well illustrated in the texts cited
below in Chapter 4, where always, "improper" sexual activity is related to
the production of improper children, while proper sexual behavior and
intimacy produce children beautiful in body and spirit. Indeed, "procreation" [Hebrew *piriya uriviya*] is often used as a synonym for sexuality
itself. We in "our" culture[9] are quick to read this concatenation as a contamination, a devaluing of sexuality, as if it were a purely instrumental
approach to the body. We readily read this view as repressive vis-à-vis
Eros itself, partly because we easily associate it with the medieval church
doctrine that sex is essentially sinful and is only redeemed by procreation
(Gardella 1985, 10). In fact, I suggest, our reading of this connection
needs to be studied anthropologically, denaturalized and accounted for. I
agree with Mopsik that we reinscribe on the desiring body the very split
between the carnal and the spiritual that determines our sense of the
body. Mopsik's brilliant insight here makes two points. The first is that in
modern culture we tend strongly to separate the functions of sexual pleasure and procreation, constructing them as, in effect, two bodies. The second point is more complex (and more directly related to the thesis of this
book). It is that the split we make between desire and procreation is the
continuance of the split between flesh and spirit for which Christianity
was the vehicle of achieving hegemony in the West.[10] This equation is
not obvious at all, for our dualism of the two bodies is ostensibly produced
as the agency of a sexual liberation, as a valorization of pleasure as opposed to its utilitarian aims, while the "Christian" split is precisely both

9. I am using "our culture" here in a sense very similar to that of Mauss (1979)
throughout his work, to refer to that generic European (Western European) formation.
See also, "But there may be another reason that it is so gratifying for *us* to define the
relationship between sex and power in terms of repression" (Foucault 1980, 6; emphasis added).

10. The reader will note that throughout my book, I have not attributed the origin
of the split, but merely its propagation, to Christianity.

the result and cause of a denigration of sexuality. We would wish, then, to see them as antitheses and not discursive allies. By exploring here the figuration of sexuality in the rabbinic culture, I hope to show why Mopsik's analysis is powerfully revealing of what the cultural stakes are in our dissociation of desire from reproduction.[11]

One of the most pervasive metaphors for sex in talmudic literature associates it with food. (See also Chapter 4.) A close reading of this metaphorical field will provide important clues to the rabbinic discourse of sexuality in general, in contrast to that of other cultural formations, in which sexuality was figured in the semantic field of elimination. For example, wives in the talmudic texts to be discussed below describe their and their husbands' sexual practice as "setting the table" and "turning it over," and the Talmud itself produces a comparison between sexuality and food—either of which one may "cook" however one pleases, provided only that it is kosher to begin with. This metaphorical association is very productive in the culture, producing (or supporting) normative determinations of various types. Reading it will, I think, help us to see the connection between the two splits that Mopsik connects genetically.

Let us think about the functions of eating in our culture. I think we all assume that its primary purpose has to do with the continuation of the vitality of the body, though we also recognize other very important functions and values for eating, including pleasure in good food, social binding from sharing food and eating together, and even ritual purposes in many groups from particular acts of eating. All of these are understood, however, as being subordinated to and generated by the primary function of eating, the continuation of life in the body. We consider absurd if not repelling such cultural practices as that of those Romans who reportedly caused themselves to vomit so that they could eat again.[12] I think that for the Rabbis, sexuality was conceived of in an analogous fashion. It was clear to them that the primary purpose for the existence of sexuality was the continuation of creation—in many senses: first and foremost, procreation. However, there were also well-understood and valorized secondary purposes for sexuality: pleasure, intimacy, and corporeal well-being. When

11. This becomes, then, another moment in the discrediting of the "repressive hypothesis," carried out so brilliantly in Foucault (1980).

12. In the Middle Ages some rabbinic thinkers would actualize this aspect of the metaphor in a way that the talmudic Rabbis never envisioned, regarding all nonprocreative sex as equivalent to eating and then vomiting (Biale 1992).

the Rabbis speak of pleasure and intimacy as leading to the conception of desirable children, then, they are simply integrating various realms of erotic life into one harmonious whole. When for whatever reason sex could not be procreative, its other purposes remained valid and valorized, for as we have seen, in this culture's normative determinations, sex was permitted and indeed encouraged with pregnant and sterile wives. And when pregnancy was contraindicated for medical reasons, contraception was permitted for the pleasure and health of the body.[13] Sexuality was primarily oriented toward the needs of the body, and the central need of the body was to continue its life, through eating and ultimately through reproducing.

Interpreting Mopsik's remark then, I would suggest that what occasions our discomfort with both the indissociable connection of sex with procreation and the pervasive metaphors of sex as eating is our desire to spiritualize sexuality itself. Still inhabiting the platonic universe of dualism, in which the body is devalued vis-à-vis the spirit, and yet desiring to valorize sexuality, the culture discovered a powerful strategy. Much of our culture has spiritualized desire, removing it from the realm of such bodily processes as becoming pregnant: the body of desire is almost not a body at all but an adjunct of the spirit. The effect is a reinscription within desire of that spiritualizing impulse of which Judith Butler speaks as transcending desire: "That sexuality now embodies this religious impulse in the form of the demand for love (considered to be an 'absolute' demand) that is distinct from both need and desire (a kind of ecstatic transcendence that eclipses sexuality altogether) lends further credibility to the Symbolic as that which operates for human subjects as the inaccessible but all-determining deity" (1990, 56). In the split of the two bodies, sexuality itself eclipses sexuality altogether by disembodying it. This is part and parcel—if a sort of reversal—of that very moralizing process regarding sexuality that Foucault has documented so powerfully in his works. Peter Gardella has documented this process in American culture: "Finally, experts on sex inherited their faith in liberation through orgasm from

13. Interestingly enough, in the early modern period when technologies of contraception became readily available, the condom was rejected as a mode of contraception by rabbinic authorities, while such devices as the pessary were deemed acceptable. The rationale advanced by at least one leading seventeenth-century rabbi was that the condom interfered with the "pleasure of one body with another," which *was the natural purpose of sex.*

Christians who had found freedom from sin in moments of religious ecstasy. The quest for ecstasy in orgasm then led people to neglect sensuality. Western mystical tradition has always known that in ecstasy the action of the senses is suspended. In America the pursuit of orgasm as the equivalent of religious ecstasy quickly became an ascetic practice" (1985, 7 and 117). According to Gardella, then, that very Christian impulse which had produced the doctrine of sensuality as sin was continued in the doctrine of a paradoxically disembodied sex.

For the Rabbis, sexuality in general was a powerful drive with very destructive possibilities but essentially a creative force in the world's life. Its proper deployment was as unproblematic as proper eating, and violation of its proper practice was similar to the eating of food that is non-kosher, a violation of the laws of the Torah, no more or less, excepting, of course, the social consequences of some types of sexual transgression, notably those that produce bastard children.[14] The hidden workings of desire have not yet become—as they would in the Middle Ages for many Jewish thinkers—the object of an intense activity of personal scrutiny and the marker of the state of the soul. Foucault could have supported his claim that "sexuality" in the modern sense, that is in the sense that someone has a sexuality, is culturally specific to our modern formation by referring to late-antique Jewish culture as well as to the Greeks and Romans.

In fine, then, what I am suggesting is that rabbinic Judaism was marked by a double discourse on human good and evil.[15] The first was a moral psychology in which a fully formed Evil Instinct contested with a Good Instinct within the breast of each human being. The goal was, of course, for the Good Instinct to defeat the Evil Instinct. There is a tendency—but only that—for the Evil Instinct to be identified with sexual-

---

14. Ironically, Gardella continues: "Marabel Morgan, evangelical author of *The Total Woman*, urged wives to seduce their husbands every day for a week. But she also illustrated the gulf that innocent ecstasy set between sex and sensuality when she wrote that 'sex is as clean and pure as eating cottage cheese'" (1985, 7). The desensualization of sex here is not in the metaphor of food but in the choice of menu. One could write as well, "Sex is as meaty and bloody as eating rare steak," a suggestion that I imagine some of my readers will find crude, thus helping me make my point.

15. I do not find any way of sorting these two discourses chronologically or geographically, between authorities or between documents. The *Yetser Hara*[c] could be the subject of an entire monograph, and I have barely scratched its surface here. Cf. Leaney (1966, 42).

ity in this anthropology, although some texts seem only to identify illicit sexuality with the Evil Instinct. In contrast to this, there is another ideology in which humans are made of only one kind of Desire. Although sometimes this tradition uses the term Evil Desire, it uses it in paradoxical ways that subvert its association with evil per se and make it refer to the destructive aspects that are inseparable from sexuality along with its creative aspects. At times, in this tradition, we find even the disappearance of the modifier "evil," and we are left with Desire alone, Desire that leads human beings both to enormous feats of creativity and love and to enormous deeds of destruction and violence as well. "To the extent that a person is superior to his or her fellows, to that extent will his or her Desire be greater also." Although the second (dialectical) tradition uses the language of the dualist tradition, it does so only to subvert it. For this tradition, the use of the term *Yetser Hara*^c does not by any means mark desire as evil but only denotes a recognition of the potential for evil that resides within all sexuality and desire.

Procreation, then, is not the "purpose" or the justification or excuse for sexuality but its very essence in rabbinic thought. Just as, for them, the very essence of eating is to continue the life of the body, so the very essence of sexuality is to continue the life of the collective body. In neither case, however, are other values and purposes excluded or even marginalized. But there is a strong construction of desire as problematic and ineluctably dangerous as well. In this reading of desire, then, rabbinic culture fits neither with medieval Christian theological notions of the sinfulness of all concupiscence, nor with modern conceptions of the innocence of all desire, but somewhere else, all its own.

The "carnality" of rabbinic Judaism did not enable the faithful simply to bypass the sexual anxieties whose spiritual and social dimensions Peter Brown explores in his great work (1988). Rather, the solutions that Christianity came up with to deal with these anxieties were not available; the body—and, specifically the sexualized body—could not be renounced, for the Rabbis believed as a religious principle in the generation of offspring and hence in intercourse sanctioned by marriage. This belief had the effect of binding men to women and women to men, making impossible the various modes of separation chronicled by Brown for Christianity and found also in various Hellenistic Judaisms. The commitment to coupling did not, however, imply any reduction of the radically unequal distribution of power that characterized virtually all of the societies of late antiquity. That inequality not only remained a fact of life for rabbinic Judaism but was confirmed in a whole conceptual apparatus, along with a complex tangle of emblematic stories, articulated in the talmudic literature.[16] But, as I will argue in the next chapter, the male perception and treatment of women did not rest on a culturally based loathing of the female body.

16. Some of the language in the last few sentences was adapted from a letter from Stephen Greenblatt to the University of California Press, November 1991.

3

Different Eves
Myths of Female Origins and the Discourse of Married Sex

Karen King has remarked that generally when male cultural products speak of women, it is sexuality that is the subject and not women. Men often think "with women" as a tool for thought about men's own bodies and their affect—fears, desires, and ideologies about sexuality. Accordingly, a misogynistic representation of woman must necessarily include at least a component, if not more, of negation of the male body as well, a negation that in effect stigmatizes it as female. Such disavowal of the body may indeed be the dominant factor in misogynist discourse, and misogyny often goes together historically with misogamy—hatred of marriage—as, notoriously, in Juvenal and throughout the Middle Ages (Bloch 1987; Wilson and Makowski 1990). I propose to test this historical thesis here by comparing two complexly related cultural formations, that of Hellenism and that of rabbinic Judaism, which operates primarily as a sort of resistance movement against Hellenism. I will try to demonstrate some fairly intricate cultural negotiations between the Rabbis and the circumambient culture around ideologies of sexuality as signified in accounts of the first woman. In the course of the discussion I will propose that the accepted characterization of rabbinic gender discourse as monolithically misogynistic is imprecise and in serious need of nuancing.

There were two types of androcentric social formations in late-antique Judaism: Hellenistic Judaism(s), in which the flesh was abhorred and women and sexuality were feared as a central theme of the culture, and rabbinic Judaism, in which the flesh was greatly valued and women and sexuality were controlled as highly prized essentials.[1] Hatred and fear of women, as

1. The distinction between Hellenistic and rabbinic Judaism is, in my view, not geographical (i.e., not Palestine versus the Diaspora) so much as chronological. I see the rabbinic movement as in large part a rejection movement against the Hellenization of much of first-century Judaism, including that of Palestine. This Hellenization, unlike the Seleucid one, did not involve the adoption of the "hedonistic"

such and as a central theme of culture, develop in Hellenistic Judaism out of a disposition toward procreation that can be traced to certain Greek cultural sources fundamentally different from the biblical one.[2] Although contending forces were also present in Greek culture itself, the themes represented and canonized in Hellenism—primarily the story of Pandora— seem to emphasize the negation and disavowal of reproduction and thence of women.[3]

PHILO'S EVE

A crucial key to all interpretations of the biblical account of the origins of the sexes is the realization that Genesis 1 and Genesis 2 have contradictory accounts, as shown above in Chapter 1. The former suggests that humanity was male and female from the beginning, while the latter seems to suggest that the first human was male, and the female came later. Most early commentators attempt to resolve this contradiction in one fashion or another, and the resolutions are ideologically significant to high degree. Philo opines that there are two different beings that the Bible calls "human," corresponding exactly to the two descriptions of creation in Genesis 1 and Genesis 2. The first is purely spiritual and androgynous in its incorporeal nature, while the second has a body and a gender that is male.[4] This second, corporeal male human being required that a female

---

sides of Hellenistic civilization so much as its dualist, spiritualist, anti-corporeal moods, as witnessed by figures as diverse as Philo, Josephus, and Paul, and by the Qumran writings. I hypothesize that as the cultural effects of this spiritualization became more and more apparent, particularly in the growing Christian movement, a significant reaction developed against it.

2. Judith Romney Wegner's excellent paper (1991), which was published after this book was substantially completed, makes the same argument from a slightly different perspective. This does not, of course, constitute an argument that misogyny is therefore not "really Jewish." Such arguments are endless, unfalsifiable, and bootless. It nevertheless helps to distinguish different cultural strands within late-antique Judaism to see which were adopting and which rejecting certain symbols and themes of Greek culture, and to evaluate the effect of all this on cultural practice.

3. For the prevalence of the Pandora story in late antiquity, see Panofsky and Panofsky 1956.

4. We will see that the theme of a purely spiritual androgyne—both male and female because it is neither—will recur in some early Christian writings of various types. Herein lies my only disagreement with Wegner's paper (1991). She understands Philo to be suggesting that male and female are different species, taking "male and female created He them," as an entirely new sentence and not as the continuation of "in the image of God, created He him." To be sure, in the passage Wegner quotes,

counterpart be created for it to assuage its loneliness and provide for continuation of the species. It is this very relationship of secondariness which is so important for Philo, for in his platonistic thought secondariness in time is a figure for lower ontological status. Accordingly, the corporeal female is twice-fallen, once from the first Adam of pure spirit and once more from the male, who in Philo's scheme represents "mind." And all this takes place, as Bloch emphasizes rightly, *before* the "apple" is eaten. The very coming into being of woman is already the Fall.[5] Describing the existence of the second man, Philo says:

> But since no created thing is constant, and things mortal are necessarily
> liable to changes and reverses, it could not but be that the first man
> too should experience some ill fortune. And woman becomes for him
> the beginning of blameworthy life. For so long as he was by himself, as
> accorded with such solitude, he went on growing like to the world and
> like God, and receiving in his soul the impressions made by the nature
> of each, not all of these, but as many as one of mortal composition can

---

Philo does write, "And when Moses had called the genus 'man', quite admirably did he distinguish its species, adding that it had been created 'male and female', and this though the individual members had not yet taken shape" (1929b, 61). I think that Wegner has slightly misread Philo here. By "genus" and "species," I think he means logical genus and species and not biological ones. Although it is still not identical to the passages I have cited above, this interpretation renders the passage less of a contradiction of Philo's explicit claim that the first human, in the image of God, was androgynous, owing to the androgyny of souls, which are both male and female because they are neither male nor female. This minor disagreement, however, does not materially affect my total agreement with the thesis of Wegner's paper.

5. As Bloch formulates it (not specifically with reference to Philo, but appropriately applied to him):

> Adam's chronological priority implies a whole set of relations that strike to the
> heart not only of medieval sign theory, but to certain questions of ontology
> that make it apparent that the Fall, commonly conceived to be the originary
> moment—the cause and justification—of medieval antifeminism, is merely a
> fulfillment or logical conclusion of that which is implicit to the creation of
> Adam and then Eve. For the woman of the Yahwist version, conceived from the
> beginning as secondary, derivative, supervenient, and supplemental, assumes,
> within the founding articulation of gender of the first centuries of Christianity,
> the burden of all that is inferior, debased, scandalous, and perverse.
> (Bloch 1991a, 25)

I would emphasize, however, that what Bloch leaves out here is the necessity of an interpretation for this set of values to be animated. The text of the Bible itself certainly does not automatically give rise to either the ontological or the axiological notions Bloch lists. I shall be dealing with this point more fully in a forthcoming article in *Paragraph*. See also n. 6.

find room for. But when woman too had been made, beholding a figure
like his own and a kindred form, he was gladdened by the sight, and
approached and greeted her. She, seeing no living thing more like herself than he, is filled with glee and shamefastly returns his greeting.
Love supervenes, brings together and fits into one the divided halves,
as it were, of a single living creature, and sets up in each of them a
desire for fellowship with the other with a view to the production of
their like. *And this desire begat likewise bodily pleasure, that pleasure
which is the beginning of wrongs and violation of the law, the pleasure
for the sake of which men bring on themselves the life of mortality and
wretchedness in lieu of that of immortality and bliss.*

(Philo 1929b, 121; emphasis added)

Two themes are combined in this passage of Philo, the two ingredients I
identify as endemic to the discourse of misogyny. The first is woman as
misfortune, not merely after the fact—contingently, as it were—but necessarily—essentially—misfortune. The second is the ontologically secondary status of the gendered human, and "woman" as the name for that
entity which produces gender. Both of these motives are absent from the
Bible, and indeed from subsequent rabbinic literature, but have anteced-
ents in canonical Greek texts and notably in Hesiod.

THE RABBIS' EVE

The rabbinic portrayals of woman's origin and role are quite different
from that of Philo and also quite varied internally. For much of the
midrashic tradition, Genesis 1:27 is interpreted as a literal statement of
the first human's creation as male and female. The first human is portrayed as physically androgynous, and what we are taught in Genesis 2:22
is that the androgyne needed to be split into the two sexes.[6] Perhaps one
of the most elegant ways of focusing on the difference in the hermeneu-

6. Bloch comments that "the suppression of the story of the simultaneous creation
of man and woman has far reaching implications for the history of sexuality in the
West. Who knows? If the spirit of this 'lost' version of Creation had prevailed, the history of the relation between the genders, beginning for example with the Fall, might
have been otherwise. Yet the priestly Genesis has been all but forgotten except for
recent attempts among feminist biblical scholars to apply the force of what is seen as
an original egalitarian intent" (1991a, 23). He thus protracts an occlusion as complete
as the occlusion of the woman and the story of equal origin for the sexes. I mean, of
course, the occlusion of the Jew and Jewish hermeneutic discourse from "the history of
sexuality in the West."

tics of Eve between the Philonic and rabbinic formations has to do with the role assigned to the snake. In Philo, the snake stands for pleasure embodied, especially the carnal pleasure that the male has in intercourse with the female.[7] Philo actually refers to the snake as "Eve's snake" (Philo 1929, 275); she is not his victim, but rather he is her agent, indeed her inevitable retinue.[8] For once Eve was created, it was inevitable that the snake (= pleasure) would threaten Adam's bliss ("it could not but be that the first man too should experience some ill fortune") and entrap him ("that pleasure which is the beginning of wrongs"). Woman, whom Philo equates with sexuality, is an ill fortune.[9] When notions such as these were combined in Philo with platonic dualism, and woman as the sign of corporeality was thereby committed to the realm of the senses, indeed construed *as* the realm of the senses, the scene was set for the production of the systematic misogyny which has plagued Western cultures ever since. Philo had an overwhelming effect on the formation of early Christian

---

7. As Philo says explicitly (1929a, 271). Dorothy Sly has pointed out that the standard translation there elides the clear sense of the Greek that it is the pleasure of the male with the female which is being spoken of (Sly 1990, 109).

8. Note that even the midrashic text cited below does not indicate that the snake is an essential attribute or companion of Eve but only that she functioned in the moment as Adam's temptress just as the snake had tempted her. The second text quoted, to the effect that Satan was created together with the woman, *is* much closer to Philo.

9. It should be noted, however, that since in the biblical text itself, Eve is positively evaluated as the "Mother of All Living," Philo does not assign her or sexuality only a negative value. Moreover, the term "Helper," for all of its connotations of subservience, is one that he can only read as having a positive valence, because help itself is clearly positively marked. On this, Dillon writes, "It seems true to say that in Philo's thought there is present the recognition of a female life-principle assisting the supreme God in his work of creation and administration, but also somehow fulfilling the role of mother to all creation. If this concept reveals contradictions, that is perhaps because Philo himself was not quite sure what to do with it" (1977, 164). Similarly, for Philo in his allegorical interpretation, "woman" is the senses, and the import is that senses are something that cannot be done without, something that has a positive role to play, however disturbing, in human life. This understanding on the allegorical level has its parallel on the literal level and even in practice, for in Philo, I think, literal women have about the same status as their signified, the senses, do in the allegorical meaning. That is, in Peter Brown's words, they are "an irritating but necessary aspect of existence" (1987, 266–67). For Philo on women in general, see Sly 1990. In this, as in other areas, Philo represents a relatively moderate position that would later be radicalized. Thus, while he ascribes spiritual meaning to the commandments, he also requires their observance and berates those who substitute the allegorical entirely for the literal observance, and while he approbates highly the celibate life of the Therapeutae, nowhere does he argue against procreation as a necessity.

thought. It is in Hellenized Judaism such as Philo's that the origins of Europe's Eve are to be found.[10]

In the midrashic texts, Eve is nearly always presented as the victim of the snake and not the victimizer of the man.[11] According to the midrash, the snake did not seduce Eve to have sex with Adam—she had already had intercourse with Adam, as we shall see—but rather, he seduced her to commit adultery with him. Thus a thrice-repeated saying of Rabbi Yohanan has it that "at the time that the snake had intercourse with Eve, he introduced filth into her. When the Israelites stood on Mount Sinai, their filth was removed" (Babylonian Talmud Yevamot 103b). Although this saying sounds like a version of Original Sin, it is such with an enormous difference. The woman is portrayed as the victim of the snake's sexual aggression, which renders her and all of her descendants temporarily impure. This impurity, however, had nothing to do with licit sexuality. According to the midrashic tradition, Adam had sex with Eve both before and after she had sex with the snake. He was not contaminated by his intimacy with a woman, nor were those who at Mount Sinai returned to their tents immediately after receiving the Torah for the express purpose, as the Rabbis claimed, of experiencing "the joy of intercourse" (Babylonian Talmud Avoda Zara 5a). The filth, then, that is transmitted to Eve's descendants temporarily is not that of sex but only of the lust for illicit sex—either adultery or bestiality or both. If there was any "original sin," it was redeemed by the Giving of the Torah at Mount Sinai, and human intercourse, even in this world, carries no stain, just as it did not for Adam and Eve. To be sure, for the time between the snake's seduction of Eve and the redemption through the giving of Torah, there was an impurity that was transmitted to all of her descendants, male and female,

10. That is, not in "an 'easy', almost self-evident, step from, say, the 'Yahwist' version of Creation," *pace* Bloch (1991a, 33). A critical hermeneutic intervention was necessary to make that step. In fact, for all of the subjugated status of women in rabbinic culture, I know of no rabbinic text whatsoever in which that status is derived from an alleged secondariness and consequent lower ontological status than that of the man, as in Timothy 2:11 or in Philo and his successors. That move is dependent not on Semitic but on Hellenic notions. I am not claiming, however, that Philo specifically has a Greek *text*, such as Hesiod, in mind, but only that the set of ideologemes concerning "Woman" that he motivates in his interpretation of Eve fit with traditional and canonical Greek literature than with the Bible. For other Hellenistic Jewish versions of Eve as the source of death and evil in the world, see citations in Sly (1990, 17) from such texts as *Ben Sira, The Life of Adam and Eve,* and *2 Enoch.*

11. Verna Harrison informs me that there are Patristic texts that hold such views as well.

but even that no longer obtains for those who stood at Sinai, both male and female and their descendants. As xenophobic as this tradition is, with its implication that those who did not stand at Sinai are still impure, it is not misogynistic.[12] "Woman," in Bible and midrash, is almost never essentialized as something evil and dangerous, as a snare to man.[13]

According to the Rabbis, there was no Fall into sexuality in the Garden of Eden. On the rabbinic readings, Adam had had intercourse with Eve from the beginning. Their intercourse is not associated in any way with the snake, the "forbidden fruit," or a Fall or expulsion from the Garden (Anderson 1989 and Pardes 1989). Licit sexuality, the intercourse of married couples, belongs not to the demonic realm of the snake but to the innocent realm of the Garden of Innocence itself. Indeed, according to Genesis Rabba 18:6 (Theodor and Albeck 1965, 168), the snake became inflamed with lust for Eve because he saw Adam and Eve having intercourse with each other, and according to 19:3 (171–72), he came and spoke to Eve while Adam was sleeping after having had intercourse with her. This narrative idea is plausibly interpreted as a quotation and reversal of prevailing pre-rabbinic interpretations by which the snake taught Eve and Adam about sex in imitation of the animals, interpretations that assimilate sexuality to the bestial and fallen (Brown 1988, 94 n. 43). This interpretation is in line with my understanding of rabbinic culture as in part a resistance movement to forces within the dominant Hellenistic formation. There is, indeed, explicit evidence of this reversal, for in another passage of the same midrashic text, we are told that the verse "Adam knew Eve his wife" means that he and she *taught the animals [caused them to know] about sex* (204–05). The snake is the aggressor. While there is illicit sexuality involved—"the snake had intercourse with Eve"—it is not female sexuality itself that is identified with the snake, as it was in Philo.

12. Indeed, I am tempted to suggest that the statement by the third-century Palestinian Rabbi Yohanan is in response to the doctrine of Original Sin, as if to say, you believe in it, you have it. Alternatively, it might represent a triumphalist claim on the part of the Rabbi that Pagans are more given to sexual immorality than Jews are—a fairly frequent rabbinic charge. In support of this latter interpretation is the fact that the Talmud cites Rabbi Yohanan's statement to support a claim by Mar Ukba bar Hamma that Pagans frequent the wives of their neighbors, and when they don't find them, they find an animal and have intercourse with it (Baylonian Talmud Avoda Zara 22b. See also Romans 1).

13. For other views, see Bal 1987. See also Mordechai A. Friedman 1990.

Pandora's Jar in Midrash: Eve as Victim

Although several rabbinic texts (some of which we shall see below) put the blame for the sin and its punishment on the woman, equally as many say the exact opposite. The most interesting of these is a text that is apparently an allusion to the Pandora story of the jar, but it assigns the role of Pandora not to Eve—but to Adam. A comparison of the story in Hesiod (the ostensible model or source of our text) with the midrashic story will provide rich material for analysis. The salient elements of the Pandora story as narrated in Hesiod's *Theogony* and *Works and Days*[14] are: Zeus becomes angry at Prometheus, whereupon Zeus hides the celestial fire. Prometheus steals fire from Zeus and brings it to men. In order to punish men for having received this illicit gift, Zeus counters with the creation of *anti pyros,* anti-fire, a "beautiful evil," who is a continuous source of harm to men (*pêma mega thnêtoisi*) (Th. 561–91). In *Works and Days* she is called Pandora (All Gifts), because the gods give her gifts to make her a beautiful pitfall and deception to men. "Her beautiful exterior, enhanced by those adornments which in Greek thought are externalized tokens of sexual allure, proves only to be a snare and a delusion" (Zeitlin 1990). Then, reports the *Works and Days*, she is sent to Prometheus's brother Epimetheus (Hindsight), who foolishly accepts her as a gift from Zeus. She opens up the jar of evil, "releasing all the evils and diseases that now silently and invisibly wander over the earth" (*WD* 56–104). Only Hope (Elpis) is left behind. Here I will compare the last part of the *Works and Days* version with its midrashic parallel. I will read the Hesiodic original first:

> And Epimetheus took no heed of Prometheus's advice
> not to receive any gift the Olympian Zeus might send him
> but to reject it lest some evil should happen to mortals.
> So he received it and learned by experience the evil he had.
> For the tribes of men had previously lived on the earth
> free and apart from evils, free from burdensome labor
> and from painful diseases, the bringers of death to men.

14. There is an entire scholarly literature devoted to the "contradictions" between these two accounts—typically for nineteenth-century scholarship, much of it is devoted to proving that one is authentic and the other spurious—but as Zeitlin remarks, "Although the two versions differ in some important details and are used to serve the differing purposes of each text, . . . they can and have been taken together as forming two halves of a single extended narrative, each providing a gloss on the other" (Zeitlin 1990). My summary, then, is a conflated version.

In the power of these evils men rapidly pass into old age.
But then woman, raising the jar's great lid in her hands
and scattering its contents, devised anguishing miseries for men.

(Frazer 1983, 99)

The text seems to manifest an internal contradiction. On the one hand, the narrative states openly that the woman is herself an evil:

Son of Iapetos, you who surpass all others in planning,
you rejoice in your theft of my fire and in having deceived me,
being the cause of great pain to yourself and men in the future.
I shall give them in payment of fire an evil which all shall
take to their hearts with delight, an evil to love and embrace

(Frazer 1983, 98)

But on the other hand, the last part of the narrative implies that Pandora loosed evils upon the world only because she opened the jar, not because she herself is evil. Furthermore, one might ask whether Epimetheus, by accepting the gift he has been warned against, is just as culpable as Pandora herself in bringing evil upon men. This elision provides strong support for the reading (Sissa 1990, 154–55; Zeitlin 1990) that the jar *is* Pandora—or rather Pandora's womb/vulva—the opening of which is the event that brings all evil into the world.[15] In Zeitlin's persuasive reading of the text, opening of the jar is breaching of Pandora's virginity, *and she is made wholly responsible, as it were, for this act as well!* The text refuses to record the first sexual act between a man and a woman, because by doing so it would have to reveal that which it seems determined to suppress, the simple fact that men are also agents in the performance of sex and thus at least equally responsible with women for whatever baneful effects sex is held to have.

Female sexuality is, on this reading, the root of all evil. The fact that it is Pandora who opens the jar and not Epimetheus is only a further displacement of any possible guilt or responsibility for "the human condition" from the male to the female. The parable in the midrash seems to depend either on the Pandora story itself (Lachs 1974), or if not directly on it, then on similar folkloristic motifs of the woman as source of evil in the world. There are, however, crucial incongruities in the relationship of this story to its intertext:

15. For a similar interpretation arrived at by other means, see Sissa (1990, 154–56).

"And he said, I heard Your voice, and I was afraid for I am naked and I hid. And he said, who told you that you are naked?" [Gen. 3:9–10]

Rabbi Levi said, This should be compared to a woman who comes to borrow vinegar, who enters into the house of the wife of a colleague.

She [the borrower] asks her [the wife], "How does your husband treat you?"

She [wife] said to her [visitor], "Everything he does with me is good, except that there is this jar, which is full of snakes and scorpions, which he does not let me control."

She [visitor] said, "All of his jewels are in there. And he plans to marry another woman and give them to her."

What did she [wife] do? She stretched out her hand into the jar.

They began to bite her.

When her husband came, he heard her voice crying out, and said, "Perhaps you touched that jar?"

Similarly [God said to Adam]: "Did you eat from the tree which I commanded you?"

(Theodor and Albeck 1965, 179–80)

Let us compare this text to its "model." As a rendering of Pandora, which the jar theme suggests that it is, or even as a parallel to it, it certainly presents some startling inconsistencies. Where Lachs sees a *corruption* of the Greek myth (Lachs 1974), I find a *parodic subversion* of that text. When we look just at the parable itself, it seems that we have a fairly close copy of the Greek exemplar. The wife, who equals Pandora, is tempted to open the jar and does so, thus releasing an evil. However, once the parable is applied to scripture, the picture changes entirely, for the equivalent to the wife of the parable is not Eve but Adam!

A midrashic parable (*mashal*) typically comes to fill in a gap in the biblical narrative with a plausibly analogous situation and especially with an exemplary one drawn from the cultural intertext. In this case, the exegetical problem is the motivation for God's accusative questioning of Adam, "How did you know that you were naked?" and its continuation, "Did you eat from the tree which I commanded you not to eat of it?" The mashal suggests that God's proof of Adam's malfeasance was precisely the fact that he was ashamed of his nakedness, thus connecting the two halves of the verse. The "Pandora" story is produced as the model for this interpretation. Just as in that story the husband accused the wife because he knew that her crying out meant she had disobeyed him, so God accused Adam because he knew that Adam's being ashamed and afraid meant he had disobeyed God. The Pandora figure of the parable is compared to Adam of the application. This interpretation is guaranteed by the statement within the midrashic text that "Similarly [God said to Adam]: 'Did you eat from the tree which I commanded you?'" The word *similarly* in a midrashic parable sets up the analogy between the parable story and the biblical narrative. The question of the husband in the parable: "Did you open the jar that I asked you not to?" is a figure for God's question to Adam, "Did you eat?" By equating this statement with the verse addressed to Adam in the Bible, the midrash says that it was he who opened the jar and was bitten, thus revealing his disobedience to the husband—God. By thus equating Adam and not Eve with the Pandora figure of the parable, the text subverts the myth of essential, female demonic evil that the Pandora story projects explicitly. Moreover, it signals that for *this* midrashic writer at least, Adam's attempts to deflect blame for his behavior to his wife are not accepted. Of course, this does not exonerate Eve of her own sin, only of the blame for Adam's. On the other hand, this text provides a powerful example of androcentrism at the same time that it subverts misogyny, for it emphasizes that the culturally significant moment is Adam's eating of the fruit and not Eve's. That is, by shifting the Pandora figure from the woman to the man, at the same time that the midrash is disabling a reading that "puts the blame" on Eve, it renders her agency in the story entirely invisible. This could almost be a paradigm for rabbinic gender relations which, while generally patronizingly solicitous toward women (as opposed to cultures which are violently misogynistic), at the same time marginalize them utterly.

There is, however, a parallel version of this midrash, in which the gender roles are not so complexly subverted. After telling the parable in more or less the same terms as in the version of Genesis Rabba, the midrash there concludes: "She put forth her hand and opened the jar and the scorpions bit her and she died. The [husband] is Primeval Adam and the wife is Eve, and the borrower of vinegar [whose gender also shifts from version to version] is the snake, for it says, 'And the snake was slyer than any beast of the field'" (Schechter 1967, 7).[16] What is crucial to note is that

16. It should be noted that even in this text, there is a version in which the Genesis Rabba inversion is maintained and the foolish wife is Adam and not Eve. I find it astonishing that when Aschkenasy cites this text she remarks on "the rabbis' attempts to reduce the stature of Eve to that of an empty-minded, jealous housewife" and does not pay attention to the fact that in most versions it is Adam who is so portrayed and not Eve (1986, 43). Aschkenasy's whole account, however, is more balanced than many in that it recognizes explicitly how rare it is to find "woman" identified as "evil incarnate" in rabbinic texts (ibid.). In contrast to Carol Meyers

even in this version of the story, which assimilates it more closely to the Pandora model, the burden of the woman's role is still entirely different from her role in Hesiod. Like Pandora, she is the victim of her curiosity and the victim of the snake, who is portrayed as having evil intent, but unlike Pandora she is not the victimizer of her husband and the world, because only she gets bitten. She does not unleash evil in the world. Adam's "self-defense" of blaming it all on Eve (in the biblical text) is not accepted.[17] She got punished for her curiosity, but he alone is responsible for his malfeasance. Indeed, according to one passage in Genesis Rabba, his attempt to blame things on Eve is cited by God later as a classic example of the ungrateful quality of human beings (Theodor and Albeck 1965, 359). In another classical midrashic text, this lack of gratitude is given as the reason that God drove him out of the Garden (Mandelbaum 1962, 284), and Rashi comments, "Because it is a shameful thing that he tries to shift the blame *onto the gift* that God gave him" (Rashi ad Genesis 3:13; emphasis added).[18] Both in Hesiod and in the Rabbis, the first woman is a divine gift to man; in one, however, the gift is a snare and in the other a true benevolence.

Misogynistic Midrashim on Eve

Other midrashic texts take a different view of Eve's complicity or guilt. Some of these are indeed quite virulent, though with few exceptions they do not ascribe to Eve the kind of evil and demonic aspect that we see in Philo's absolute equation of Eve with sexuality, the source of all evil from the very start.[19] The only exceptions that I know of in early rabbinic texts are from a single context in Genesis Rabba, where Rabbi Aha explains the name Eve (Hebrew *Hawwah*) as being related to the Aramaic *Hiwiah*, snake. He has Adam say to her, "The snake was your snake, and

---

(1988, 74–75), who conflated the early rabbinic interpretative tradition with that of non-rabbinic Jews and Christians, Aschkenasy writes, "As we have seen, unlike in Christian Bible exegesis, the figure of Eve in Judaic tradition did not take on the aspect of cosmic evil" (Aschkenasy 1986, 50).

17. See below, however, for another tradition of rabbinic hermeneutics, which does blame it "all on Eve."

18. I know of one dramatic exception to this pattern in classical midrashic literature and will discuss it below. Compare, for instance, Ambrose, "Well does the Scripture omit specifying where Adam was deceived; for he fell, not by his own fault, but by the vice of his wife" (cited in Higgins [1976, 644]).

19. Philo (1929a, 275), among many examples. See also Sly (1990, 109).

you were my snake," as the justification for her name (Theodor and Albeck 1965, 195). In a similar vein we find, in the same context, "Rabbi Haninah the son of Rabbi Idi said, 'From the beginning of the book and until now, there is no letter *s*. When the woman was created, the Satan was created with her'" (ibid.).[20] These exceptions to the cultural pattern, while not insignificant, only draw further attention to the much more common discourse that opposes them. The most extended piece of contempt for women produced in the midrash is from Bereshit Rabba, and even here the discourse is complicated; despite the open misogyny of the passage, once it turns to procreation, the emphasis is positive:

> They asked Rabbi Yehoshua, "why is the male born face down and the female is born face up?" He said to them, "the male looks to the place from which he was created [the earth], and the female looks to the place from which she was created [the rib]."
>
> "And why does the woman have to perfume herself, and the man does not have to perfume himself?" He said to them, "Adam was created from the earth, and the earth never smells rotten, but Eve was created from a bone. If you leave meat for three days without salt, it will smell bad."
>
> "And why does the voice of a woman carry but not that of a man?" He answered, "It's like a pot which if you fill it with meat, its voice will not carry, but if you put one bone in it its voice carries."[21]
>
> "Why is it easy to pacify a man, but not a woman?" He said to them, "Adam was created from the earth, once you put on it a drop of water, it immediately swallows it up. Eve was created from a bone; even if you soak it for several days, the water will not be absorbed."
>
> "Why does the man pursue the woman, and the woman does not pursue the man?" He answered, "To what is the matter similar, to a person who has lost something; he seeks the lost object, but the lost object does not seek him."
>
> "Why does the man deposit seed in the woman, but the woman does not deposit seed in the man?" He answered, "It is like one who had a valuable object; he searches for someone who is reliable to deposit it with."
>
> (Theodor and Albeck 1965,
> 158–59)

20. It would be a mistake, however, to read this last passage in the light of later notions of the Satan. I thank Ilana Pardes, who reminded me of this last passage.

21. For the persistence of these misogynistic topoi, cf. the medieval French text quoted by Bloch (1987, 18), "Why are women more noisy, full of foolish words, and more garrulous than men? Because they are made of bones and our persons are made of clay: bones rattle louder than earth."

Up till here, Rabbi Yehoshua's remarks, while obnoxious in tone, do not necessarily depict vicious contempt for the female. Indeed, the last of the sentences is generally consonant with the argument of this chapter to the fact that rabbinic essentialization of women was owing to their desire to ensure that their procreative role not be compromised in any way. Rabbi Yehoshua's diatribe, however, continues:

> "Why does the man go out bare-headed but the woman with her head covered?" He said to them, "it is like one who has committed a sin, and he is ashamed in front of others; therefore she goes out covered."
>
> "Why do they go first to the dead?" He said, "since they caused death in the world, therefore they go first to the dead."
>
> "And why was she given the Commandment of menstrual separation?" "Because she spilled the blood of the First Adam, therefore she was given the Commandment of menstrual separation." "And why was she given the Commandment to sacrifice the first portion of the dough?"[22] "Because she spoiled the First Adam, who was the first portion of the world, therefore she was given the Commandment to sacrifice the first portion of the dough." "And why was she given the Commandment of lighting the Sabbath candle?" "Because she extinguished the soul of the First Adam, therefore she was given the Commandment of lighting the Sabbath candle."
>
> (ibid; cf. Schechter 1967, 117)

Open misogyny like that of Rabbi Yehoshua is rare indeed in the rabbinic corpus, certainly by comparison with Philo, on the one hand, or Patristic culture on the other.[23] This sort of misogynistic catalogue would become, however, endemic in medieval Judaism, as it was in medieval culture generally (Bloch 1987). Moreover, even this text does not project a conceptualization of female sexuality per se as dangerous and threatening, though it certainly suggests that possibility lurking in the background.

"The Three Sins for Which Women Die in Childbirth" and Rabbinic Dissent

Rabbi Yehoshua's nascent idea that Eve is the origin of death is amplified in the Palestinian Talmud's reading of a famous mishnaic passage: "There are three sins for which women die in childbirth: a lack of care with

22. When baking bread, a portion of the dough is set aside as an offering for the priests. Since such offerings to priests are always from the first of the fruit of the dough, and Adam was the first human, he is compared to the first of the dough.

23. To the best of my knowledge, the two texts cited here from a single place in Genesis Rabba are the only examples of such misogynistic diatribe in all of the

regard to menstrual separation, the separation of the dough-offering, and the light of the [Sabbath] candle" (Shabbat 2:6). These are precisely the commandments to which Rabbi Yehoshua refers, suggesting a genetic tie between the two utterances, one that makes these three "female" commandments a sort of punishment rather than privilege. In the Palestinian Talmud's interpretation of this Mishna, this assertion of the Mishna is associated with a midrash similar to Rabbi Yehoshua's, "The First Adam was the blood of the world . . . and Eve caused him death; therefore the commandment of menstrual separation was given to the woman. Adam was the first pure dough-offering of the world. . . . and Eve caused his death; therefore she was given the commandment of the dough-offering. Adam was the candle of the world, for it says 'the soul of Adam is the candle of God,' and Eve caused him death; therefore the commandment of lighting the candle was given to the woman" (Palestinian Talmud Shabbat 2:6 8b).[24] However, even though this tradition blames the entire sin and its consequential death on Eve, it does not project that sin as owing to her sexuality. Eve's act was indeed a sin, and it created the need for her "daughters" to have a means of atoning it, but there is no hint, whatsoever, that the sin is repeated. or continued in the sexual life. Moreover, the fact that the three commandments are linked together in this way shows something else of importance. The menstrual separation is not given special emphasis here nor treated differently in any way from the two commandments of the dough-sacrifice and the lighting of Sabbath candles. If there were an a priori opportunity to identify women's sexuality with death, danger, or demonic powers, it would have been here, and even in the misogynistic text we are reading here, that option is refused.

The Babylonian Talmud goes much further by completely undermining the gender-asymmetric force of the Mishna and by rejecting Rabbi Yehoshua's misogynistic midrash. The Talmud begins by raising the possibility of a sexual interpretation of the Mishna—the very interpretation that seems, at first glance, to be so obvious:

> For [not being careful] about menstrual separation, what is the reason?
> Rabbi Yitzhaq said, "She spoiled things with her sexuality [lit., her
> inner parts]; therefore she will be smitten by her inner parts."

---

classical rabbinic literature. See also below for a catalogue of other misogynistic expressions in the texts. I hope that I have not missed anything significant.

24. This text may even be simply a citation of Rabbi Yehoshua's midrash.

This view would of course canonize Rabbi Yehoshua's misogynistic read-ing. The Talmud, however, immediately rejects such an interpretation—because it does not square with the other commandments mentioned, namely the dough-offering and the lighting of Sabbath candles—and of-fers another reading. Indeed, this hegemonic commentary deflects the issue from one of gender entirely:

> As a certain Galilean interpreted: I have put into you a portion of blood; therefore I have given you a commandment having to do with blood. I called you the "firstling"; therefore I have given you a com-mandment having to do with the first [dough]. The soul which I have given you is called a candle; therefore I have given you a command-ment having to do with candles. If you keep them well and good, but if not I will take away your soul.
>
> (Babylonian Talmud
Shabbat 31b–32a)

These commandments, according to the Babylonian Talmud, like any others belong in principle to the whole people, male and female alike. But these are particularly given to women because they belong particu-larly to women's sphere as understood by the rabbinic culture, to her body, cooking, and the comfort of the house, just as other command-ments, which belong to the "male" spheres of public life and worship, are restricted to men.[25] The Talmud then asks, "Why then at the time of giv-ing birth?" to which the answer is that the time of danger is when a per-son is tested for righteousness. The text next asks when men are tested, and the answer is given that they are tested when passing over bridges and in similar moments of danger.[26] For the next two pages, the Talmud

25. Compare the reading of this text in Wegner (1988, 155–56). I can see no rea-son whatsoever for her determination that "the three cultic duties listed here, like other biblical precepts, are primarily incumbent on *men*" (155). These are precisely examples of cultic duties that in mishnaic law are incumbent on women just as on men. So violation of the laws of menstrual sexual separation is just as much a violation for the female as for the male partner, as is the eating of untithed food or a possible violation of the Sabbath. These are not, even technically, in the category of time-contingent positive precepts incumbent only on men.

26. Wegner's statement, then, that "women's performance is encouraged by threatening them with death in childbirth for failure to carry out the rites in question" (155), while accurate for the Mishna, certainly is not an appropriate description of the rabbinic practice in general. It is the case that women have a "double dose" of testing, since they presumably cross bridges equally as frequently as men, but this does not materially affect the argument that the danger is de-essentialized from something par-ticularly female here.

goes on to list commandments that fall on men and women alike and punishments that result from laxity with regard to them. Thus, even a potential discourse positing an essential relationship between women's sexuality and death is countered by the classical culture text, the Talmud, and precisely where it could have been expected to be activated, with regard to menstruation.[27]

Nor was this contestation only Babylonian; the Palestinian midrash on Ecclesiastes also "emends" the text, as it were, to read "For three things women die in childbirth, and for three things men die" (Kohellet Rabba

---

27. At least in the classical rabbinic period, this was not understood as an essential manifestation of demonic evil associated with blood, death, birth, or sexuality and was certainly not an association of woman per se with impurity or contamination, *pace* Wegner (Shaye J. D. Cohen 1991, 281).

Other evidence cited by Wegner for her claim that rabbinic Judaism manifests an atavistic fear of women also seems to me to be misread, or at least to allow for another reading. Wegner's argument from the prohibition of a man from being alone with two women when a woman is not prohibited from being alone with two men simply does not establish her point that "the sages' androcentric perspective blames the dangers of private encounters between the sexes on women's moral laxity rather than on men's greater susceptibility to arousal" (Wegner 1988, 159–61). The same argument can be made with reference to other rabbinic sexual "hedges," for example, the prohibition on a man hearing a woman singing if she is not his wife. Here again, there is no reason to assume that moral laxity of women rather than arousability of men is at all at issue. Indeed, this latter interpretation can be strengthened considerably when we remember that men are not supposed to look at the colored clothing of women *on the clothesline*, lest they be aroused by it, a situation in which moral laxity of women could hardly be the issue. These talmudic practices do propose some essential difference between men and women, and presuppose a social hierarchy, but they do not provide compelling or even persuasive evidence for a perception of women as dangerous and contaminating.

Similarly, I do not think that the evidence cited by Nehama Aschkenasy supports her claim that in rabbinic culture, "Woman is seen primarily as a sexual being whose moral weakness is coupled with sexual power which she puts to evil use" (1986, 40), still less for her suggestion that "woman in general is condemned by the Midrash as immodest and voluptuous, especially in connection with the story of Creation" (ibid., 74). Aschkenasy gives three references to support this claim for what "the Midrash" holds. As for the evidence from Genesis Rabba, it is apposite but not typical. I have already cited it above and evaluated its extent there. I see nothing on Sota 19b that supports such a claim at all and assume that the reference must be misprinted. The third text cited is The Fathers According to Rabbi Nathan 1. A careful reading of that entire passage supports only an argument that Eve was more susceptible to being deceived by the Serpent than Adam, no more than that. Moreover, the text explicitly blames even this on Adam, when it says, "What led to Eve's touching the tree? It was the hedge that Adam put around his words"—that is, his exaggeration in reporting God's interdiction on eating from the tree caused Eve to be deceived. God had said not to eat, but Adam's report that he had said not even to touch the tree enabled the snake to fool her (Goldin 1955, 9–10).

3:3). Furthermore, in the midrash on the gynecophobic verse of Ecclesiastes 7:37, "And I found the woman more bitter than death," where a commonplace theme of essential feminine evil or danger could have been expected to surface, all we find is a statement to the effect that *sometimes* a woman is so demanding of her husband that she leads him into a bitter death and an anecdote illustrating such an occurrence (Kohellet Rabba 7:37). Androcentric, to be sure; gynecophobic, no. These rabbis are not willing to consider either woman per se or sexuality a negative or threatening element in the world. But any social hierarchy, however "benign," seems to carry within itself the seeds of a potential discourse of contempt, and such discourse was likely hovering just below the surface of the rabbinic attempt to produce a discourse of female confinement that was not misogynistic in character. Indeed, as many critics have argued, and as Bloch has shown most recently, any *male* discourse that essentializes women and their roles, whether "negatively" or "positively," ultimately leads to misogyny. But Bloch himself would formulate this differently; he argues that any predication of the form "women are" or "woman is" is already misogynistic (Bloch 1991, 4–5). I am impressed by his argument. This approach has the salutary effect (in my opinion) of completely cutting out the ground from a certain kind of apologetic discourse that I am also trying to avoid, namely, a discourse that argues that rabbinic Judaism was not sexist because it often "praised" women, but it makes it harder to see and describe real cultural differences in the representation of women, body, and gender in different cultures. So I prefer to weaken the formulation somewhat by suggesting that any "positive" predication of this form easily slides into its opposite, that "putting women on a pedestal," for instance, as in the Victorian period, leads easily to violence against women, and that the rabbinic discourse of great valuation of sexuality and the female body leads just as easily and naturally into the genuine and open misogyny of much of medieval Jewish discourse, as we shall see below.

The "Other Woman": Lilith and Woman's Sexuality as Demonic

In what were almost his last words Foucault said: "My point is not that everything is bad, but that everything is dangerous" (Dreyfus and Rabinow 1983, 232). Virtually any cultural practice can have multiple social meanings.[28] A similar point has been made with regard to menstrual taboos by the anthropologists Buckley and Gottlieb:

> In much of the literature, when women have been described as being prohibited from contact with something in the male domain—a man's hunting gear, say—it has been interpreted as an indication of male dominance manifested by women's exclusion from prestigious activities. Conversely, however, when it is forbidden for men to have contact with something in the female domain—such as menstrual blood—it has been interpreted in an opposite manner, as a sign of female inferiority. The two kinds of actions, or taboos, would seem parallel, yet the anthropological interpretation of them has been binary.
>
> (Buckley and Gottlieb 1988, 14)

Only specific analysis of specific historical situations reveals the specific meanings of a practice within the particular formation, and, of course, even within a given cultural formation the same practice can have multiple and contradictory meanings. If I have argued, then, that within rabbinic Judaism of the talmudic period, even menstrual taboos did not constitute an essentialized fear and hatred of women as defiling, such interpretations and understandings were certainly latent and easily derived from the practices.

In another set of Jewish myths about the origin of woman we do find representation of the woman as demonic figure. I am referring, of course, to the Lilith myths, which appear in literature only *after* the rabbinic period, first being attested in the *Alpha-Beta d'ben Sirah*, a text of the eighth century (Yassif 1984). This story tells of a first wife created for Adam who wanted to "be on top" and whom he divorced. She lives on as a succubus, sleeping with men at night (her name means "Night Demon") and producing demon children from their nocturnal and masturbatory emissions. As Yassif points out, the classical midrashic texts know of a motif of a "First Eve," who "returned to her dust" (Theodor and Albeck 1965, 213). This may be the trace of a longer narrative that contained the entire story of a woman who was created and rebelled, demanded sexual parity, and lives on as a demon. But the evidence for such a construction is meager indeed. Genesis Rabba does, in fact, mention the sexual demons who come in the night, but in a context that completely

---

28. I wonder what the limits of this claim are. Instinctively, I put them at practices that cause death or grave bodily harm.

undermines the story's later cultural valence. When Adam and Eve were driven from the Garden of Eden, in mourning they refrained from sex for one hundred and thirty years. During that time, he was visited by succubi *and she by incubi,* and both produced demon children (Theodor and Albeck 1965, 195). And indeed, the Talmud refers to the very ancient (see Milgrom 1988, 226–29 and cited literature) "Lilin and Lilioth," both male and female demons of the night—both male and female in incantations from the period as well (ibid., 231). By the Middle Ages, this motif has become, "Know and understand that when Adam separated himself from Eve for one hundred and thirty years and would sleep alone, the first Eve, that is Lilith, would find him and she lusted after his beauty, went and slept with him, and from here there went out demons, spirits and night demons" (Yassif 1984, 65 and literature cited there). A gender-neutral statement of how demons exploit celibates has become by a subtle shift a representation of demonic female sexuality.

In the rabbinic period, such legends, fears, and terrors of women's sexuality apparently persisted below the consciousness of the official textuality and culture. The evidence for the existence of such legends in the rabbinic culture comes only, however, from their denial or repression in the "official texts." The rabbinic culture (understood strictly here as the culture of the Rabbis themselves) did not countenance them. But from the early Middle Ages on, they become well entrenched in rabbinic culture and official religion, paralleled exactly by similar changes in the discourse of menstruation from cultic disability to near-demonic contamination (Shaye J. D. Cohen 1991, 281 and 284–85). The development of such demonized images of women and demonization of menstruation is, moreover, paralleled by a growing anxiety about sexuality itself in the Jewish Middle Ages (Biale 1992). We could argue, then, that misogyny was a latent and predictable effect of the disenfranchisement of women and even more so of the menstrual taboos themselves. We must not, however, read the texts of classical rabbinic literature through the fear and hatred of women characteristic of the later period, running the risk, by doing so, of further canonizing that misogynistic position.[29] In this domain it seems clear that the Rabbis are much closer to the biblical than

29. As a case in point, I would cite the notoriously misogynistic modern Hebrew poet, H. N. Bialik, who in his anthology of rabbinic lore on marriage cited extensively the most misogynistic texts and virtually nothing else (Bialik 1951, 480–99).

to the Hellenistic worlds. Once again, comparison of myths of female origins—this time, between Hesiod and the Bible—provides an important key.

Eve and Pandora

Although Pandora is occasionally referred to as the "Greek Eve" (Séchan 1929), the comparison is somewhat misleading. The difference between these two myths goes back to the beginning, for as Froma Zeitlin has shown in a recent paper (Zeitlin 1990), the narrations are already sharply differentiated in the biblical version itself of Eve's origin.[30] Zeitlin has analyzed well the differences between this myth and the biblical myth of Eve: In the Hesiodic myth, woman is not a natural being, nor consubstantial with man, but an artificially constructed creature, "a technical invention, the result of a premeditated action, an artisanal product and even a work of art—in short, an artifice in every sense of the word" (Zeitlin 1990). Next, "Woman is not created as a companion to assuage man's loneliness, as for example, the Biblical account of Adam and Eve tells us, but rather as a punishment." Third, woman is not presented as a partner in the "conduct of mortal existence," but as a drone and a drain on the man, sitting "within the house, 'filling their bellies up with the products of the toils of others' [*Th.* 599]" (Zeitlin 1990). This contrast between the production of Pandora and the creation of Eve extends to the respective representations of sexual life. Thus:

> We note that in Hesiod, far from "cleaving together and becoming one flesh" as the Biblical account tells us, or even "mingling in love -(*philotês*)," as the canonical euphemism in Greek texts (and elsewhere in the *Theogony*) would have it, man and woman remain distinctive and disjoined entities, engaged in an unequal transaction by which woman actually steals man's substance, both alimentary and sexual, and by her appetites even "roasts man alive and brings him to a premature old age" (*WD* 705). Her beautiful exterior, enhanced by those adornments which in Greek thought are externalized tokens of sexual allure, proves only to be a snare and delusion. . . . The dangers of sexuality as encroachment on the autonomous male body and the potential imbalance of its humors, the limitations/qualifications set to its unrestricted enjoyment, its separation from a specified love object, and the

---

30. I am grateful to Zeitlin for sharing a copy of this paper with me.

unbridled (extravagant) sexual appetites attributed to women are characteristic and recurrent features of Greek attitudes. Later medical and philosophical texts will spell out the dangers to men's health in taking sexual pleasure . . . but the framework is already in place in Hesiod, particularly in the context of woman's creation as an *anti pyros*, a "fire" that takes the place of the one that was stolen.

(Zeitlin 1990)

Zeitlin makes another very significant point. The Hesiodic text manifests an extraordinary ambivalence even about the role of woman as producer of children. Nothing in the text suggests that woman has the function of fecundity, as would be found, for instance, in "orthodox Greek representations of fertility" (Loraux 1981). Perhaps the clearest marker of this difference in the stories is that Eve is referred to as "The Mother of All That Lives," while Pandora is only the ancestress of the race of women (*genos gynaikīn*). As Zeitlin remarks, Hesiod even reverses the meaning of her name from "Bestower of All Gifts," an epithet of Gaia, to "Recipient of All Gifts." Finally, there is no recognition of the woman's painful productivity in the bearing of children.[31]

Zeitlin emphasizes that in the biblical story, for all of its gender asymmetry, the picture is entirely different. There, once the expulsion from the Garden has been enacted, there is a certain complementarity (if not equality) of the positions of the man and the woman. They are presented as partners, each toiling and suffering to continue human life. This distinction between Genesis and Hesiod becomes even clearer when the Genesis story is read in accordance with some important feminist interpreters, who have taught us that even Genesis 2, with its creation of Eve out of a part of Adam, is not necessarily a myth of origin to justify female subordination.[32] In any case, the sexuality of Adam and Eve is affirmed as the joining together of a single flesh, and the production of children is an unmitigated good, a blessing or even a commandment. Zeitlin goes on in her essay to inquire into the reasons both for the production of the wholly

31. Carol Meyers (1988, 100–109) disagrees with interpretations of Genesis 3:16 that see it as mentioning the pain of childbirth; however, I remain unconvinced by this argument. I think that the man and his travail in bringing forth agricultural fruit from the earth is proposed as analogous to the woman's travail in bringing forth reproductive fruit. I do not believe that this slight disagreement significantly changes the meaning of Meyers's overall corrective to the traditional misreadings.

32. See Trible 1978, Bal 1987, Meyers (1988, 85 and especially 114–17), and Boyarin 1990d.

negative Hesiodic description of woman's origin and woman's role and, even more significantly, for "the fact that the Hesiodic texts become canonical in Greek thought."

> The particularities too of Hesiod's extreme negativity towards woman, while open to compromise and mitigation in other texts and other spheres of interest, still remain the touchstone of an underlying attitude concerning this intrusive and ambivalent "other" who is brought into another man's household and forever remains under suspicion as introducing a dangerous mixture into the desired purity and univocity of male identity, whether in sexual relations or in the production of children.
>
> (Zeitlin 1990)

For our purposes here, the most significant point of contrast that she draws between the Hesiodic and biblical formations is the extreme ambivalence toward reproduction which was seemingly endemic to "the economy of scarcity, parsimony, and anxious surveillance over what man has patiently accumulated by himself and for himself" in Greece in contrast to the unqualified enthusiasm typical of the "economy of abundance, proliferation, and expansiveness" of Hebrew culture.[33]

Zeitlin's argument is an important corrective to a tendency to elide the fact that while all known ancient Mediterranean societies were thoroughly androcentric, there was nevertheless a wide range of gender ideologies in them. These different ideologies do not *necessarily* indicate differences in other categories of social practice, however. I am not going to make any claim for essential differences in social practice between the represented cultures "in the background of" particular literary works, still less between entire social formations. Thus, to claim that one or the other culture's canonical texts construct woman as evil, scary, weak, gentle, nurturing, etc., while those of the other do not, teaches us very little about how women lived in the cultures. As the late John Winkler wisely remarked, such representations may be only "male palaver." Caroline Bynum has also made the point that we cannot take what texts say about women's position in society at face value (Bynum 1986, 258). Nevertheless, what the canonical texts themselves say is an important social practice in its

---

33. It is not completely clear from Zeitlin's text whether she considers this superstructure on an actual difference in the economic base or whether the economic terms are functioning for her as metaphors for cultural/ideological phenomena.

own right, and it is that practice which I seek here to understand. There are major differences between the Bible and the texts of Greek culture that were canonical, or at any rate were transmitted as canonical to the world of late antiquity, especially the Pandora story (Panofsky and Panofsky 1956, 3–13).

The role of women in biblical literature is subordinate, dominated, and non-autonomous, but the functions of women, whether social or sexual, productive or reproductive, are valued highly and represented not as an evil that has befallen "man" but as a mark of God's benefice to man. In Hesiod's version of Greek culture (which, while not universal there, was the one transmitted to late antiquity and the Middle Ages), woman is a mark of evil and a source of danger for man and indeed essentially evil in her very nature. The economy is male in both cases; the difference is the place of woman in that economy. I argue, then, that in rabbinic literature this biblical cultural pattern and ideology were essentially retained, while in Hellenistic Judaisms the essential components of the Hellenistic ideology of women were accepted and even abetted. I postulate that at the root of Western ideologies of woman lies Pandora superimposed on Eve.

Women's Ornaments:
Divine Gift or Divine Trap?

The distinction between Eve and Pandora as the signs of two different configurations of androcentrism can be delineated sharply in the contrast between the Rabbis and Tertullian on clothing and cosmetics. In contrast to the categorical denunciation of feminine adornment typical of the Fathers, in the rabbinic culture, ornamentation, attractive dress, and cosmetics are considered entirely appropriate to the woman in her ordained role of sexual partner. Thus a bride even in mourning is permitted to use makeup, for otherwise she might become unattractive to her husband. Women are also permitted to put on makeup on holidays, although painting and drawing are forbidden, because the use of cosmetics is considered a pleasure for them and not work (Babylonian Talmud Moed Katan 9b). In the view of Rabbi Akiva, even a menstruant may wear her makeup and jewelry. That is to say, her sexuality and the external signs of her sexual allure are not suppressed even when menstruating. This is hardly a discourse of "atavistic fear of women," as a recent writer has characterized it, but it is one of subordination of women almost entirely to the needs of men.

According to legend, the same Rabbi Akiva wishes to give his beloved and self-sacrificing bride a "golden tiara in the shape of Jerusalem" as they lie together in a hay-barn (see Chapter 5). Almost as if in direct contradiction, Clement of Alexandria—the most "pro-marriage" of all of the early Fathers—writes, "Just as the serpent deceived Eve, so, too, the enticing golden ornament in the shape of a serpent enkindles a mad frenzy in the hearts of the rest of womankind, leading them to have images made of lampreys and snakes as decorations." The opposition between the discourses could not be clearer. In the Father's view, the jewel is identified as having the shape of the very noxious beasts that are the symbols of Eve's allure, while in the rabbinic formation that exemplary female ornament is the Holy City.

A passage of the Palestinian midrash on Genesis, Genesis Rabba, brings this out elegantly, as it provides an almost exact analogue for a Hesiodic (in fact, generally Greek and Hellenistic) motif and yet, once more, reverses its valences. I will begin by quoting the Hesiodic text:

> And the goddess gray-eyed Athena girdled and dressed her
> in a silver-white gown and over her head drew a veil,
> one that was woven with wonderful skill, a marvel to look at;
> and over this a garland of spring flowers, bright in their freshness.
> Pallas Athena set on her head, a lovely adornment;
> and a gold crown, encircling the brow, she put in its place,
> which had been made by the famous Lame-legged One himself.
> Using the skill of his hands, gladly obliging Zeus Father.
>
> ———————
>
> When he had finished this beauty, *this evil to balance a good,*
> Hephaistos brought her among the other gods and men,
> glorying in her adornment by the gray-eyed daughter of Great Zeus.
> Then the gods and mortals were struck with amazement when they
> beheld *this sheer inescapable snare for men.*
>
> (Frazer 1983, 66; emphasis added)

We have in the midrash exactly the same motif that is found in Hesiod's Pandora story, divine adornment of the first woman:

> R. Aibo and some say it in the name of R. Banaya and some in the name of R. Simeon the son of Yohai, "He ornamented her like a bride and brought her to him. There are places where the braid is called a

"construction."[34] Said R. Hama in the name of R. Hanina, "Do you suppose, that he simply placed her under a carob or a sycamore tree, rather
he ornamented her with twenty-four ornaments and then brought her
to him, as it says, 'When you were in Eden, the Garden of God, every
precious stone was your decoration: carnelian, chrysolite, amethyst,
beryl, lapis lazuli, jasper, sapphire, turquoise, emerald, and gold'"
[Ezekiel 28:3].

(Theodor and Albeck 1965, 161)

Although there is no reason to assume that the midrash here is in any
way dependent on Hesiod, the comparison of the treatment of the motif
of women's ornaments gives us a very neat contrast in the cultures. We
can easily see that the valence of the motif is exactly turned on its head
here. God does not adorn the woman in order to trap the man but in
order, rather, to enhance the beauty of the first wedding night, of the first
erotic encounter between husband and wife. Once more, as in the motif
of the divine gift, we see the same narrative element but with its values
precisely overturned.

As Zeitlin has remarked in a passage quoted above, there can be little
doubt that these adornments are "externalized tokens of sexual allure."
Thus, the opposite values that they are assigned in the two discourses represent the diametrically opposed valuations of women's sexuality in the
two cultural practices. The Hesiodic text reflects a discursive practice of
contempt for clothing, cosmetics, and jewelry, which was a commonplace
in both Roman and Greek literature. It is not biblical in origin, nor is it
current in rabbinic culture, but it does appear in a Jew like Philo, in such
Hellenized Jewish texts as the Testaments of the Twelve Patriarchs,[35] and

---

34. [= *banayta*]. In other words, when the Torah says "And he constructed a
woman," it can be read as "And he braided the woman's [hair]."

35.

For women are evil, my children, and by reason of their lacking authority or
power over man, they scheme treacherously how they might entice him to
themselves by means of their looks. And whomever they cannot enchant by
their appearance they conquer by a stratagem. Indeed, the angel of the Lord
told me and instructed me that women are more easily overcome by the spirit
of promiscuity than are men. They contrive in their hearts against men, then
by decking themselves out they lead men's minds astray, by a look they implant
their poison, and finally by the act itself they take them captive. . . .

Accordingly, my children, flee from sexual promiscuity, and order your
wives and your daughters not to adorn their heads and their appearances so as
to deceive men's sound minds.

(Kee 1983, 784)

in Christians like Tertullian and Clement.[36] In the midrashic text, not only are Eve's ornaments a positive gift of God to the man but they are invested with the most positive symbolism that the culture can muster. The "you" in the verse from Ezekiel is Israel herself, here identified with Eve, and the time in the Garden is referred to as a sort of honeymoon period of God's relations with Israel. Female ornaments—i.e., sexuality— are thus represented in a manner almost identical to the way that they were depicted above in the story of Rabbi Akiva, as, for the Rabbis, the very symbol of their sancta, the exact antithesis of their value in Hellenic and Hellenistic Jewish cultures.[37] For the rabbinic text, female sexuality is the image of Jerusalem, while for Clement, it is the image of a snake.

In Tertullian, as in Jerome and many others in the Patristic tradition, Woman is identified with all that is artificial and merely decorative and thus counter to the purpose of God (Bloch 1987, 11–12; see also Lichtenstein 1987):

> That which He Himself has not produced is not pleasing to God, un-less He was unable to order sheep to be born with purple and sky-blue fleeces! If He was able, then plainly He was unwilling: what God willed not, of course, ought not to be fashioned. Those things, then, are not the best by nature which are not from God, the Author of nature. Thus they are understood to be from the devil, from the corrupter of nature: for there is no other whose they can be, if they are not God's; because what are not God's must necessarily be His rival's.
>
> (Tertullian 1989b, 17)

Familiar by now is the association of women's decorations with the devil. For Tertullian, indeed, the evil of women's adornment lies precisely in that it is inappropriate to the "ignominy of the first sin" (Tertullian 1989b, 14), that is, for her who is after all "the devil's gateway" (ibid.).[38]

---

36. Tertullian seems aware of the contested nature of the topos, which he cites from the Enoch books and then remarks: "I am aware that the Scripture of Enoch, which has assigned this order (of action) to angels, is not received by some, because it is not admitted into the Jewish canon. . . . By the *Jews* it may now seem to have been rejected" (Tertullian 1989b, 15–16).

37. Indeed, stimulated by a question of Froma Zeitlin's, I am led to speculate whether the number twenty-four for the jewels is not an allusion to the twenty-four books of the bible or to the jewels on the High Priest's breastplate, which were arrayed in rows of twelve, corresponding to the twelve tribes.

38. Cf. the similar remark of R. Yehoshua quoted above who (alone among the Rabbis) also relates aspects of women's dress to the "sin of Eve," however, paradoxically

Most important for my argument is Tertullian's insistence that female ornamentation is the gift to women of the fallen angels:

> For they, withal, who instituted them are assigned, under condemna-
> tion, to the penalty of death—those angels, to wit, who rushed from
> heaven on the daughters of men; so that this ignominy also attaches to
> woman. . . . they conferred properly and as it were peculiarly upon
> women that instrumental mean of womanly ostentation, the radiances
> of jewels wherewith necklaces are variegated, and the circlets of gold
> wherewith the arms are compressed, and the medicaments of orchil
> with which wools are colored, and that black powder itself wherewith
> the eyelids and eyelashes are made prominent. What is the quality of
> these things may be declared meantime, even at this point, from the
> quality and condition of their teachers; in that sinners could never have
> either shown or supplied anything conducive to integrity.
>
> (Tertullian 1989b, 14–15)

I think that I am not unjustified in seeing in these fallen angels a powerful echo of the gods and goddesses who in Hesiod decorated Pandora as a
trap for man. The discourse of contempt for women's adornments and
their deceptive nature is, of course, endemic throughout Greek thought,
but the specific narrative element of the jewelry as a deceptive gift from
divine beings is particular, I think, to the Pandora story.

A similar but even more powerful reversal of values is shown in a parallel to the above midrashic text, in which we are told that God led Eve
by the hand to Adam, to which can be compared the leading of Pandora
to Epimetheus in the *Works and Days* version of the story. However, in
the midrashic text, this is referred to as a proof of God's steadfast love for
the human couple!, and "Happy is the citizen who has seen the king taking his [the citizen's] bride by the hand and leading her to his [the citizen's] house to him" (Tanhuma Buber Hayye Sarah), while in Hesiod,
"when he had completed this sheer inescapable snare, Zeus Father had
her led off as a gift to Epimetheus" (Frazer 1983, 98–99). Once more, I
think that the midrashic text is an allusion to the motif in the Pandora
myth of the woman given to the man by the god as a trick, a trap, and a
punishment. But in the midrashic text, the valence is explicitly reversed;
God is not a trickster, and his activities are only benevolent. In the

---

to explain why women do adorn themselves. The argument is just as obnoxious but
nevertheless significant of the directly opposite roles that objectification of women
play in the two cultures.

androcentric economy of the midrash, the woman is God's greatest gift to the man, not his revenge. The midrash emphasizes over and over that the creation of sexuality and God's participation in the wedding, as it were, signify his "steadfast love" for humans both male and female—steadfast love, as opposed to the anger and jealousy manifested by Zeus. The very excessiveness of this repetition serves, I would suggest, as an index to the energy that is being mobilized to reverse the meaning of the Hesiodic motif. Moreover, in the midrash, both man and woman are subjects, and both recipients, of God's graciousness to them in the marriage relationship.

Woman exists only to be a marriage partner, but as such, her attractiveness and pleasure are warmly appreciated, not reviled as snares and deceptions, and her ornaments and decorations are also positively valued. God himself acts the bridesmaid and prepares her for the nuptial night. Woman is not a deviation from humanity but rather its completion, for as the Rabbis proclaim, "One who is not married is not a whole human." Sin and its punishment, according to the Rabbis, initiate not sexuality but sexual shame. In describing the rabbinic ideology of sex and gender an important set of distinctions made by anthropologist Sherry Ortner in a classic paper will be very useful (1974). She identifies three different versions of female inferiority in different cultures:

> (1) elements of cultural ideology and informants' statements that explicitly devalue women, according them, their roles, their tasks, their products, and their social milieux less prestige than are accorded men and the male correlates; (2) symbolic devices, such as the attribution of defilement, which may be interpreted as implicitly making a statement of inferior valuation; and (3) social-structural arrangements that exclude women from participation in or contact with some realm in which the highest powers of the society are felt to reside. These three types of data may all of course be interrelated in any particular system, though they need not necessarily be.
>
> (1974, 69–70)

My claim is that an ethnography of rabbinic culture would find that the first two categories are *not* dominant in this formation, i.e., that explicit devaluation of women, while certainly present in the texts, is not in them a key symbol (Ortner 1973). Moreover, as I have tried to show here, even practices such as menstrual defilement do not necessarily reflect a general attribution of defilement to women or female sexuality and that within the classical rabbinic period—as opposed to medieval Judaism—they, in fact, do not. If, however, Ortner's first two categories of female inferiority—

devaluation of women and attribution of essential defilement—do not prominently obtain for the rabbinic culture, the third category—"social-structural arrangements that exclude women from participation in or contact with some realm in which the highest powers of the society are felt to reside"—does so with a vengeance.

In summation, then, rabbinic culture is gender-asymmetric. Women are imagined as enablers of men by providing for their sexual and procreative needs (which is not to deny women's independent subjectivity or rights as persons in many areas, including the right to pleasure). Such androcentric (and indeed egocentric) constructions of gender roles, however, do not imply demonization or a view of women as impure and contaminating, as I hope to have shown here. Marriage and sexuality accordingly are seen in this formation as wholly positive, as they were not, of course, in either Philo or the patristic and medieval church. The Rabbis continue a biblical sense of the essential good of sex and procreation, while the negative valence given to sexuality, the body, and in particular the woman's body, in Hellenistic Judaism and its Christian successors, continues and transforms the classical Greek ambivalence about sexuality and procreation. The rabbinic tradition rejects the characteristic ontological move of western gender discourse by which "the masculine pose[s] as a disembodied universality and the feminine get[s] constructed as a disavowed corporeality" (Butler 1990, 12). Because the Rabbis do not disavow their corporeality, they do not construct it as feminine. In the next chapter, I shall attempt to analyze something of the discourse of sexual desire and interaction in marriage, particularly as it affects the differential power of men and women in the culture.

4

Engendering Desire
Husbands, Wives, and Sexual Intercourse

The object, in short, is to define the regime of power-knowledge-pleasure
that sustains the discourse on human sexuality . . . to account for the
fact that it is spoken about, to discover who does the speaking, the
positions and viewpoints from which they speak, the institutions which
prompt people to speak about it and which store and distribute the
things that are said. What is at issue, briefly, is the over-all "discursive
fact," the way in which sex is "put into discourse." Hence, too, my
main concern will be to locate the forms of power, the channels it
takes, and the discourses it permeates in order to reach the most tenuous and individual modes of behavior, the paths that give it access to
the rare or scarcely perceivable forms of desire, how it penetrates and
controls everyday pleasure—all this entailing effects that may be those
of refusal, blockage, and invalidation, but also incitement and intensification: in short, the "polymorphous techniques of power."

(Foucault 1980, 11)

My purpose in this chapter is to begin the charting of the operations of
power over and within the forms of pleasure and desire in the talmudic
culture, the power of the rabbinic class over the sexual practices of married couples, and the power of men over women in sexual life. The
Foucauldian critique of the "repressive hypothesis" will serve us well here
in looking at the complex modalities of power and production within
which rabbinic texts on sexuality function. I will be looking at texts that
have been read until now as the very origin and sites of a repressive discourse, but my aim will be to show that their actual function is quite different from what has usually been portrayed. The text often cited as the
marker of a controlling force that the Rabbis claimed over the conduct of
married sexual practice can be read precisely as a renunciation of such
control. In several ways, through several textual practices, the Rabbis
removed from the Torah's purview the actual practices of married couples
in the bedroom, and their extreme codification of the necessity for privacy during sexual activity makes actual sexual practice invisible and thus

uncontrollable. The area over which the Rabbis do wish to retain control is paradoxically the emotional, affective state of relations between the husband and wife at the time of sexual contact, which they codify as requiring intimacy, harmony of desires, and mutual arousal and pleasure. This point will raise serious questions regarding a commonly held view that woman is a sexual object and not subject in rabbinic culture. While the only voices heard in the talmudic and midrashic texts are male ones, among those male voices many are earnestly empathic of female need and desire.

Indeed, this ironic double stance of both genuine empathy for women and rigid hierarchical domination of women is endemic in the talmudic discourse. Perhaps its most sardonic moment comes in a text that I will analyze in the next chapter, where a husband who has spent more than a decade away from home to study Torah refers to his wife as "that poor woman," *because he has been away for more than a decade studying Torah!* In general, however, women are held to be in the category of virtually powerless people who need to be dealt with in a solicitous fashion. Thus, in a talmudic passage dealing with the ineluctable moral power that wronged people have when they pray to God, most of the examples deal with the treatment of wives by husbands:

> Said Rav: A man should always be careful not to grieve his wife, for since her tears are nigh, [the punishment for] her grief is nigh.
>
> Rabbi El'azar said: From the day that the Temple was destroyed, the gates of prayer have been shut, as it says: *Even though I call out and shout, he shut out my prayer* [Lamentations 3:8]. But even though the gates of prayer were locked, the gates of tears were not locked, as it says: *Hear my prayer, O God; listen to my supplication. Do not be silent [in the face of] my tears* [Psalms 39:13].
>
> (Baba Metsia 59a)

Wives are represented as virtually powerless creatures, whose only weapon is tears—tears which, to be sure, guarantee an automatic divine response. It is nevertheless the case, however, that the force of this discourse, far from authorizing men to mistreat women as their property, is rather to encourage men to be very solicitous (even patronizing) of women. The text goes on:

> And Rav [also] said: He who follows the advice of his wife, will fall into Hell, for it says: *But there was none like Ahab, who gave himself over to do what was evil in the sight of the Lord, as Jezebel his wife had incited him* [1 Kings 21:25].

But, said Rav Pappa to Abayye: Don't the people say, "If your wife is short, bend down and whisper with her"?!

There is no difficulty; one case refers to worldly matters and the other to domestic matters, or some say, one case refers to heavenly matters and the other to worldly matters.

The same Rav who just above produced a strong statement and a strong incentive for husbands not to cause their wives tears, now equally as strongly counsels them to ignore their wives' advice. Here is an almost perfect emblem of a benignly patronizing formation. On the other hand, this latter statement is challenged by Rav Pappa, and, interestingly, the challenge comes from a popular proverb that indicates that a man should pay very great attention to what his wife is saying. The two resolutions that the Talmud provides for the apparent contradiction are themselves instructive, as one gives the wife voice only in domestic matters, while the other gives her voice in all secular issues, only constricting her from having anything to say about religious issues. Although we will see some breaks in this pattern in following chapters, this structure is emblematic of rabbinic gender discourse. Women are rendered nearly powerless, and then the Rabbis, the very same ones who (as Rav here) produced the discourse of male domination, ameliorate its effects somewhat by inducing men not to take advantage of their wives' powerlessness and, indeed, to be highly solicitous of them. The same pattern obtains with regard to sexual practice as well.

MALE DESIRE

In the Babylonian Talmud Nedarim 20a–b, we find the following very famous text in which the question of "how sex is put into discourse" is thematized directly. What is usually claimed to be the site par excellence of rabbinic repression of sexual practice even within marriage will be read as its exact opposite:

It has been taught: *In order that His fear shall be upon you* [Exod. 20:20] —This is modesty. *In order that you not sin* [ibid.]—teaches that modesty conduces to the fear of sin. From hence they said: It is a good sign about a person that he [or she] is modest. Others say: Anyone who is modest does not quickly sin, and as for one who does not have modesty of demeanor, this is a sign that his ancestors did not stand at Mt. Sinai.

Rabbi Yohanan the son of Dabai said—The Ministering Angels told me:

Why are there lame children? Because they [their fathers] turn over the tables.[1]

Why are there dumb children? Because they kiss that place.

Why are there deaf children? Because they talk during intercourse.

Why are there blind children? Because they look at that place.

And we challenged [that tradition with the following tradition]: They asked Imma Shalom [Mother Peace], the wife of Rabbi Eliezer, "Why do you have such beautiful children?" She said to them, "He does not have intercourse with me at the beginning of the night, nor at the end of the night, but at midnight, and when he has intercourse with me, he unveils an inch and veils it again, and appears as if he was driven by a demon." I asked him, "What is the reason [for this strange behavior]?" And he said to me, "In order that I not imagine another woman, and the children will come to be bastards."[2]

There is no contradiction. One refers to matters of sex, and the other to non-sexual matters.

Rabbi Yohanan [a later one—not the same as Yohanan the son of Dabai] said: These are the words of Rabbi Yohanan the son of Dabai, but the sages say, "Anything that a man wishes to do with his wife, he may do, analogously to meat that comes from the shop. If he wishes to eat it with salt, he may; roasted, he may; boiled, he may; braised, he may. And similarly fish from the store of the fisherman."

Amemar said: Who are the Ministering Angels? The Rabbis, for if you say literally: Ministering Angels, then why did Rabbi Yohanan say that the law is not like Rabbi Yohanan the son of Dabai? After all, they certainly know embryology! And why does he call them "Ministering Angels"? Because they are excellent like the Ministering Angels.

A certain woman came before Rabbi [an honorific title of Rabbi Yehudah the Prince], and said to him: Rabbi: I set him a table, and he turned it over. He said to her: My daughter, The Torah has permitted you, and I, what can I do for you?

A certain woman came before Rabbi. She said to him: Rabbi, I set him the table, and he turned it over. He said: How is the case different from fish?

And you shall not wander after your hearts [Num. 16:39]—From hence Rabbi said: Let not a man drink from this cup and have his mind on another cup.

---

1. "Turning the tables" may refer to anal intercourse, or to vaginal intercourse from behind, or even just to vaginal intercourse with the woman on top. The male, understood in any case as the active partner, is the one "held responsible." The next sentences make clear that the male partner is the subject here, because "that place" always refers to the female genitals.

2. This latter part of the text is quoted in Chapter 1 above. Rabbi Eliezer's behavior, which is not my theme here, is interpreted there.

Ravina said: It was not necessary [to say this], except for even when both of them are his wives [i.e., when the women are not both his wives it is obvious that he must not think of another woman while he sleeps with his wife, but this comes to teach us that even when he is married to both of them, he is forbidden to have his mind on one while he has sex with the other].

And I will remove from you the rebellious ones and the criminals [Ezek. 20:39]—Said Rabbi Levi: These are nine categories:

Children of fright; children of rape; children of a despised woman; children of excommunication; children of exchange; children of strife; children of drunkenness; children of one whom he has divorced in his heart; children of mixture; children of a brazen woman.

Indeed? But did not Shmuel the son of Nahmani say that Rabbi Yohanan[3] said: Any man whose wife approaches him sexually will have children such as were unknown even in the generation of Moses. . . .

That refers to a case where she arouses him [but does not explicitly and verbally request sex].

This is, perhaps, the single most extended and important text on the techniques of married sex in the talmudic literature. It is an excellent demonstration, moreover, of the dangers of quoting a talmudic citation out of the dialectic context in which it is embedded. The text has to be read in two modes. At one level, it has to be read for the ideology of the redactor[s], but at the same time, the contrary ideologies of the sources cited and problematized by those redactors have to be taken into account.

The Talmud here thematizes two kinds of control over sexual behavior in the conjugal bed. One has to do with the actual practices engaged in and the other with the affective state of the couple. The first type of control is renounced by the text, while the second is strongly supported. In addition, as we will see below, the two types of control are actually thematized as mutually oppositional to each other. After a general statement of the requirement of modesty for Jewish people, both men and women, the Talmud cites a source that is ostensibly a prescription for the enactment of modest behavior. This text has one strikingly unusual feature, namely, that it is a report of a conversation with the Ministering Angels. In all of the Talmud, there is no other report of an attempt by the Ministering Angels to impose their halakhic or moral ideas on human beings. Indeed, in the only places in the Talmud where knowing the speech of angels is referred to as part of the knowledge of an outstanding sage, this

3. Variant: Yonathan.

knowledge is placed way down on the list, something on the order of knowing the speech of demons, as opposed to the various branches of Torah-knowledge proper, including knowledge of the Oral Torah and the aggadah, which are placed very high on the list.[4] The citation, by placing its statements in the mouths of angels, is not codifying them as Torah-knowledge, that is, as normative statements, but as "scientific" or practical knowledge. The form of the assertions themselves implies this pragmatic orientation, for instead of saying that it is forbidden to engage in such activities and relating that the punishment will be such and such, the assertions merely claim that these sexual practices give rise to certain undesirable procreative results. The type of control attempted here fits Foucault's descriptions of the modern discourses of medical control of sexuality better than it does the way that the medieval church exercised its control (Foucault 1980, 37–38) through canon law and the system of penances.

Rabbi Yohanan rejects, however, both the content of Rabbi Yohanan the son of Dabai's statement and, implicitly, its claims to scientific status. He promotes it from the category of "good advice" from a knowledgeable source to the level of Torah discourse, that is, to the discourse of the forbidden and permitted according to religion, but he does so in order to *reject* its religious validity. While Amemar's explanation seems farfetched, in a sense it is necessitated by Rabbi Yohanan's intervention, because the latter had introduced a discontinuity into the discursive frame by saying, "The halakha is not like Rabbi Yohanan the son of Dabai," as the latter had ostensibly not made a halakhic statement at all. In any case, the upshot of Rabbi Yohanan's pronouncement is to disqualify Rabbi Yohanan the son of Dabai's statement twice, as lacking both the scientific status of angelic knowledge and any correctness as Torah-knowledge. The Torah disqualifies itself from any interference in the private sexual practices of married couples, who may behave sexually as they please with each other. Moreover, as if Rabbi Yohanan were not authority enough, the Talmud backs up this judgment with an authority even greater than his, that of Rabbi—the author of the Mishna itself, who, in actual practical situations advises two women that they have no recourse or complaint to the rabbis against their husbands' desire for an "unusual" form of intercourse—either woman on top or, somewhat less likely, anal penetration (see below)—because the Torah has permitted it. Note

4. See Sukkah 28a and Baba Bathra 134a.

that according to Rabbi Yohanan, not even non-procreative acts are condemned by the Torah. In other talmudic texts we learn, moreover, that anal intercourse is permitted as well. According to this view, at any rate, "wasting of seed" takes place only in masturbation, not in sexual intercourse of even non-procreative varieties.

FEMALE DESIRE

Until this point, I have purposely evaded an issue that must now be directly addressed. In interpreting that both Rabbi Yohanan and Rabbi permit *couples* to engage in whatever sexual practices *they* wish, I have tacitly been ignoring the obvious fact of gender asymmetry in this text. These rabbinic voices—i.e., those attributed to Rabbi and Rabbi Yohanan—only specify and relate to the will of the man and not to that of the woman. The "reciprocal" interpretation given thus far tends, therefore, to mystify the effects of gender inequality in sexuality as in most areas of the culture. One could even imagine, in fact, that what is encoded here is permission to the male to exercise his will upon the body of the woman without reference to her desire. This misogynistic interpretation seems well warranted by the text: we have here a metaphor that apparently compares the woman to a piece of meat or fish, seemingly an object for the satisfaction of the man, and we also have Rabbi's explicit declaration that he can do nothing for the women who come to him expressing their wish that their husbands be censured, since the Torah has permitted such sexual practice. This view of Rabbi and of his student Rabbi Yohanan stands in sharp contrast, however—in fact, in direct contradiction—to the rest of the talmudic discourse on this topic, which unambiguously forbids all sexual coercion, including verbal, of a wife by her husband and raises a joining of wills and desires to a very high value in its hygiene of sexual intercourse.

In contrast to the more usual situation, then, where I identify a counter-voice that I choose to animate and mobilize for a future of gender politics, in this case it is the counter-voice that I wish to leave as inactive. The dominant—in terms of both the text itself and the "reception" of this text—unambiguously militates against the notion of the wife as object in sexual relations. Thus, in distinction to the *rejected* angelic proscriptions on various sexual practices, as leading to physical defects in the children, the Talmud *accepts* the statement of Rabbi Levi that affective disorder in the sexual relation leads to moral faults in the offspring. The affective disturbances listed, moreover, are ones that take very seriously indeed the desire of the wife. The first two on the list are children of fear and children of rape—that is, offspring of situations in which the husband coerces his wife into having sex with him by being aggressive to the point that she is too frightened to say no or, even worse, is actually raped. This note is strengthened dramatically by a parallel passage in the Talmud Eruvin 100b, where the following pronouncement occurs:

> Rami bar Hama said that Rav Asi said: It is forbidden for a man to force his wife in a holy deed,[5] for it says *One who presses the legs is a sinner* [Prov. 19:2]. And Rabbi Yehoshua ben Levi said: One who forces his wife in a holy deed will have dishonest children.
>
> Said Rav Ika the son of Hinnena: What is its verse? *Also without will, the soul is not good* [ibid.]. And so we have learnt in a tannaitic tradition as well: What is the meaning of *Also without will, the soul is not good?* This is the one who forces his wife in a holy deed. *And one who presses the legs is a sinner?* This is one who has intercourse twice in a row.
>
> Can that be? But did not Rava say: If one wants all of his children to be male, he should have intercourse twice in a row.
>
> There is no difficulty: One refers to a case where she does not agree, and one to a case where she does agree.

Because the Talmud both here and in the parallel passage strongly condemns one who has intercourse with his wife against her will, and indeed codifies such behavior as "forbidden" even when it is procreative, then the proscription against force should be all the stronger in a nonprocreative situation, such as oral or anal intercourse. This opinion that one may not force one's wife is not at all an isolated or minority view; it is the generally held and authoritative position both of the Talmud and of later Jewish law. Indeed, far from treating a wife as a piece of property or mere object for the satisfaction of the husband's sexual desire, talmudic law may be the first legal or moral system that recognizes that when a husband forces his wife the act is rape, pure and simple, and as condemnable and contemnable as any other rape![6] Another attempt to enact

5. The literal translation is "in the matter of a commandment." There is no doubt, however, that the reference is to sexual intercourse, as Rashi points out. It is indeed interesting that the talmudic discourse uses *commandment* without further definition to refer to sexual intercourse and *transgression* without further definition to refer to sexual sin.

6. For the *present* situation of American law, see Chamberlain (1991, 122). I remember reading somewhere (but unfortunately not where) that an American court had cited the Talmud as a legal precedent for treating wife-rape as rape. In this

a control over the act of sexual intercourse itself—namely that it should not be repeated immediately, presumably because the second act would not be procreative—is transmuted by the Talmud into yet another and stronger prohibition of wife-rape. Even if she has agreed to a first act of intercourse, he may not presume her agreement to a repeated act on the same occasion but must know explicitly that she wishes it.

Furthermore, several of the other elements of Rabbi Levi's list also regard the affective relation between husband and wife as of primary importance in the propriety of sexual relations. If the husband hates his wife, has decided to divorce her, is drunk and "cannot pay attention to his wife's needs" [Rashi], or even if the pair have had a quarrel and not properly made up after it, then sexual relations are forbidden between them, and the fruit of such improper unions will be rebellious and wicked children. Indeed, even if he believes that he is sleeping with one of his wives and is actually with another, that alone is enough to produce such undesirable offspring, because the intimate emotional relations required for appropriate sexual joining are absent. This is marked even more explicitly in a parallel text, which adds "the children of a sleeping woman" to the list. All this is totally irreconcilable with a notion that a wife is a sexual object and not a subject in talmudic culture.

The most obvious way to read Rabbi Yohanan and Rabbi's utterances is that these passages, at least, explicitly treat a wife as instrument and object of the husband's sexuality. Their statements are, then, in this regard, the counter-voice within the talmudic text, and, as such, *may* represent a minority ideology that did objectify wives. The method of reading employed in this book often involves the identification of a point of tension or conflict between the voices of the texts that the Talmud quotes and the ideological interests of the redactors. If we accept this reading, that which I have just identified as the most obvious one, then we have such a point of sharp conflict here. While all the rest of the text here and other textual resources in the Talmud insist that sexual practice be only in accord with the wife's will and desire, these statements seem to represent a different position, one that encodes a wife not so much as a human

---

context, I would like to note that Wegner's repeated insistence that a wife's sexuality is the property of her husband in talmudic law is extremely misleading (Wegner 1988, 19 and passim), particularly in the legal context of her discussion. Virtually none of the legal definitions of ownership apply. A husband may not make use of her sexuality without her consent; he may not alienate it; he may not dispose of it. The definition seems to me, therefore, entirely invalid.

subject but as meat or fish. Just as I have often identified contesting voices in the Talmud that I find attractive, I would recognize here the presence of a contesting voice that I find simply appalling. We may have here evidence even of a development in talmudic ideology from an earlier position that did not recognize the relevance of female desire to a later one that made it central. The Talmud's citation of these voices, as on the one hand a refutation of Rabbi Yohanan the son of Dabai's repressive views, and on the other hand just before the strong prohibition of rape in Rabbi Levi's statement, would be understood along this line of interpretation as the Talmud's attempt to neutralize the implication that wives are sexual objects but preserve the point that sexual practice itself is not controlled by the Torah.

On the other hand, we must reckon as well with the possibility that just as "apologetic" readings may be playing false with the text for our purposes, so also a reading that makes these rabbinic voices so unpalatable may also be an anachronism that grows out of our own cultural presuppositions. Is it possible to read Rabbi Yohanan's and Rabbi's statements otherwise? Perhaps yes. Rabbi Yohanan simply says nothing at all about the wife's desire, because that is not at issue for him here. His project is rejecting the attempt of Rabbi Yohanan the son of Dabai to promulgate a rigid code of sexual behaviors between husband and wife with everything forbidden but the "missionary position." The issue of her consent is simply not raised here, but that does not mean that it is irrelevant. Only a few lines later the Talmud makes its strong statement against wife-rape. To be sure, his statement is addressed to men and about men—"whatever a man wishes"—but this is a reflection of the overweening androcentrism of the discourse as a whole, not *necessarily* a statement that husbands do not need to take account of their wives' needs. In other words, this may simply be an androcentric way of saying that husbands and wives are free to do in the bedroom whatever *they* wish, since sex is kosher between them, just as one is permitted to cook kosher meat in whatever way one wishes. Nonetheless, the force of the metaphor and the implied equation of the woman's body to food cannot be denied. But even this extremely offensive utterance does not translate into a statement that a woman is a pure sexual object, a mere "piece of meat" for the satisfaction of her husband's desire, but only that the Torah does not get involved in the bedroom. The eating metaphor here must be read within the context of the rich field of metaphors in which sex and eating are mutually mapped onto each other in the talmudic culture with eating the quintessential signifier of that which is both pleasurable and necessary for health and well-being. Within this field, the notion of consuming or devouring does not seem dominant, and here the primary metaphorical comparison is with the fact that while there are many categories of foods which are forbidden, those that are permitted may be enjoyed in any manner. Similarly, while there are sexual connections that are forbidden, those that are permitted may be enjoyed in any fashion. The overtone of male dominance is here and cannot be gainsaid or whitewashed, but it does not, on this reading, constitute the primary thrust of the metaphor, nor is the point of the statement that men can do whatever they want *to* their wives. The food metaphor in itself does not turn women into food. The Talmud also uses the metaphor of eating to refer to the woman's sexual experience. Thus the Mishna at Ketubbot 5:9 reads that a wife has the right to eat with her husband every Friday night, and in both Talmuds this is understood to mean to have sexual intercourse with him.[7] There are even places in the talmudic text, moreover, where children are referred to with food metaphors as well, and children are certainly not objectified as "consumables." This complex usage of the metaphorical field militates against the notion that its function is to define woman as "sex object."[8]

The stories about Rabbi and the wives are much more resistant to reinterpretation, because they *do* relate to the wife's desire and do so in a negative way. Rabbi certainly seems to indicate that the Torah has nothing to say about proscribing certain sexual practices, even when the activities involved are distasteful to the wives. But, strangely enough, the redactor of the Talmud did not seem to feel that there was any tension between Rabbi's stories and the emphatic prohibition of wife-rape which comes just after them. Although the redactorial level of the Talmud often "harmonizes," tacitly reducing tensions that I wish to emphasize, in cases of direct (and felt) contradiction it *explicitly* attempts to reduce the contradiction. In this case, given the enormous rhetorical force of the prohibitions on wife-rape that this redactor encodes, it seems then that he, at any rate, did not consider these stories as being cases of rape. In both

7. I am grateful to Mordechai Friedman for reminding me of this reference.

8. My colleague Chana Kronfeld reminded me of this usage. Note that wives and children are in some sense figured as "property" of the patriarch for his enjoyment, but for his enjoyment as human beings in his world, not as objects to be used.

situations the wife indicates that she was interested in having sex, and her only objection was to the position. It seems to me that much turns on the exact meaning of the term "turning over the tables," which as a sexual practice is unfortunately obscure. The most plausible interpretation on philological grounds is intercourse with the woman on top, in which case Rabbi's response is a relatively innocuous: The Torah allows that practice, so negotiate it with him. In support of this reading—at least as the one that the Talmud's redactors fostered—stands the absence of anything in the text's rhetoric or structure that would indicate that they understood Rabbi's position to be antithetical or adversative to their own unequivocal stand against wife-rape. If one is forbidden to have intercourse with one's wife a second time without her explicit consent, and to do so is considered wife-rape by the Talmud, it hardly seems possible that it would be normative that forcing her to have, e.g., anal intercourse is permitted.[9] Rabbi may simply have understood, therefore, that the women's concern was somehow related to the propriety of sexual intercourse with the woman on top—and there might indeed have been some reason for anxiety, since according to some traditions, Lilith's sin was her desire for such sex. Note the irony: The men are demanding a sexual practice which is otherwise taken as a signifier for female insubordination, as it were; their wives are objecting, and the Rabbi indicates that it is permitted.

9. A reader of the manuscript suggested that my reasoning was faulty here, and that the reason that the Rabbis do not proscribe these acts against the will of the wife is precisely because they are non-procreative and therefore of no concern for the Rabbis. This reading makes the following assumptions: (1) that the Rabbis' only concern about sexuality was the quality of progeny; and (2) that they believed that what is wrong with rape is that it is not conducive to the conception of proper children, and not what seems to me to be the obvious interpretation, namely, that *since* rape is ethically wrong, *therefore* the punishment will be immoral children. Although neither of these assumptions is impossible, neither is suggested by anything in the talmudic text, and the question is why one would want to begin with premises that ascribe the worst possible motives to *any* group of people, thus violating the hermeneutic principle of charity. Two further arguments can be brought to bear against this interpretation. First: it violates Ockham's razor as well. Given my interpretation, we understand why rape would produce undesirable children, namely, as a punishment for the rape, but if we assume that rape is only forbidden because it produces undesirable children, then from whence comes the notion itself that rape leads to bad progeny? We would have to assume this as a further, otherwise unattested and uncontextualized notion of the culture, thus violating the principle that the simplest explanation is to be preferred. Finally, the notion that bad action leads to bad results is firmly anchored in the almost ubiquitous topos of rabbinic culture, namely: measure for measure. Unless we are prepared to posit that in general these structures of crime and punishment are a smokescreen, why would we do so here?

Rabbi is, in effect, assuring them that such sex is permitted, and they need fear no repercussions from God. Alternatively, we might read him somewhat less charitably and assume that he (and the talmudic redactors) might have understood that once a woman has consented to sex, then her lack of consent to a particular position does not constitute rape. Note that according to this reading, "permitted you" is to be interpreted as the Torah has permitted you to engage in this practice. If, on the other hand, the practice referred to is indeed anal intercourse, then, it would seem, engaging in it without the express desire of the wife does constitute a rape—not, I hasten to add, because of the "unnaturalness" of anal inter-course but simply because penetration of a different orifice seems much greater a violation of the woman's will than the arrangement of the bod-ies. According to this reading, "permitted you" would mean the Torah has permitted you to him—the Hebrew supports either construction. According to this latter reading, then, Rabbi's position is once more sharply antithetical to the rest of the text.

If we adopt the first reading, namely, that the wife desired sex—as she indicates herself—and that all the husband proposed was to have her on top, then it is clear why Rabbi is not represented as referring to the very halakha which forbids a husband to have any coercive sex with his wife. If the other view is adopted, then it seems perhaps that there is a relic here of a position that did not recognize wife-rape as forbidden. I cannot claim that the more generous interpretation is a "better" or more truthful one than the first.[10] There very probably was dissent within the rabbinic culture, here as in so many other situations. In any case the Talmud cites the emphatic halakha against wife-rape to its implied male audience, so that those readers, at any rate, cannot misunderstand and derive from here permission to treat their wives as objects. What can be said to be established, therefore, is that whatever the view of Rabbi or Rabbi

10. For an excellent account of decision criteria for interpretations in a feminist-critical context, see Bal (1987, 11–15). My second, more generous, interpretation observes the convention of unity, a convention that I am otherwise opposed to throughout, so this cannot serve as a criterion in its favor. On the other hand, it may also serve to render the text more useful in the sense that Bal articulates: "One modest and legitimate goal has always been a fuller understanding of the text, one that is sophisticated, reproducible, and accessible to a larger audience. As long as by 'a fuller understanding' one means having found a more satisfying way of integrating the read-ing experience into one's life, more possibilities of doing something with this experi-ence, such an approach is a justifiable critical practice. . . . These criteria are basically pragmatic. Far from having anything to do with standards of 'scientificity', they deal with what readers can find of use" (12–13).

Yohanan, the Talmud makes crystal clear the point that a man may not force his wife to have sex with him and that to do so is rape. The reason that the Talmud cites their views here is not to permit sexual objectification of a wife, as the context makes abundantly clear, but to indicate that the Torah does not interfere in the details of sexual practices, of positions and pleasures between husband and wife, any more than it prescribes whether to boil or fry (kosher) foods. Nevertheless, the decision *not* to interfere when a situation is potentially repressive implicitly supports the status quo. While banning rape, the text still implies that male dominance in sexual matters is protected by the law, because the law will not interfere to put checks on it or provide the woman with protection or with a procedure to attain her own desires and exercise her own free will. The prescriptions repeatedly provided by the Talmud for the creation of conditions for mutual arousal, intimacy, and mutual satisfaction exclude the interpretation that the purpose of the citation of the Rabbi stories is to permit wife-rape, since that very practice is condemned so severely only a few lines later, but they still leave the husband firmly in control. It is worth noting, moreover, that this interpretation of the text is the one that came to be codified in medieval and later Jewish law; wife-rape was absolutely forbidden and recognized as sin, and all that was learned from Rabbi Yohanan and Rabbi was that the Torah does not prescribe nor proscribe any particular sexual practices between husbands and wives.

The theme of the necessity for intimacy between the husband and wife at the time of sexual intercourse is expressed throughout the passage in different ways.[11] Thus, even with regard to the ambivalent story of Rabbi Eliezer's sexual practice that Imma Shalom tells,[12] while we must concede a great deal of ambivalence in association with the Rabbi's behavior we must also not ignore the explicit statement that the purpose of his behavior

11. My interpretations here are much influenced by the doctoral dissertation of my student Dalia Hoshen (Hoshen 1990), from whom I have learned a great deal. She is not, of course, responsible for the exact nuances of my interpretations, which are sometimes in open conflict with her positions.

12. It should be emphasized that I am not denying ideological conflict and ambivalence about sexuality among the Rabbis. My position is somewhat between that of the "apologists," who have blithely characterized rabbinic Judaism as pro-sex, this-worldly, and non-ascetic and those of the "revisionists," which seek to characterize it as very similar in its sexual anxieties to the late-antique pagan and Christian world around and among the Jews. In Chapter 1 above, I have detailed this in-between point of view.

was to prevent him from thinking of another woman. That is to say, whatever the "true" meaning of Rabbi Eliezer's sexual behavior, the narrator, through the speech of Imma Shalom, inscribes it in the intimacy code. Moreover, it is consistent with at least three other moments in the text. First, the function for which the story of Rabbi Eliezer and Imma Shalom is cited is explicitly as an objection to the statement by Rabbi Yohanan the son of Dabai that a couple may not converse during intercourse.[13] The Rabbis who cited this source here understood that the conversation between Rabbi Eliezer and Imma Shalom took place during sexual intercourse. Moreover, the resolution of the apparent conflict between the texts is also highly significant. What the angels intended to forbid, according to the talmudic resolution, was speaking of other and distracting matters during the sexual act. Even the angels permit couples to speak of sexual matters, which is what Rabbi Eliezer and Imma Shalom did. According to the redactorial level of the talmudic text, then, one is permitted to speak of sex during sexual activity, as it is considered conducive to the creation of intimacy and warmth between the partners. This is, then, consistent with the stated reason for the Rabbi's behavior.

Let us read this story a bit more closely. It is important to know at the start that the word that Imma Shalom uses for "intercourse" is "talking." Literally, what she says to the Rabbis is, "When he talks to me, he does not talk to me at the beginning of the night, nor at the end of the night, but at midnight." I think that the linguistic echo is significant, because the story, like the entire talmudic passage, is about the *discourse* of sex, that is, at least in this case, about *talking* about sex.[14] Rabbi Yohanan ben Dabai's angelic communication has been cited as illustration of the principle that modesty is vitally important. Accordingly, the conversation that takes place between husband and wife during intercourse (which in English, too, means conversation!) is an example of immodesty according to that tradition. It is that notion that the text of Imma Shalom is motivated here to counter.

However, at first glance, one would think that far from countering or opposing Rabbi Yohanan ben Dabai's tradition, the story of how Rabbi Eliezer conducted his sexual life would seem to support that tradition. If

---

13. That is, *mirabile dictu*, the text is cited as a permissive one!

14. I do not agree with David Biale (1989) who sees here a misunderstanding of the word and claims that the Talmud cites this as an objection on the basis of a literal understanding here of "talking."

he did not undress her or himself, uncovering only the bare necessary minimum, then he certainly did not "look at that place," let alone kiss it. Nor, seemingly, could he have taken the time to talk to her at all, since he was conducting himself as if driven by a demon. What does the Talmud mean, then, by citing the story as an objection to Rabbi Yohanan ben Dabai? The Talmud understands that she asked him to explain his strange behavior (and note that by this it is marked as strange) during the act itself, and, moreover, that he answered her at the same time. They spoke to each other during sex, which is what constitutes the apparent refutation of Rabbi Yohanan ben Dabai. In any case, according to the Talmud's refutation and resolution of the apparent contradiction, this problem disappears: the only sort of speech that is forbidden is speech that distracts from the intercourse, not speech that enhances it, and even that restriction is rejected in the end with the total rejection of Rabbi Yohanan ben Dabai. According to the talmudic passage, in fine, the Torah seeks control not over the physical aspects of married sex but only over the emotional side of it.

The Contradiction of Discourses

As the Talmud explicitly argues, in fact, the two attempts at control of married sex contradict each other, for repression of visual, tactile, and conversational intimacy would have a chilling effect on that very closeness of the partners' desires and wills that the other voice wishes to promote. We have two contradictory discourses—the discourse of control in the conjugal bed and the discourse of free intimacy. By citing the Rabbi Eliezer and Imma Shalom story dialectically, the Talmud makes sure that we realize this point, for indeed, otherwise this citation is irrelevant, nothing but a local objection and modification of an utterance by Rabbi Yohanan ben Dabai that the Talmud intends to reject entirely. But it makes this very point—that such control and intimacy are in opposition to each other.

In another place, the Talmud cites one more story that supports the contradictory nature of these two discourses, as well as giving us a "real-life" vignette of the sexual practice of a Rabbi who was one of the most authoritative figures of the entire culture:

Rav Kahana entered and lay down beneath the bed of Rav. He heard that he was talking and laughing and having sexual intercourse. He said, "The mouth of Abba [Rav's name] appears as if he has never tasted this dish."[15] He [Rav] said to him, "Kahana, get out; this is not proper behavior!" He [Kahana] said to him, "It is Torah, and I must learn it."

This is a fascinating, complex, and rich text. It almost explicitly raises the issue of the "panopticon," the surveillance of private sexual behavior on the part of a culture. Although it does so in a surprising direction—from below to above, from student to teacher—this fact does not materially change its operations, for if the teacher is to be observed having sex by the student, then sex is being controlled, just as effectively as if the students were to be observed by their teachers. The surveillance is, however, vigorously rejected. There is no evidence whatsoever that Rav or the Talmud itself accepted Rav Kahana's declaration here that "it" is Torah that he must learn, but in the meantime the text has managed to reveal precisely that which it ostensibly seeks to conceal, namely, that Rav "was talking and laughing" intimately with his wife as they had intercourse, thus further supporting the thought presented by the Nedarim text that such verbal behavior as enhances the intimacy and pleasure of sex is permitted and praiseworthy.

We have, indeed, explicit evidence that it was Rav's behavior here that was considered normative. In the Babylonian Talmud Hagiga 5b, we read:

> Rabbi Ila was going up the staircase of the house of Rabba the son of Shila and he heard a child reciting: For behold, He creates the mountains and creates the wind, and tells a man about his conversation [Amos 4:13]. He said: A slave whose master tells him about his conversations, has he any remedy?
>
> *What does "about his conversation" mean?* Rav said: Even the superfluous speech between husband and wife is reported to the man at the time of his death.
>
> *Can that be? But Rav Kahana was lying under the bed of Rav, and he heard him conversing and laughing and having intercourse. He said, "The mouth of Rav appears as if he has never tasted this dish." He [Rav] said to him, "Kahana, get out; this is not proper behavior!"*
>
> There is no difficulty. This is a case where he has to arouse her, and this is a case where he does not have to arouse her.

---

15. This also serves as an argument for the conclusion reached above, namely, that in the figurative usage of eating for sexual intercourse, the food is the sex and not the wife. Certainly, Rav Kahana was referring to Rav's ebullience and enthusiasm for sex and not implying that he was behaving as if this were the first time with her.

I have quoted the entire story again, because I think it is significant that Rav Kahana's defense that "It is Torah, and I must learn it" is omitted from this version (or was added in the other version). What is quoted as normative is Rav's behavior with his wife, and this is raised as an objection to his declaration that all superfluous speech, including intimate speech between husband and wife, will be answerable for at death. The Talmud's response is that when he needs to arouse his wife, when she is not "in the mood for love," then it is entirely appropriate and indeed required that he do so with words of intimacy and play. This, then, fits perfectly the picture that I have drawn on the basis of the Nedarim passage alone, that the requirement to arouse the desire of the wife and the intimacy and harmony of the couple are what become codified as the purview of Torah, according to the Talmud, and not the details of the physical act itself, which are left to their desires.

However, in accord with the method of reading in this book in general, we cannot ignore the fact that the text also incorporates Rav Kahana's voice claiming that this *is* Torah, and that he has the right (duty, obligation) to observe it. This voice correlates with the voice of Rabbi Yohanan ben Dabai and his angelic interlocutors, who also wish to place the details of the sexual practices between lawful husband and wife under scrutiny and control.[16] Moreover, within the text itself it is thematized as directly contradictory to Rav's desire for intimacy and spontaneity in the sexual relations with his wife. Indeed, possibly we could detect a tension between the two citations of the story within the Talmud itself. As I have noted above, Rav Kahana's response—"It is Torah and I must learn it"—does not occur in the version cited in Hagiga, in which Rav's behavior is being cited as definitive. An argument can be constructed, in fact, that this phrase has been added in the Berakhot version. Immediately before this story there, two tannaitic stories are presented about pupils who fol-

16. To be sure, we are not told what aspect of sexual behavior Rav Kahana desired to learn about, nor what he considered to be Torah. My argument is not, then, that Rav Kahana literally held the view of Rabbi Yohanan ben Dabai but that the very fact that he wished to observe the sexual behavior implied the existence of a right way and a wrong way to do "it." One could argue that the right way is precisely the one that I am identifying as what the Rabbis wish to maintain, namely the affective, intimate aspect of sexual intercourse, but precisely that, of course, would be made impossible by observation! We have a kind of Heisenberg uncertainty principle with a vengeance. Hence, it is this aspect of the sexual behavior of the teacher that the student comments upon negatively. In order to ensure intimacy, the Rabbis have to be prepared to leave intimate behavior as intimate. Sometimes power can only function by withdrawing itself. The continuation of my argument will bear out this reading.

low their masters into the toilet and, upon being reprimanded for not having the proper respect, reply, "It is Torah and I must learn it." In both of those stories, the pupil is not rebuked after this reply. It is not implausible, therefore, to assume that the editor who incorporated the Rav Kahana story here and added (according to this hypothesis) the student's reply in imitation of the earlier tannaitic traditions, did so in order to give weight to the act of Rav Kahana, thus providing in this context a sort of censure of Rav's behavior, for as we have seen, the two are in a conflictual articulation with each other. Be that as it may, we see that there were two opposed notions of the discourse of sexuality within the cultural formation of, at least, the Babylonian Talmud, with the weight of hegemony going, however, to the one that renounced vision and thus control over the sexual practices of the couple but insisted on mutual desire and intimacy in the conduct of relations. Rav Kahana's attempt to institute a panopticon for sex is rejected.

Sex in the Dark

Continuing the theme of the passage that throws the Rabbi out of his teacher's bedroom, the most insistent group of controls over sexual practice within marriage are those that encode extreme privacy for the sexual act.[17] Even these regulations, which at first glance appear to be repressive, hold some surprises for us. The Babylonian Talmud in Niddah 16b–17a produces the following discourse:

> Said Rabbi Shim'on the son of Yohai: There are four things that the Holy, Blessed One hates, and I do not like them either: one who enters his house suddenly—and it is unnecessary to say "the house of his fellow"—, one who holds his penis while urinating, one who urinates naked in front of his bed,[18] and one who has intercourse while any living creature is watching.
> Rav Yehuda said to Shmuel: Even in front of mice.
> He said to him: Wise-guy,[19] No, it refers to those like the household of John Doe who have intercourse in front of their male and female slaves.

17. David Biale reminded me of the importance of this material in this context.

18. The first of these regulations is apparently intended to prevent a man from catching the women of his house nude; the second is aimed at avoiding a possible temptation to masturbate; the purpose of the third is mysterious to me.

19. This is apparently a somewhat pejorative endearment that Shmuel used with this sometimes overly clever student of his. Literally, it means "toothy," which may be a reference to overly sharp scholastic teeth.

And as for them, how did they justify their practice biblically?
Sit here with the donkey [Gen. 22:5]—with the people that is like a
donkey.
Rabbah the son of Rav Huna used to ring the bells around the bed
[*another reading*: drive away the horse flies]. Abbaye drove the flies
away. Rava drove away the mosquitoes.

Rabbi Shim'on the Palestinian holy man established an extreme rule for
privacy during sex. No living creature should be present. While Shmuel
(an early Babylonian authority) seemingly attempted to ameliorate this
rule, the later Babylonian Rabbis endorsed it unequivocally. Shmuel
regards it simply as an attack on the Roman practice of having intercourse in the presence of slaves, a practice that indeed involved the assumption that slaves are not somehow human (Veyne 1987, 72–73).
However, his successors understood "living creature" quite literally and
vied with each other to drive away smaller and smaller living creatures
before having intercourse with their wives. The first view, that of Rabbah
the son of Rav Huna, is ambiguous, because of a difference of reading
between different talmudic manuscripts. According to our received text,
endorsed and interpreted by Rashi, he drove away the human beings by
ringing a bell indicating that he was going to sleep with his wife, showing
that his view was like that of Shmuel, but according to Eastern manuscript traditions, he drove away horse-flies, manifesting support for Rav
Yehuda's position. In any case, two of his fellows vied with each other:
Abbaye drove the flies away and Rava even the much smaller mosquitoes.
We cannot know, of course, precisely what Rabbi Shim'on's position was
(or indeed what he said), but it is certainly possible that the statement
was made in reaction to prevailing Roman practices of treating slaves as
virtual non-persons, who were often privy to their masters' sexual behavior. The interpretations of the other Rabbis would then represent a much
more extreme version of that reaction.[20] Now, there may be no doubting
that these regulations were understood as promoting that rabbinic ideal of
"modesty"; however, the very extremes of privacy that were encoded in
the practice also promoted the notions of intimacy and freedom in sexual
behavior. Veyne points out that the Roman practice amounted to constant surveillance (ibid). In sharp contrast, the rabbinic reaction to that

20. It could be, however, that the Babylonian Rabbis, for whom the custom of
Romans having sex with their servants present was unknown, simply misunderstood
Rabbi Shim'on's dictum and took it literally to mean "any creature."

practice produced (willy-nilly?) an extreme renunciation, once more, of surveillance of the conduct of the marriage bed. Rav Kahana's practice of "It is Torah" is also totally excluded by this principle.

In what follows in the talmudic passage, once more a law that seems to encode a "puritanical" sexual hygiene and attitude is reinterpreted by the Babylonian Talmud to encode instead the ideal of intimacy that I have explored here. My point is not, of course, to deny the presence of the ascetic voice in the text but only to show how it is systematically opposed to another voice from within the culture, indeed to a voice with at least as much claim to hegemony as the prudish one. The same text continues:

> Rav Hisda said: A man may not have intercourse during the day, for it says *And you shall love your friend as yourself* [Lev. 19:18]. Said Abbaye: What is the meaning of this? Perhaps he will see in her something which is ugly, and she will become unattractive to him.
>
> Rav Huna said: Israelites are holy and they do not have intercourse by day.
>
> Said Rava: But if it was a dark room, it is permitted, and a scholar may darken the room with his garment and have intercourse. . . .
>
> But come and hear [a contradictory position]: "The household of Munbaz the King used to do three things, for which they were praised: They used to have intercourse during the day. . . ."
>
> We see that it is taught that they had intercourse during the day [and that it was considered praiseworthy]!
>
> I will emend it that they would examine their beds during the day, and I have proof for this. For if you think that the text reads "had intercourse," why would they be praiseworthy for this? [i.e., at best, it is neutral behavior].
>
> Indeed, because of the force of sleep, she would become unpleasant to him.

This is indeed a remarkable text, once more for the way that it encodes explicit and extreme cultural struggle in the hegemonic culture-text itself. Once again, it is nearly obvious that there was a tradition that encoded a rather extreme and restricting notion of modesty requiring that intercourse take place only at night. This was countered on the halakhic level by Rava, however, who limits the condition to any darkened room, including (for Torah-scholars!) one darkened merely by curtains. However, it is on the interpretative level that the ideological opposition is expressed even more clearly. Rav Hisda implicitly and Abbaye explicitly turn this apparently inhibiting sexual rule into yet another prescription for enhancing intimacy between married lovers. Should they make love in full daylight, perhaps he would see some blemish on her body and she would not be attractive to him any more. Of course, here as always, the androcentric perspective is unquestioned, but nevertheless, one also finds clearly encoded again and again that the telos and enabling condition of proper sexual intercourse between married couples is harmony, desire, pleasure, and intimacy. We find the same theme repeated in another place in the Babylonian Talmud, where we are told that it is forbidden for a man to marry a woman until he has seen her to assure that she is attractive to him, for otherwise he will be violating the command to "love his friend as himself" (Kiddushin 41a).[21] The emphasis on intimacy is, moreover, continued in the text with the analysis of the tradition regarding the rabbinic approval of the practice of the household of Munbaz. One of the interlocutors cannot believe that the Rabbis actually considered it praiseworthy to have intercourse by day, so he argues that they must have said [or meant] something else, to which the reply comes that it is indeed praiseworthy to have intercourse by day, for then he is not sleepy. If he has intercourse while sleepy, she may be unpleasant to him, i.e., he may do it out of duty and *not for pleasure*, and then the intimacy of the married lovers is destroyed. As Rashi remarks, "Since he is overcome with sleep, he does not desire her so much, and he has intercourse only to perform the commandment of regular intercourse or to please her, and then he is repelled by her, *and this is one of the nine categories mentioned in Nedarim.*" Rashi's interpretation seems well justified here by the entire context and particularly by the cited topos of loving one's friend as oneself. Male sexual desire and pleasure are as crucial as female sexual desire and pleasure in the conduct of conjugal relations, for sex is only proper when it is the product and producer of intimacy. Over and over in these texts, the discourse of surveillance and control is placed into opposition with a discourse of intimacy and sexual pleasure and mutual desire, and surveillance is renounced in favor of desire—to be sure, only the legitimated desire of husband and wife. Given the androcentric nature of the texts and the culture, we still need to ask further questions about the status of female desire.

21. This is, incidentally, the reversal of a misogynistic topos repeated over and over in the Roman and Christian anti-marriage discourse that one should not marry, because one examines any purchase but that of a wife (Bloch 1991a, 20)

Speech and Female Desire:
Patriarchal Concern for Female Well-being

The permission that the husband has to speak in order to "arouse" his wife is indicated by precisely the same verb the Talmud used with reference to what a wife may do to ask for sex without speaking directly and "brazenly." The Talmud had objected to the notion that a "brazen woman," by which they understood one who openly asks for intercourse, will have improper children: "Indeed? But did not Shmuel the son of Nahmani say that Rabbi Yohanan said: Any man whose wife approaches him sexually will have children such as were unknown even in the generation of Moses." And they answer: "That refers to a case where she arouses him." She is not called a brazen woman if she stimulates and invites her husband by signs and signals that arouse his desire, but only—according to this text—if she openly asks for sex. Female desire itself is not stigmatized, only open, explicit use of language to express that desire. He, on the other hand, is enjoined to use speech precisely for the purpose of arousing her. He is required to use his speech to arouse her desire, for without that arousal he must not have intercourse with her. The gender asymmetry is not so much, then, in rights to sex, as in the rights to speech, who has control over the situation and who is "being taken care of."

It is generally taken to be an absolute that female desire in talmudic culture must be silent. Indeed, this is usually taken as the "curse of Eve" in rabbinic writings. It is startling to find, therefore, that not only was it not a monolithic notion among the Rabbis that female desire may not be spoken, but that there was at least one voice that held that its utterance was of the highest value. We have already seen an allusion to that voice at the end of the Nedarim passage. The very text condemning wife-rape that I have cited above continues by thematizing this issue directly:

> Rav Shmuel the son of Nahmani said in the name of Rabbi Yohanan:[22] Any man whose wife asks for sex will have children such as were unknown even in the generation of Moses, for in the generation of Moses it is written, *Get yourself intelligent, wise and renowned men* [Deut. 1:14], and then it is written, *And I took as the heads of the tribes renowned and intelligent men* [Deut. 1:16], but he could not find "wise men," but with regard to Leah it says, *And Leah went out to him, and said 'You shall sleep with me tonight, for I have hired you'* [Gen. 30:16]

22. Variant: Yonathan.

and it says, *The children of Yissachar were acquainted with wisdom*
[1 Chron. 12:34]. . . .

Rav Shmuel's tradition praises the woman who requests sex openly in as
vivid and strong terms as the rabbinic tradition knows by claiming that
such a woman would have children better than even the children of that
paragon generation, the generation of Moses. This principle is derived
from a typically clever midrashic reading. Moses is sent by God to search
for a certain kind of person to be the tribal leaders, but when the results
of that search are reported, one of the qualifications is absent. The midrash, with its usual literalness, assumes this to mean that he could not
find people who had that quality: wisdom. On the other hand, the Bible
tells us explicitly that Leah requested sex openly of Jacob, when she had
paid her sister for the right to have him that night, and with regard to
her children we are informed in another place in the Bible that they
possessed exactly that characteristic found lacking in the generation of
Moses. The inference is drawn that it was the open expression of their
mother's desire to their father that produced that wisdom.

The Talmud goes on to raise a challenge to this proposition, however:

> Can that be so? But didn't Rav Avdimi say that Eve was cursed with
> ten curses, for it says, *And to the woman He said: Greatly I will multiply*
> [Gen. 3:16]: These are the two flows of blood, the blood of menstrua-
> tion and the blood of virginity. *your pain:* This is the effort of rearing
> children. *and your conception:* this the effort of pregnancy. *in pain shall
> you bear children:* as it sounds. *and to your man will be your desire:*
> teaches that the wife desires her husband when he goes on a journey.
> *and he will rule over you:* that the woman bids [for sex] in her heart,
> while the man with his mouth.
> That which we said is [praiseworthy] is when she arouses him.

Once again, as in the passage from Nedarim, the view of Rav Shmuel is
attenuated by the Talmud. He had boldly stated that the ideal is a woman
who openly asks for sex. The Talmud has some problem with this view in
both passages and dilutes it by interpreting it to mean that she may by
verbal and other signals arouse her husband's interest and hint to him
that she wants sex, but she may not speak openly of her desire. We are
not bound, however, by the Talmud's desire to harmonize all views whenever it can, so from our perspective we can see that even on this point the
culture was not monolithic. There were views that denied to women the
speaking of their desire, but also another view that not only "granted"

them their speech but even exuberantly praised the speaking of female desire. Still, the dominant tradition remained, to be sure, the one that suppressed the open speaking of desire by women.

But emblematic of the ideology of gender in the rabbinic culture is the fact that this interdiction on speaking her desire on the part of women was *not* supposed to create conditions of suffering and deprivation for her, but rather to impose a special obligation on her husband to be attentive and sensitive to her subtle signals. The fact that she desired him especially when he was about to go on a journey, *which is one of the curses with which she was cursed*, does *not* mean that therefore she must suffer frustration but that he must sleep with her before he leaves:

> Rabbi Yehoshua the son of Levi said, "A man is required to sleep with his wife when he is about to go on a journey, for it says *And you shall know that your tent is peace and you shall pay attention to your dwelling, and thus you will not sin*" [Job 5:25].
>
> Does it in fact derive from that verse? Doesn't it derive from *And unto the man is her desire* [Gen. 3:16], which teaches that the woman desires her husband when he goes on a journey.
>
> Rav Yosef said, "It was not necessary [to cite the other verse] except for the situation in which she is close to her period [when normally sex is forbidden, but this prohibition is lifted when he is going to go on a journey]" [Yevamot 62b].

The "curses" are women's state, not their estate. Not only is the curse not a justification for causing her to suffer, it is that very curse that creates the obligation for the husband to "take care of her." Once again it is clearly the case, however, that the gender relations are asymmetrical, that the position of women in sexuality is subordinate, and the position of men is dominant. The very consideration that *he* is supposed to show *her* is the marker of this magnanimous but confining patriarchy. As the Talmud says explicitly in the continuation, "She is a mattress for her husband."

TRUTH AND DESIRE

At the bottom of this (inter)textual complex, I read, then, an intricate strategy for "putting sex into discourse," and at the same time for limiting the discourse of sexual control. Foucault has contrasted two relations of sexuality to truth as characteristic of two cultural formations, that of the ancient Greeks and "ours":

> In Greece, truth and sex were linked, in the form of pedagogy, by the transmission of a precious knowledge from one body to another; sex served as a medium for initiations into learning. For us, it is in the confession that truth and sex are joined, through the obligatory and exhaustive expression of an individual secret. But this time it is truth that serves as a medium for sex and its manifestations.
>
> (Foucault 1980, 61)

What, then, is the link between truth and sex in the textual complex that we have been reading here? That is, how shall we describe the talmudic culture on the scale of Foucault's taxonomy? Certainly, neither of the alternatives that he proposes to describe the two formations with which he deals are adequate for describing this culture, for sex is not the medium of a *paideia*, and confession is not a mode of producing truth in this culture. It would seem, indeed, that what the Talmud is telling us is that the truth of sex (that is, the Torah of sex) is concerned with two aspects of sexuality only: that the objects of sexual interaction be appropriate, and that the connection between wife and husband be marked by warmth, intimacy, exclusiveness (even in polygyny!), and respect for the desire and pleasure of the subordinate female partner. The actual deployment of bodies and pleasures lies outside of the purview of Torah.

The rabbinic culture thus occupies a position somewhere "between" Foucault's Greek and Christian cultures. On the one hand, there is a near-explicit rejection of the model of the panoptical surveillance of sexual behavior between husbands and wives; on the other hand, sexuality itself is not seen as an area entirely out of the realm of socio-cultural legislation. The Talmud achieves diverse (and not always compatible) discursive objectives through this complicated strategy. The "repressive" discourse is made available—and indeed, later cultural forces will mobilize it—but it is rendered counter-normative and marginalized. The net effect of such textual tactics is that out of the ashes of a rejected *scientia sexualis* a very embryonic *ars erotica* is produced.[23] The (male) reader of the text now knows that it is possible to derive pleasure from looking at his wife's genitals, from kissing them, from "turning the tables," and most of all, from conversing with her, laughing and playing while making love.

23. The terms are, of course, those of Michel Foucault, whose influence pervades this chapter (Foucault 1980, 67). To be sure, they are only partially appropriate in the present context, but Foucault himself allows that the binary opposition between the two may be deconstructible.

This is a perfect illustration of Foucault's point that power/knowledge "penetrates and controls everyday pleasure—all this entailing effects that may be those of refusal, blockage, and invalidation, but also incitement and intensification" (Foucault 1980, 11). The husband has certainly been taught, moreover, that respect and honor for his wife's desire and pleasure are integral to an appropriate conduct of sexual life, and that he will be rewarded for such consideration with the type of children that he desires. This discourse, however, and my reading of it, should not be misunderstood as a celebration of the gender relations that it presupposes and enforces.

In studying the complex of texts around the subject of the speaking of female desire, we see a continuation of the cultural pattern of gender politics that we observe throughout this book. On the one hand, there is an enormous respect for women's rights to physical well-being, to an absence of male violence toward them, to satisfaction of their physical needs, including especially the need for sex, but on the other hand, they are always in an absolutely subordinated position vis-à-vis the dominant, if normatively considerate, male. A quintessential representation of this situation is the halakhic requirement (analyzed in the next chapter) that is addressed to men as to how frequently they must sleep with their wives— only if, of course, the wife desires sex, the implication being, once more, that the man is in control and that the wife needs to be patronistically cared for. As patronistic as this is, however, it is in contrast with another mode of relating to women, which would propose simply that their needs are irrelevant. In the next chapter, a complex of texts will be read in which the concern for the fulfillment of female desire, and indeed for its legitimacy, is significantly weakened in one part of the rabbinic world, as it is seen to conflict with other values within the culture, namely, the complete devotion to the study of Torah. At the same time, we discover a vivid oppositional voice to that weakening of empathy for the needs, desires, indeed the subject-hood of rabbinic wives.

5

Lusting After Learning
The Torah as "the Other Woman"

Rabbi Akiva says, Anyone who commits murder diminishes the image of God, as it says, *One who spills blood of a human, for the sake of the human his blood will be spilt for in the image of God, He made the human* [Gen. 9:6].

Rabbi Elʿazar ben Azariah says, Anyone who does not engage in procreation diminishes the Divine Image, for it says, *In the image of God, He made the human* [Gen. 9:6], and it is written [immediately following], *And as for you, be fruitful and multiply*.

Ben-Azzai says, Anyone who does not engage in procreation is a murderer and diminishes the Divine Image, for it says, *One who spills blood of a human, for the sake of the human his blood will be spilt, for in the image of God, He made the human, and as for you, be fruitful and multiply*.

Rabbi Elʿazar ben Azariah said to him, "Ben-Azzai, words are fine when accompanied by practice. There are those who interpret well and behave well, and those who behave well but do not interpret well. You interpret well, but do not behave well." Ben-Azzai said to them, "What shall I do? My soul desires Torah. Let the world continue by the efforts of others!"

(Tosefta Yevamot 8:7; compare
Babylonian Talmud Yevamot 63b)

The absolute and contradictory demands of marriage and commitment to study of Torah remained one of the great unresolved tensions of rabbinic culture. The text thematizes that tension by "personifying" its poles.[1] The Rabbis are commenting on the biblical text: "One who spills blood of a human, for the sake of the human his blood will be spilt, for in the image of God, He made the human. And as for you, be fruitful and multiply." Rabbis Akiva and Elʿazar disagree on the interpretation of the context.

---

1. This is to be taken as neither an assertion nor a denial of the biographical, historical "reality" of these Rabbis and their discourse, but only as an interpretation of the function that the text plays, in my reading, in rabbinic culture.

Rabbi Akiva understands that the clause referring to the "image of God" has to do with the murderer who diminishes the human image of God, while Rabbi El'azar reads it as pertaining to the continuation of the text and thus referring to procreation. Ben-Azzai reads the entire text as one context and thus derives his strong principle that non-procreation is equivalent to both murder and diminishment of the Divine Image. Rabbi El'azar, quite naturally, attacks the celibate Ben-Azzai for hypocrisy, to which Ben-Azzai replies that much as he would like to be able to fulfill the commandment, he cannot, because his soul has such desire (the verb used is exactly the verb used in erotic contexts) for study. All of his erotic energy is devoted to the love of Torah; there is none left for a woman.[2] This reading, however, seems merely to imply that Ben-Azzai is a complicated hypocrite. We must read him, therefore, to be saying that he knows that he ought to be performing the commandment to be married; indeed, he knows that he is both a murderer and a diminisher of the Divine by not doing so, but his lust for Torah will not let him. His argument is the exact analogue of the self-justification of the lecher who says he knows that he should not be a-whoring, but he cannot help himself.[3] In fact, Ben-Azzai's self-defense is modeled on that kind of statement, and the erotic terminology used by Ben-Azzai, the terminology of desire, strengthens this reading. In this story, then, we find the perfect representation of the extreme internal conflict set up by contradictory demands that one be married, have children, and also devote oneself entirely to Torah. Both Ben-Azzai's self-justification and Rabbi El'azar's condemnation of him are left to stand in the text, suggesting how lively the contest was in rabbinic times. But it should be emphasized that Ben-Azzai is a limit case, truly an exception that proves the rule. Virtually all of the other Rabbis are represented as married; marriage was a nearly obligatory norm for the Rabbis as well as for the populace, but also obligatory for the Rabbis was constant attention to Torah.

The privileging of virginity in the Church and some late-antique Jewish religious groups allowed for the division of humanity into two classes: the religious, who were able to be wholly devoted to the spirit, and the householders, who married and reproduced (Fraade 1986, 266–68; An-

2. On Ben-Azzai's self-justification, see also Daube (1977, 37–38).

3. For similar contradictions between the theory and practice of Hellenistic (Stoic) sages, see Griffin (1976, 340).

derson 1989, 140). This solution was available to the Rabbis as well, but they vehemently rejected it. The story of Ben-Azzai is an index of how much energy was required to combat the attractiveness of the celibate life.[4] Extravagant praise of the married state, which occurs over and over in rabbinic texts, is a marker not of how happily married the Rabbis were but of how much pressure against marrying there was in their world. Celibacy provided an attractive "out" from the world's pain, and, moreover, the life of the purely spiritual seeker of wisdom was the ideal of much of the circumambient culture, both Jewish and non-Jewish.[5]

Rabbinic culture, accordingly, is beleaguered with a constant unresolved tension—almost an antinomy—between the obligation to marry and the equal obligation to devote oneself entirely to the life of Torah-study (Fraade 1986, 275). In contrast to other cultural formations, both Jewish and non-Jewish, which formulate the problem as a conflict between body and spirit, the Rabbis do not set this up as a hierarchy of values. The activities of the "lower" (reproductive) body were considered as important as those of the "upper" (speaking) body, but were acknowledged at the same time somehow to conflict with them, at the very least in that both activities competed for time and energy.[6] Unless we remain aware of both poles of this tension, it will be difficult to account for many of the features of rabbinic culture. Rabbinic texts provide several attempts to produce social practices that would resolve the tension between marriage and the study of Torah, between sex and the text. We will see, however, that all of the proposed resolutions roused great opposition within the culture, as we can determine from oppositional discourses captured in the very texts that produce the "solutions."

A RABBINIC ROMANCE

The Babylonian Talmud relates the following "biography" of one of its greatest heroes, Rabbi Akiva, a Palestinian authority of the second century:

4. Cf. David Biale 1989 for a reading along somewhat similar but differently nuanced lines. He provides further evidence for the attractions of celibacy and even castration for late-antique Jews.

5. Peter Brown's book is the most eloquent evocation of that pain and the response to it among early Christians. See also the important comments of Jeremy Cohen (1989, 114 n. 177).

6. For a somewhat different, partly complementary and partly contradictory account of these matters, see Eilberg-Schwartz (1990b, 229–34). See also David Biale 1989 and Eilberg-Schwartz 1990a.

Rabbi Akiva was the shepherd of Kalba Savuaᶜ. The daughter of Kalba
Savuaᶜ became engaged to Rabbi Akiva. Kalba Savuaᶜ heard and cut
her off from any of his property. She went and married him in the winter. They used to lie in the hay-barn, and he would take hay out of her
hair. He said to her, "Were I only able, I would give you a 'Jerusalem of
Gold!'"[7] Elijah the Prophet came and appeared to them as a person crying out at the door. He said, "Give me some of your hay, for my wife is
giving birth and I have nothing for her to lie down on." Rabbi Akiva
said to his wife, "You see, there is someone who doesn't even have
hay." She said to him, "Go and sit in the House of Study." He went for
twelve years and studied with Rabbi Eliezer and Rabbi Yehoshua. At
the end of twelve years, he came home. He heard from behind his
house, a certain rogue saying to his wife, "Your father treated you suit-
ably. First of all, he [Rabbi Akiva] is not of your kind, and moreover he
has left you a grass widow all of these years." She said to him, "If he
were to follow my wishes, he would remain for another twelve years."
He said, "Since she has given me permission, I will go back." He went
for another twelve years. He came with twenty-four thousand pairs
of disciples. Everyone came out to receive him, and she also came
out to meet him. That rogue said to her, "Where do you think you
are going?" She said, "'The righteous man senses the need of his pet'
[Prov. 12:10]."[8] She came to show herself to him. The Rabbis were
pushing her aside. He said to them, "Leave her be. That which is mine
and that which is yours is really hers!" Kalba Savuaᶜ went and asked
to be relieved of his vow, and he was released. In six ways Rabbi Akiva
became wealthy from the property of Kalba Savuaᶜ.

                    (Babylonian Talmud Nedarim 50a)

This text may be seen to show several of the generic characteristics of
romance. We have the topoi of the marriage for love obstructed by soci-
etal strictures and parental opposition, the triumph of the young lovers
who resist the thwarting of their desires, and their eventual vindication
even in the eyes of the original opponent of their love. Even so, it is
impossible, of course, to read the story as either a representation of actual

---

7. A particularly precious sort of tiara.

8. "Pet" is not a literal translation, as pethood is an institution specific to modern
culture. However, this translation comes closest to conveying the connotations of the
relation between a shepherd and sheep in the pastoral Jewish culture, including the
erotic overtones thereof. For the erotic associations of pet-keeping, see Shell 1985.
"Beast" would be a more strict rendering, but would be misleading in its connotation.
The use of this verse implies the solicitous (patronizing) care of a superior in the hierarchy for an inferior, not an ascription of bestiality. Thus, for example, it is used in
Tanhuma on Noah 7, paragraph 1, to refer to the fact that God knew that Noah was
righteous from among all of the human beings who existed then. I shall further develop these points in my reading of the story below.

historical-biographical reality or a literary version of a "kernel" of bio-graphical truth.[9] However, it is not *just* a romance either, not just a fic-tional tale about made-up characters, but a highly charged story about a central culture hero. Why is this story told about Rabbi Akiva? What is the cultural work that is done by making the hero of the "romance" specifically a great scholar and martyr and more specifically Rabbi Akiva? To attempt an answer to these questions, let us have a look at some rab-binic discursive practices that can be made to inform our reading of the biographical narrative, and especially the genre of halakhic (ritual legal) controversy.

HALAKHA

Which Precedes: Marriage or Torah?

The first halakhic text that seems relevant for the narrative of Rabbi Akiva's romance is the discussion in Babylonian Talmud Kiddushin 29b of the appropriate timing for marriage; the question is which comes first, study or marriage:

> The sages have taught: On studying Torah and marrying a woman?
> He should study Torah and then marry, but if he cannot manage with-out a wife, he should marry and then study Torah. Said Rav Yehudah that Shmuel said, "The *halakha* is that he should marry and then study Torah." Rabbi Yohanan said, "A millstone around his neck and he will study Torah!?" *And they do not disagree; that is for us and that is for them.*

First of all, some simple commentary. The text begins with a *baraita*—that is, an early Palestinian halakhic tradition—which in the absence of a controverting text from the same period is normally halakhically au-thoritative. Despite this theoretically definitive statement, the later Baby-lonian authority Shmuel is reported as having held that the young scholar should marry and then study Torah. His equally authoritative Palestinian counterpart and contemporary, Rabbi Yohanan, holds the opposite view,

---

9. The historical reading is problematic, that is, beyond the bare facts that there was an Akiva, that he was married, and that apparently he and his wife suffered great poverty while he studied Torah. This much of the story seems so frequently told as to be established historically, though given the nature of rumor, one may even wonder at this. If we only find significance, however, in the historically "true," then, we will be left with very little to read in rabbinic literature.

expressing himself in what seems to be a proverbial formulation, that the responsibilities of marriage are a millstone around the neck of the young scholar, who cannot be free, then, for the study of Torah. The Talmud—that is a later stratum thereof—comments that in fact they do not disagree with each other, but each is referring to the situation of a different community, presumably each to his own (that is, Shmuel to Babylonia and Rabbi Yohanan to Palestine). Presently I shall undertake to interpret this difference, but for the moment let us note that there is, as expected, no disagreement on the obligation to marry for Torah-students, only on its antecedence to study. Moreover, even Rabbi Yohanan, who expresses himself so strongly to the effect that Torah comes first, does not project an essential contradiction between the holiness or spirituality of Torah-study and sexuality but only a pragmatic contradiction (however caustically expressed by Rabbi Yohanan) between the responsibilities of marriage and full commitment to the study of Torah. Quite the opposite: the idea is that being married and having a sexual outlet is productive of "one who studies Torah in purity," as explicitly stated in Babylonian Talmud Yoma 72b (and see Pesachim 112b and Menahot 110b). One who is *unmarried* cannot study Torah purely. This concept is, moreover, well supported in other rabbinic texts, such as the requirement that only married men should be the leaders of prayer (Babylonian Talmud Taanith 16a).[10]

---

10. This enables us to understand better a passage (already quoted above) in the Persian Church Father Aphrahat, which puzzled Gary Anderson somewhat:

> Aphrahat declares that one Jew has asserted that Christians are unclean because they do not take wives. He writes:
>
>> I have written to you, my beloved, concerning virginity and holiness because I heard about a Jewish man who has reviled one of our brethren, the members of the church. He said to him, "You are impure for you don't take wives. But we are holy and more virtuous for we bear children and multiply seed in the world."
>
> Aphrahat's understanding of holiness is significant. He correctly distinguishes the Jewish understanding of the term, as reflected in rabbinic documentation, from the Christian. Jews understood the term to refer to the state of marriage. Syriac Christians understood the term to refer to sexual continence. Aphrahat's identification of sexual abstinence with uncleanness might seem unusual. The Rabbis never placed the sexually abstinent individual in the legal category of unclean.
>
> (Anderson 1989, 122–23)

We can see, however, that Aphrahat's allusion is exactly correct. For the (Babylonian) Rabbis (the ones that Aphrahat's congregation would have been in contact

The difference between the Babylonians and the Palestinians seems to be predicated on a cultural division in the understanding of male sexuality. While the Palestinians seem to have adhered to the general Hellenistic notion that sexuality was something that a human being could do without, and all that was required was self-control, *sophrosyne*, the Babylonians apparently did not think so (Gafni 1989, 20–21).[11] This suggestion is supported strongly by the continuation of the text itself, which proceeds with a story that clarifies both the intensity of the Babylonian allegiance to early marriage and the reason for it:

> Rav Huna [the Babylonian] said, "Anyone who is twenty years old and not married, all of his days are sinful." Can you really think that he is sinful? Rather I will say, "All of his days are in thoughts of sin." Rava said, and thus also the One of the House of Rabbi Ishmael teaches, "Until the twentieth year, the Holiness, May it be blessed, waits for the man; when will he marry. When he is twenty and unmarried, He says, 'Blast his bones!'" Rav Hisda said, "I am preferable to my fellows, for I married at sixteen and if I had married at fourteen, I could have said to the Satan, 'An arrow in your eyes!'"[12]

The discourse of these two major Babylonian Rabbis suggests strongly that the primary motivation (or, at least, *one* primary motivation) for marriage as understood by the Babylonians is that sexual activity is necessary for people from the age of puberty on (fourteen), and that without sex they would find it impossible to concentrate on their studies.[13] More-

---

with), someone who was unmarried was impure, on the assumption that he would necessarily engage in impure thoughts or more probably seminal emissions, which would, of course, produce impurity in the technical sense.

11. I find it exciting that Gafni, whose article came out while this book was being written, came to such similar conclusions about Palestinian and Babylonian differences on the question of sexuality.

12. Rashi: "I could have challenged him (and Satan is the Evil Inclination), and I would not have been afraid that he would cause me to sin."

13. The text here only addresses the question regarding male people. Note the difference between this and Paul's notion of marriage as a defense against lust in 1 Corinthians 7. For Paul, this is a concession for those "not gifted" by being able to transcend sexuality, and he argues that it is not to be accounted a sin for them to marry, while for these Babylonians *everyone* is prey to lust and should marry. The ability to renounce sexuality cannot be taken as any sort of barometer of the person. (I am, of course, aware that some interpret Paul's remarks as being addressed solely to the apocalyptic situation; I think, however, that the anthropological and psychological implications remain the same.) See next note. My colleague Anne Drafthorn Kilmer has informed me that the notion that sex is necessary for everyone seems to have been current in the Babylonian *Kulturgebiet* from very ancient times. In the epic *Atrahasis*,

over, it is at least possible that there is a suggestion here that an unmarried adult male will either masturbate or have nocturnal emissions, both of which were considered as leading to moral impurity in ways that marital intercourse did not. This story should be understood, then, as commentary on the talmudic passage that precedes it. The Babylonian rabbinic community strongly encodes its own self-perception that adult males cannot live without sex, and therefore the young scholar should marry and then study.[14]

We are left to account for the view and practice of "them"—the Palestinians—also encoded in our text. Presumably, "they" have a different understanding from "us" of the nature of men and the function of marriage. Rabbi Yohanan's case for delaying marriage is based on the impossibility of full commitment to Torah-study while exercising the responsibilities of marriage. Moreover, he seemingly does not share the Babylonians' concern that an unmarried man could not possibly study Torah "in purity." If the Babylonians understood marriage as the means to fulfillment of a universal need and as a defense against pollution, and

---

after the flood, the priests and priestesses are forbidden to bear children, but not to have sex!

14. By "self-perception," I mean that it reflects a judgment by Babylonian Rabbis on themselves, as well as on others. While this does not in itself constitute a positive appreciation of sexuality per se, as opposed to procreation, it does make it impossible for the capacity to withdraw from sex to be understood as a barometer of the spirit, as it is in several Hellenistic traditions:

> A man must not treat his wife as he would a mistress, Seneca admonishes, and Saint Jerome cites him approvingly. His nephew Lucan was of the same opinion. He wrote an epic, a sort of realistic historical novel, in which he describes in his own fashion the story of the civil war between Caesar and Pompey. He shows Cato, model of the Stoic, taking leave of his wife (the same wife he lent for a time to a friend) as he prepares to go off to war. Even on the eve of such a lengthy separation, they do not make love, as Lucan is at pains to point out, explaining as he does the doctrinal significance of the fact. Even that semigreat man Pompey, although no Stoic, does not sleep with his wife on the farewell night. Why the abstinence? Because a good man does not live for petty pleasures and is careful about every action. To give in to desire is immoral. There is only one reasonable ground for a couple to sleep together: procreation. It was a question not of asceticism but of rationalism.
>
> (Veyne 1987, 47)

In addition to the fact that a Jewish husband is *required* to sleep with his wife on a farewell night, the fundamental difference here is that according to the rabbinic cultural formation, fulfilling desire (within the bounds of the permitted) is in no way censorable and cannot, therefore, serve as a barometer of virtue.

therefore were opposed to putting it off at all, the Palestinians who supported delayed marriages must have had a different conception of marital
teleology. It would seem a priori that the most obvious candidate for such
a role is procreation, which can be postponed without being entirely subverted. This hypothesized emphasis on procreation is consistent with
general cultural trends in the Greco-Roman world (Brown 1988, 5–7).
David Daube has shown how the twin notions of the duty of procreation
and the denial of any value to sex other than procreation are offspring of
the marriage of platonism and Stoicism in Hellenistic culture (1977, 29.
See also David Biale 1989, 7). The Palestinians, then, provide a model of
a partial resolution of the antinomy between full commitment to marriage
and to Torah by organizing them into different stages in the life of the
Torah-student. Since it is impossible to fulfill both at the same time and
possible to fulfill them serially, that is precisely what is proposed.[15]

In Babylonia, this solution was excluded by the assumption that a man
without a sexual outlet will inevitably sin, or at least be constantly occu-
pied with "thoughts of sin." If the Palestinians hold that Torah-study can
best be fulfilled by remaining unmarried for a time, the Babylonians
counter that the state of celibacy renders it nearly impossible to do so "in
purity." The text proposes then a sort of utopian solution, which allows
for both marriage and total commitment to Torah-study, namely, marrying early and then leaving home for extended periods of time to study
Torah. In short, the solution of the Babylonian culture was to create a
class of married monks, men who had the pleasure and benefit of marriage
for parts of their lives but who would absent themselves from home for
extended periods for study. However, problems arise for this "solution"
from another halakhic requirement.

The Marital Debt Rabbinic Style
(Ketubbot 61b ff.)

In addition to the aspect of sexuality as an obligation that the man owes
his own body, as it were, the married man was considered by talmudic law

---

15. Rashi and Tosafot, the classic medieval commentators on this talmudic passage, interpret the difference between the Babylonians and Palestinians as having to
do with putative differences in the distance from the scholars' homes to their *yeshivoth*,
places of study. Aside from the fact that these two come to precisely opposite theories
of both the material base and its reflection in the superstructure here, the geographic
difference does not seem to be thematized as the issue in the Talmud itself, while the
ideological difference does seem to me present in the text.

under a legal-contractual obligation to sleep with his wife regularly for her pleasure and benefit. This obligation was derived by the Rabbis from the verse of the Torah that, speaking of the taking of a second wife, says that he must not "reduce the flesh, covering, or seasons" (Exod. 21:10) of the first wife. This philologically puzzling list was variously interpreted in the midrash, but the hegemonic opinion is that "flesh" means food, "covering" refers to clothing, and "seasons" refers to regularity of sexual intercourse.[16] This obligation was also made contractual in the standard rabbinically approved marriage contract, which reads, "I will feed you, clothe you, and have intercourse with you, in accordance with the customs of Jewish husbands." In this context, the Mishna discusses the exact definition of "regularity," i.e., what constitutes fulfillment of the husband's sexual debt to his wife.

The Mishna reads:

> If one takes a vow not to sleep with his wife; Bet Shammai say two weeks, and Bet Hillel one week.[17] The students may go away from their homes for study of Torah without permission for thirty days and laborers for one week. The "season" [required frequency of intercourse] which is mentioned in the Torah: for the *tayyalin*,[18] *it is every day; for laborers twice a week; for donkey drivers, once a week; for camel drivers once in thirty days; for sailors once in six months; these are the words of Rabbi Eliezer.*

The talmudic commentary on this Mishna is revealing in the manner in which it vacillates and contradicts itself. Thus, close reading of the text will provide us with symptomatic evidence of the unresolvability of the cultural problem of tension between marriage and Torah-study within the Babylonian rabbinic system.

The Talmud discusses the exceptional "permission" afforded by the Mishna for a student to be away from his wife for thirty days without the agreement of the wife:

---

16. The linguistic basis for this identification is complex. The root 'ny, from which 'onah (the word that I have translated as "season") is derived, is often used in sexual contexts to mean "have intercourse with." In that sense, it is unrelated linguistically to the word that means "seasons." I think, however, that the Rabbis have conjoined the two senses into one and thence derived the complex meaning of "regular intercourse."

17. I.e., these are the maximum times he is permitted to vow not to sleep with her. If he takes a vow for longer, he must divorce her and pay her the divorce settlement.

18. This is a difficult term that means something like idlers; it may mean those who spend all of their time in study.

> *The students may go away from their homes for study of Torah without permission for thirty days and laborers for one week:* With permission, how much? As much as he wants. But what is the correct behavior? Rav said, one month here [studying] and one month at home, for it says, "In the matter of the labor brigades, one goes and one comes month by month for the months of the year" [1 Chron. 27:1]. Rabbi Yohanan says, one month here and two at home, for it says, "One month they will be in Lebanon and two months at home" [1 Kings 5:28].

The issue here is that although a wife is sovereign to permit her husband to spend as much time away from her as they mutually agree upon, it is recognized that an unequal power relationship exists between them. The husband will very likely be able to prevail upon her to "permit" him to go away for longer periods of time, and then, in the words of Rashi, he will be "sinning" against his wife.[19] The Talmud establishes, therefore, if not a strictly legalistic proscription, a strong moral one on being away from home for longer than thirty days. Two of the most dominant of talmudic authorities are cited to that effect, the only difference between them involving how much time the husband will spend at home once he returns. According to the Babylonian Rav, the married man would spend one-half of his time studying Torah, but according to the Palestinian, Rabbi Yohanan, he would spend two-thirds of his time with his wife.

The continuation of the talmudic text on the next page switches gears in a startling contradiction of the previous section:

> [*The students may go away from their homes for study of Torah without permission for thirty days . . .*]; *these are the words of Rabbi Eliezer:* Rav Bruna said that Rav said: The halakha is in accordance with the view of Rabbi Eliezer. Rav Ada the son of Ahva said that Rav said: Those are [only] the words of Rabbi Eliezer, but the sages hold that the students may go away for the study of Torah for two or three years without permission. Rava said that our Rabbis have relied upon Rav Ada the son of Ahva and indeed practice in accordance with his view.

We find here a relatively late Babylonian tradition, which, in contrast to all earlier authorities, reverses the ruling of Rabbi Eliezer that the married scholar may not absent himself for more than thirty days from his wife and permits absences of several years.[20] This reversal demonstrates power-

---

19. To be sure, this is not the only possible interpretation of this passage, but it is, interestingly enough, the interpretation of Rashi and the Tosafists, the canonical commentators on the Talmud.

20. "Two or three" is a conventional Semitic expression for "several."

fully how much pressure the halakhic requirement that a husband must sleep regularly with his wife brought to bear on the entire socio-cultural system.

There is here, to be sure, an apparent self-contradiction. On the one hand, I have claimed on the basis of fairly explicit Babylonian texts that these men held that adults cannot do without sex and that therefore they must marry early. On the other hand, I am arguing that to solve problems occasioned by those same early marriages, some of them promulgated a system of exceedingly long absence of husband from wife. The contradiction is, I think, internal to the system and not an artifact of my reading. Several solutions seem possible. One is that the understanding was that very early marriage would dampen sexual desire forever.[21] A perhaps more plausible suggestion would be that the men were not expected to be celibate during these long absences from home. There are two stories in the Talmud itself about prominent rabbis who, upon arriving in a strange city, would go into the marketplace and seek a "wife" for the night (Yoma 18b; Yevamoth 37b). As Gafni (1989, 24–25) has already argued, this practice bears a remarkable similarity to the well-attested later Iranian institution of temporary marriage for pleasure (Haeri 1989), an institution that also seems to attest to the persistence of the notion of the necessity for sexual outlets in this cultural area. If indeed there was a widespread practice of such temporary marriages for rabbinical students far from home (and this possibility is quite speculative), it is much easier to understand why the Talmud would have represented the primary problem here as being the wife's sexual needs and not the husband's! Another possibility would be to read this as another example of "thinking with women," the notion that men often talk about women when referring in fact to their own sexuality, such that here the requirement of a certain frequency of intercourse because of the needs of women becomes, ipso facto, a means of giving men permission to enjoy that frequency of intercourse themselves. It is important, however, to note once more that at least in the rabbinic formation, the need of women for sex is not described in pejorative terms.[22]

21. For evidence of such notions among Jews at a much later period, see David Biale 1986.

22. In partial contrast to this, a modern Orthodox rabbi who requires a greater frequency of intercourse for rabbinic scholars than does the Talmud argues for it in the following terms:

Because of the promiscuity of this generation and jealousy for another woman's

Whatever the solution to that structural contradiction, this dissenting tradition of what Rav had said is identified as definitive, in marked contrast to the drift of the entire discourse up until this point, which had been strongly oriented toward the responsibility of the husband to satisfy his wife regularly. Without, of course, suggesting that Rav Ada's tradition is fabricated, it is nevertheless remarkable that this tradition became accepted as authoritative in spite of the fact that it contradicts the Mishna and contradicts another tradition of Rav's own view.[23] The Palestinian Talmud, on the other hand, knows of no such "qualification" of the Mishna's position, and the law there is established that the husband may not leave home without permission for more than thirty days.

The Babylonian Talmud's report of Rava's declaration—"our Rabbis have relied upon Rav Ada, the son of Ahva and indeed practice according to his view"—constitutes evidence for a change in social practice that is associated by the tradition with Rava, that is, with the leading Babylonian rabbinic authority of the fourth century, though to be sure, such attribution is not necessarily to be taken literally. It would seem, however, that the attempt to institute this change in marriage practice met with substantial opposition in spite of Rava's hegemonic prestige. The talmudic text, at the same time that it is ostensibly recording the support for this innovation, reveals sharp dissension from it. These oppositional voices encoded within the text, I suggest, are intimations of the social conflict outside the text.

CONTESTATION IN THE TEXTS

Conflict Within Babylonia: Covert Contestation

The Talmud proceeds to cite a story, which, while overtly claiming to be a precedent for the practice of the "Rabbis" who stay away from their

---

lot, a woman feels desire and erotic passion more often than once a week. Therefore, her husband is obligated in this respect.

(Rabbi Moshe Feinstein, cited in Rachel Biale 1984, 134)

What is fascinating about this text is that despite manifesting no open recognition of the fact that male sexual needs may have changed owing to the promiscuity of the generation, it provides, in line with classical rabbinic practice, not for greater sexual abstemiousness but for more frequent sexual satisfaction for everyone, in the disguise of the obligation of men toward women.

23. It further contradicts the statement above in the names of both Rav and Rabbi Yohanan to the effect that *even with permission a man should not stay away from home*

wives for two or three years, is plausibly read as an index of ambivalence and opposition to this practice:

> Rava said that our Rabbis have relied upon Rav Ada the son of Ahva and indeed practice in accordance with his view. As in the case of Rav Rehume who was a disciple of Rava's in Mahoza. He would regularly visit his wife every year on the Eve of Yom Kippur. One day, his studies absorbed him. His wife was waiting for him, "Now he will come. Now he will come." He did not come. She became upset, and a tear fell from her eye. He was sitting on the roof. The roof collapsed under him and he died.

As I have said, on the overt level of the structure of the Talmud's argument, this text is cited as a support for Rava's contention that the Rabbis depend legitimately on Rav Ada's tradition and practice accordingly. However, it does not take a very suspicious hermeneut to read it against the grain. The story, in fact, encodes a very sharp critique of the practice of married Rabbis being away from home for extended periods. First of all, let us note that it is clear from this story that the Rabbi did not study at any great distance from his home, for had he done so, one day of slightly extended study would not have made such a difference and prevented him from getting home for Yom Kippur. This consideration only enhances the irony to which Yonah Fränkel has pointed in the phrase "would *regularly* visit his wife on the Eve of Yom Kippur" (Fränkel 1981, 101). Further, the fact that he is portrayed as being so unmindful that he even forgets the one time of the year that he goes to visit his wife can only be read as an extremely critical and ironic representation of this Rabbi's behavior. It is possible that the name of the protagonist also is ironically emblematic of his character, for his name, *Rehume*, means "lover" or "merciful one," and he demonstrates that he is neither. Another possible, and indeed very attractive, interpretation is that Rav Rehume is indeed a lover, a lover of Torah.[24] That is, we would have here actuated once again a version of the topos that we saw above with regard

---

for more than a month, a fortiori, without permission. However, it is possible to understand that statement differently, to wit: that thirty days away from home can be described as normal practice, or even that the discussion focuses really on what happens after the return home of the one who goes away for thirty days without permission, in which case Rav and Rabbi Yohanan are merely questioning how long he must stay home before leaving again. The argument is not definitive.

24. The name itself is otherwise attested in the Talmud approximately eight times. My suggestion is that choosing precisely this figure as the hero of this story is not accidental.

to Ben-Azzai of the life of a Torah-student as erotic abandonment to Torah, such that the wife becomes a rival to the beloved Torah. The Rabbis certainly figured their attachment to Torah as erotic, referring to the Torah as being "like the narrow sex of the gazelle, for whose husband every time is like the first time" (Babylonian Talmud Eruvin 54b), so also for those who study Torah, every time is like the first time.[25] Reversing the Hellenistic topos of the wife and the seductions of this world as a danger to the philosopher, we have here the seductions of Torah as a threat to fulfillment of the Torah-sage's responsibilities to the world, especially with regard to his sexual debt to his wife. This reading renders the story less a moral condemnation of the Rabbi himself and more a cautionary tale in general to beware being overly inundated in the erotic pleasures of Torah-study.[26]

In either case, the empathetic depiction of the eagerly waiting wife is calculated by the narrator to lead the reader/hearer of this story to a position of identification with her, a moral judgment that is confirmed on the explicit level when the Rabbi is punished by death. To be sure, there is nothing in the overt narrative that condemns the practice of being away from home per se. The implication is that had he fulfilled at least his habit of visiting once a year, there would have been no stain on his behavior. Nevertheless, I would claim that the way that the entire story is presented provides rather a strong condemnation of the practice at the same time that it is overtly supporting it. We will find this strain between overt support and covert contestation in other texts as well.

The Talmud continues its halakhic discourse with another statement that seems to strongly contest Rava's claim that it is legitimate for the Torah-scholars to be away from home for extended periods:

> What is the "season" of the Disciples of the Wise? Rav Yehuda said that Shmuel said, from the Eve of Sabbath till the Eve of Sabbath [i.e., the Torah-scholar should at the least come home and sleep with his wife every Friday night]. *The one who gives his fruit in its time* [Psalms 1:4]; Said Rav Yehuda—and there are those who say Rav Huna, and those who say Rav Nahman—this refers to one who sleeps with his wife every Eve of the Sabbath.

---

25. And note that the word for the sex or vagina of the gazelle is from the same root as the name Rehume, the lover!

26. In Boyarin 1992, I consider more unambivalently positive connotations of the religious life as erotic. As this book was going to press, Michael White informed me of Greek texts in which courtesans complain of philosophers who seduce their lovers away from them. Our stories may very well be formed, once more, as parodic appropriations of these narratives.

The Talmud then tells us a tale of one who regularly came home on such a schedule and met dire consequences when he missed this appointment one time:

> Yehuda, the son of Rabbi Hiyya, was the son-in-law of Rabbi Yannai. He went and sat in the House of Study. Every Friday at twilight he would come to his wife, and when he would come they would see in front of him a pillar of fire. One day, he became engrossed in his study and did not come. As soon as they did not see the sign [the pillar of fire], Rabbi Yannai said to them, "Turn over his bed, for were Yehuda alive, he would not fail to fulfill his sexual obligation," and it was *like an error from the mouth of a ruler* [Eccles. 10:5], and Yehuda died.

This story not only encodes opposition to the practice of extended absences of Rabbis from their wives, it also encodes in narrative the ideological significance of sexuality which is the reason for the opposition (Fränkel 1981, 102–04). Fränkel notes that the pillar of fire functions in the tale as a hermeneutic key. Were we not to have this element, it is conceivable that the story could be understood as a story of conflict between the sacred and the secular, and that its point is render unto Caesar, as it were. However, the fact that Yehuda's procession to his home is preceded by a pillar of fire, the very sign that led the Jews in the Wilderness and brought them to the Promised Land, is a strong indication that we are not to read the narrative as a conflict of values. Both the study of Torah and marital sex are holy acts. Moreover, the "pillar of fire" is highly charged as an erotic symbol, since it is phallic in shape and since fire has strongly erotic associations. If the previous story encodes the erotic nature of Torah-study, this one complements it by strongly encoding a sacred status for marital sex. The nexus between the Sabbath and sexual intercourse also promotes this connection. To put it in structural terms, in both cases, sex and Torah, or marriage and the study-house, are set up as equal but opposed alternatives in complementary distribution.[27]

Yehuda, who should be equally willing to fulfill both religious obligations, seems, however, to perform the obligation of study with zeal and joy, while his coming home to sleep with his wife seems almost against his

---

27. I owe this formulation to Alan Dundes. Although this text encodes equal status, as it were, to the wife and the Torah, it also removes women entirely from the sphere of Torah through this complementary distribution. Another way to put this would be that the woman is raised to the status of Torah and therefore prevented from engaging in Torah—analogous to the status of women as art objects in "Western" culture, which has barred them from being artists. See also Moi (1990, 6). In the next chapter I will analyze at length a discontinuity in the discourse of gender that allows women access to study of Torah, as well as further explaining this structural issue.

will and only out of a sense of obligation. That is what trips him up and leads to his death. His father-in-law is sure that only death could have prevented Yehuda from fulfilling the commandment, and he therefore enacts a rite of mourning for him—turning over his bed. The performance of the rite, however, turns out to cause his death. As the citation from Ecclesiastes implies, a sentence of capital punishment given by the king, even in error, may not be revoked in certain legal situations. So here, performing a rite that indicated death is held to have caused the death. The fact that this rite is precisely a turning over of the bed is most evocative, as Fränkel acutely notes: he who ignored the responsibilities of the bed is punished by the bed, as it were. Without a doubt, the point of the story is, as Fränkel claims, that the Rabbi suffers a divine sentence of capital punishment because of his failure to perceive that the obligation to sleep with his wife is as holy a commandment as the obligation to study Torah. The story, like the previous one, remains an eloquent testimony to the unworkability of the utopian solution of the halakha requiring the husband who studies to nevertheless come home regularly. The tension and contradiction remain.

At this point in the text of the Babylonian Talmud, the story of Rabbi Akiva and his romance with Rachel is produced.[28] We are now in a position to read that story. Both the immediate textual context and the larger cultural intertextual context suggest that this romantic narrative is the ultimate Babylonian attempt at a utopian resolution and justification for the local practice, attested to in the name of Rava, of husbands spending enormous quantities of time away from home to study Torah. It will be remembered that this practice is contrary to the express moral injunctions of both early Palestinian and Babylonian supreme authorities, who said that even with permission, husbands should not be away for more than a month at a time.[29] It stands, also, in contradiction to the view of Shmuel,

28. For a sensitive analysis of the differences between the two versions (which are irrelevant for my reading here), see Weller (1989, 101–05). I find implausible, however, her assumption of a "nuclear story" that was elaborated in the two texts.

29. This contradiction was already remarked by the twelfth-century talmudic commentators, the Tosafists, who were puzzled at the fact that the Rabbis stay away from home for two or three years, in direct contradiction to the views of both Rav and Rabbi Yohanan. They reinterpret the clear meaning of the text in order to escape from this contradiction, while in my view the whole function of these stories is to neutralize Rav and Rabbi Yohanan, as explicitly noted by Rava himself, who is presented as citing the first one.

another major Babylonian authority, to the effect that a Rabbi should sleep with his wife at least once a week. It is not surprising that, given the weight of halakhic and moral authority to be overcome, symbols with great cultural authority were necessary, and there is none greater in Jewish tradition than Rabbi Akiva. The thoroughly romantic quality of the story of his marriage to Rachel underscores dramatically how extremely disrupting the practice must have been—a disruptiveness that is allowed place in all of the other stories but completely suppressed in the story of Rabbi Akiva. Twice, the story emphasizes the fact that the Rabbi had been given "permission" by his bride to be away for so long. The "solution" that the Babylonian Talmud produces is to create a system of enormous socio-cultural pressure on women to "voluntarily" renounce their rights. As we shall see below, this Babylonian innovation was vigorously contested from Palestine on near-feminist grounds.[30]

Close reading of the story will show how it performs as narrative its ideological and cultural function of female subjugation and how its deployment of the romance genre is crucial as well. The key to my reading is the name, Rachel, which the tradition has universally (and with good textual warrant, as we will see) assigned to Rabbi Akiva's wife. This name, while quite common for Hebrew women, is also the usual word for ewe.[31] The entire story of the romance of Rabbi Akiva and Rachel is generated by one root metaphor: Akiva as the shepherd and Rachel as a ewe. Rabbi Akiva's relationship with his wife is figured in several ways as the relationship of a shepherd to a beloved ewe-lamb; the very site of their erotic idyll is a barn. Rachel's declaration that the "righteous [shepherd] knows the soul [desire] of his animal" is, in fact, the key moment in the story. The metaphor of male lover as shepherd and female beloved as ewe is, in fact, common in biblical discourse, used frequently as a figure for the relationship of God and Israel and appearing often in the Song of Songs. The story of Rabbi Akiva and Rachel is thus a plausible narrative development of a common biblical erotic metaphorical model.

30. That is, the opposition grows out of a representation of women's subjectivity (not that it is a presentation of actual women's subjectivity). See also below, n. 40.

31. Since Rachel's father, the quintessential fat cat, also has an emblematic name in this text, "Satisfied Dog," I do not think that reading Rachel's name as emblematic is overdrawn. Note that her name is only hinted at in the talmudic text, but so strongly that the tradition univocally understood that her name was Rachel. The very absence of explicit reference becomes, accordingly, almost a means of drawing attention to the symbolic value of the name. See further support for this point below.

The relationship between shepherd and ewe is an extraordinarily poignant and marked liaison within the context of the pastoral culture. As obnoxious as we may find the status of wife that is encoded in this metaphor, we will not be able to understand it or its power to persuade without taking seriously the cultural context in which it was generated. In order to get some feel for what this relationship might have evoked in the rabbinic culture, a vivid biblical text will be helpful. The text is the famous parable of the Poor Man's Ewe-Lamb in 2 Samuel 12:

> And God sent Nathan to David and he came to him and said to him: "There were two men in the city, one rich and one poor. [2] The rich man had very great flocks and cattle. [3] The poor man had nothing but one small ewe-lamb, which he had acquired and which he sustained and she grew up with him and with his children together; from his bread she would eat, and from his glass she would drink, and she would lie in his arms and was a daughter to him. [4] And a guest came to the rich man, and he didn't want to take from his flock or herd to cook for the guest who had come to him, and he took the ewe-lamb of the poor man and cooked it for his guest." [5] David was horrified, and said to Nathan, "That man should be executed."

This is an extraordinary picture from the point of view of our cultural stance. The animal is adopted into the family as a foundling child would be. Note as well the explicit class-coding in the story; the poor man feeds and cares for the animal as if human; the rich man thinks of the animal (and of the poor man!) as only an instrument to fulfill his economic needs. There is, moreover, a powerful erotic valence to the word-picture of the man sharing his bed with the ewe, an overtone the talmudic Rabbis do not miss: "By sleeping in his arms, she is a daughter?! Rather, a wife" (Megillah 13a). The midrashic comment is based on a linguistic subtlety; the word for daughter is *bat*, while the word for house, often used to mean wife, is *bayt*.[32] The context in which this parable is told makes this erotic overtone inescapable: David, the king with many wives, is accused of stealing the one beloved wife of his servant Uriah. The biblical text encodes a very vivid picture of an ideal marriage as like the love of a

32. The slippage between wife and daughter is not accidental; "my daughter" was a common mode of address used by the Rabbis toward their wives and other adult women. Moreover, as Chana Kronfeld remarks, erotic love is often figured in biblical (and later Hebrew) parlance as kinship, thus "my sister, my bride" in the Song of Songs.

shepherd for his only ewe-lamb. The wife is the ewe, in the biblical parable, as well as in our parabolic life of Rabbi Akiva and Rachel.

There is another important biblical intertext here, the story of Jacob and his marriages. There also, the hero is a shepherd in love with his master's daughter. There also, the father opposes the match. There also, the shepherd works for two periods of a number of years to win her, and there also, the daughter is named Rachel. Moreover, that shepherd's name, Ya‘qov, is an almost perfect anagram of our hero's name, spelt in Hebrew ‘Aqyva. We have, accordingly, very strong support for the suggestion that the pattern of Rabbi Akiva's marriage and particularly the shepherd-ewe relationship is being encoded in this story as a marriage ideal for Jews.

I have gone on at some length to establish the cultural emotional background of the association of husband with shepherd and wife with ewe on which the talmudic story is built. As subservient as the ewe-wife is, she is not denigrated or despised in this encoding. Indeed, she is both loved and honored when she knows her place. The text recognizes her subjectivity; at least in theory she has the power to accept or reject the absence of her husband for study. She chooses, of course, to accept. Indeed, she is the original motivating force for him to go away to study Torah. This moment constitutes a crisis as well as a crux in the story.[33] Up until then, Rachel is the agent of the narrative. It is she who "becomes engaged to Rabbi Akiva," she who marries him in the winter, not he who marries her. This is a reflection of the class-coding of the story; she as the patrician holds the upper hand. He is a poor shepherd, while she is the daughter of his master. However, at the moment that he reveals his potential as a Torah-scholar by drawing the proper moral of the incognito advent of Elijah, she exercises her agency for the last time by abdicating it. She sends him to study. From here on, the class code is superseded by the learning code, which is (almost ineluctably) a gender code. At this point he becomes, as it were, her pastor. It is self-understood and beyond question that what a Jewish wife desires is a husband learned in the Torah.[34] The love of Rabbi Akiva for her is marked twice in the story, in very powerful ways, in the poignant wish of the poor shepherd to give his

33. Some critics have in fact suggested that two originally unconnected texts have been joined here. In good formalist tradition, I will argue that the story is a unity, and the gap in the sujet is homologous with a sharp transition in the fabula.

34. See also Fränkel (1981, 113) on this point.

bride a very expensive gift and then in the dramatic statement to the students, that: "That which is mine and that which is yours is really hers!" It is this double effect—on the one hand, encoding a self-abnegation on the part of women, but on the other hand rewarding that self-abnegation with great prestige—that enabled this story to have the normative effect that it had in Jewish culture. A formation that did not offer powerful social rewards to women for behaving in this way could not have been as successful in achieving the hegemony that this role model for women did achieve among Jews.

A coda, added in the version of the Rabbi Akiva story in Ketubbot, makes even more explicitly manifest the political function of those stories:

> The daughter of Rabbi Akiva also behaved in this manner towards Ben-Azzai. And this fits the popular saying, "Ewe follows ewe—as the mother, so the daughter!"

This remark makes explicit for the first time the pun on the name of "Rachel" meaning "ewe." More to the point, however, is the ideological work that this little epilogue is performing. First of all, the story solves the problem of the recalcitrant Ben-Azzai, who refused to marry because his soul desired Torah, by domesticating him. Even he got married in the end and became a married monk. There really is no tension, the text implies, between marriage and lust for learning; all you need is the right kind of wife. The story encodes the extreme model of Rachel as an ideal for Jewish womanhood and not as an exception, and indeed the practice of husbands leaving their wives for very extended periods to study Torah was current in some communities (and a theme of literature) until the early twentieth century, since when it seems to have been abandoned.[35] In any case, in certain circles of traditional Jews, the story of Rachel still remains a powerful ideological force, as witness the following recent statement by a prominent and popular Orthodox teacher: "Much of what happened to Rachel remains in obscurity, as she herself preferred. Her joy was in his triumph, which, in barely twenty years, exceeded all that she could ever have imagined" (Steinsaltz 1988, 165). The romance of Rabbi Akiva

35. Note that this notice of Rachel's daughter as the wife of Ben-Azzai contradicts the text cited above and other traditions that hold that Ben-Azzai remained unmarried; the discrepancy only emphasizes all the more the ideological function of the stories.

and Rachel is thus historical in precisely the sense that Eva Cantarella
argues that the Homeric epics are historical:

> For all the centuries of the so-called Hellenic Middle Ages, the *aidoi*
> and *rhapsodoi*, singing the deeds of their ancestors, fulfilled not only a
> recreational function but an important pedagogical one as well. They
> taught the Greeks what to feel and think, what they should be, and
> how they should behave. As men learned from the *epos* to adapt them-
> selves to the model of the hero, so women listening to the poets
> learned what sort of behavior they should adopt and what they should
> avoid. It is in this sense that the *Iliad* and the *Odyssey* are considered
> historical documents.
>
> (Cantarella 1987, 25)

Our romantic historical fiction is a historical document in precisely this
sense. The romance of Rabbi Akiva and Rachel is foundational for the
two-edged sword of European Jewish patriarchal culture, which often gave
women much power and prestige in the "secular" realm while denying them
participation in the religious sphere. My great-grandmother ran a large
lumber business while her husband devoted himself to the study of Torah.
Such is the cultural power that the figure of Rabbi Akiva commands.[36]

All was not smooth, however, in the innovation of the practice of the
married monk. The Talmud itself shows us the cracks just under the surface of the utopian solution. The amount of conflict that the new social
practice engendered is marked by the astonishing final story in the collection, which is truly one of the most appalling stories of a Rabbi's behavior
in the Talmud. After reading it, we are not at all surprised at the cultural

---

36. He lived, at any rate, at home, but into the nineteenth century (!) many
young husbands were sent to study away from their wives in perfect imitation of the
story of Rabbi Akiva (Biale 1992). (I wonder to what extent the practice of a wife
"putting a husband through graduate school," widely practiced as recently as my own
formation—and by us—is a fossilized relic of this Jewish cultural practice. The contribution of Jewish culture, both positive and negative, to post-Reformation European
marriage practice has not yet been investigated. Given the wide knowledge by
Gentiles in the early modern period, such as Milton, of rabbinic literature, I think this
issue is not trivial.)

Finkelstein (1964, 80) also sees that this story of Rabbi Akiva is crucial in estab-
lishing the practice of married students staying away from home for years on end, but
he takes it to mean that Rabbi Akiva actually established the practice, while I, of
course, see it as a later Babylonian story that enforces the practice instituted there. For
another example of the power of stories about Rabbi Akiva in forming Jewish practice,
see Boyarin 1989.

energy that was required to institute such an extreme practice, nor at the necessity to utilize Rabbi Akiva for its production:

> Rav Yosef the son of Rava was sent by his father to the House of Study to study with Rabbi Joseph. They set for him six years of study [i.e., he had been married and it was decided that he would be away from home for six years]. After three years, on the Eve of Yom Kippur, he said, "I will go and visit my wife." His father heard and went out to meet him with a weapon. He said to him, "You remembered your whore?"[37] They fought, and neither of them got to eat the final meal before the fast.

This shocking tale, with near-unique violence of language and more than a hint of violent behavior between a father and a son, testifies eloquently to the extent of the conflict aroused by the Babylonian innovation associated with Rava's name in his own community of Babylonia. Representing the strife as between Rava and his own son makes that conflict vividly real.

Critique from Without: Palestinian Rejection

The two communities of the Rabbis, in Babylonia and Palestine, were by no means sealed off one from the other. Any cultural currents in one would have been felt as waves in the other. We have already seen that in the Palestinian Talmud no extreme marriage patterns such as that of the Babylonians are contemplated. There is, indeed, further evidence that the Babylonian ideal of rabbinic marriage was not even countenanced. Our Babylonian talmudic text contains three more narratives of rabbis who married and then left their wives for periods of twelve years or more, one of which occurs both in a Babylonian version and in a Palestinian version in Bereshit Rabba. This narrative offers an elegant testing ground for my hypothesis that the practice of marrying and leaving one's wife for extended periods was much more heavily stigmatized in Palestine than in Babylonia. To facilitate comparison, I will present the two stories side by side:

Palestinian Version	*Babylonian Version*
Hananiah the son of Hakinai and Rabbi Shimon the son of Yohai went to study Torah with Rabbi Akiva in Bnei Berak.	Rabbi Hananiah the son of Hakinai was going to the House of the Rabbi [the study-house] at the end of the wedding of Rabbi

37. A variant in the text reads, "You remembered your dove?" The difference in Hebrew is but one letter. Not surprisingly, the glossator could not stand to leave the text as it was.

They were there for thirteen years.

Rabbi Shimon the son of Yohai used to send letters to his wife, and used to know what was happening to his family. Hananiah the son of Hakinai did not send letters to his wife and did not know what was happening to his family. His wife sent to him, "Your daughter is grown; come and find her a match." Rabbi Akiva perceived with the Holy Spirit and said, "Anyone who has a grown daughter should go and find her a match."

[He wished to enter his house but found that it was turned in a different direction.] What did he do? He went and sat by the well. He heard the voices of the water-drawers saying, "Daughter of Hakinai, fill your pitcher and ascend."

She went, and he went after her, until he came into his house. Just as his wife saw him, her soul left her.

{There are those who say that it returned.}

(Theodor and Albeck 1965, 1232)[38]

Shimon the son of Yohai. He [Shimon] said to him, "Wait for me until I can come with you." He did not wait.

He went and sat for twelve years in the House of the Rabbi.

By the time that he arrived, the streets of the town had changed and he did not know the way home. He went and sat by the bank of the river. He heard that they were calling a girl: "Daughter of Hakinai, Daughter of Hakinai, come and fill your pitcher, and come let us go." He said [to himself], "One can derive from this that this girl is mine."

He followed her. His wife was sitting and sifting flour. She lifted her eyes, saw him, was filled with desire; her soul departed. He said before Him, "Master of the Universe, Such is the reward of this poor woman?" He prayed for her and she lived.

Precisely the evident fact that we have the *same* story in front of us in two versions here enables us to perceive the different cultural work that each version is doing, thus providing clues for differences between the two cultures that produced them. Looking first at the Palestinian version, we see that it is entirely oriented toward condemnation of the behavior of Hananiah (note that he is not even awarded his title of "Rabbi" in this version!). We have here a portrayal of an extreme, a married man who

---

38. The curly braces indicate that the last sentence is a very late addition to the text, on which see next note.

becomes so involved with his studies that he does not know whether he has a daughter, or if he does, forgets her existence entirely. Even after his wife writes to him—after thirteen years—and requests his aid in caring for his daughter's future, he does not respond until explicitly commanded to do so by the head of the yeshiva, none other than Rabbi Akiva, whose cultural prestige is being mobilized here for a purpose quite different from that in the Babylonian text. The original story ends with the bitter consequence of his behavior, the death of his wife. There is nothing in this version that ameliorates in any way the critique of the practice of long absences for study of Torah, unless it be the implicit contrast with Rabbi Shim'on, who at least stayed in constant touch with his wife.

In stark contrast to this version is the Babylonian rewriting of the story. Here, the elements of critique of Rabbi Hananiah are relatively muted. We are not told that he did not contact his family, or that he only decided to go home when forced to either by the wife or by the teacher. When his wife dies, he is horrified and intervenes with heaven to restore her to life. What I am claiming is that the Babylonian version is a revision of the story, which is explicitly designed to provide a utopian solution to the enormous moral and halakhic contradictions involved in the practice of husbands being away from their wives to study Torah for years on end, as if to suggest that, in our contemporary language of utopia, you can have it all. The Babylonian reteller, struggling with a Palestinian story that, not surprisingly, reflects the strongly critical position of that culture against the practice, mutes that critique dramatically by leaving out certain elements of the narrative. His provision of the deus ex machina of a miraculous resurrection only emphasizes the failed utopian resolution of the story even more. This happy ending rings as false as the ending of *The Tempest* or *Midsummer Night's Dream,* with everyone well married. This comparison is not intended, of course, as an aesthetic comment, but rather a statement of the way that the very resolutions typical of the comic literary text often betray rather than provide solutions for the underlying socio-cultural conflicts.[39]

---

39. A glossator has added a line to the Palestinian version as well, to the effect that the wife's soul returned; it is clear, however, that this is only a later addition to the text, and perhaps one that is based on the Babylonian story. Fränkel makes the same point. The version in the equally Palestinian Wayyiqra Rabba 21:8 text also includes an ending in which the outcry of Rabbi Hananiah causes a miraculous resurrection, but I am virtually certain that this also is a later scribal addition imitating the Babylonian talmudic version. There are three reasons for this judgment. First, the very fact that the two Palestinian texts, otherwise almost identical, have entirely different

If in Babylonia the practice of extended absence of rabbinic husband from wife was contested, in Palestine it seems, then, to have been simply rejected. I am not arguing for greater asceticism in Babylonia than in Palestine; quite the opposite, I think that in Palestine there was more of a sense that it is possible and desirable for men to separate themselves from sexual desire at least in part, either by remaining unmarried for extended periods of time or by ascetic sexual practice within marriage. However, together with that notion, there seems also to have been an understanding in Palestine that once married such asceticism cannot be imposed on a wife.[40] Support for this claim can be found in the tannaitic midrash on Miriam's complaint against her brother Moses (Numbers 12 and Sifre ad loc.). This narrative tells of a complaint that Miriam lodged with and against her brother Moses and the strong rebuke and punishment which she received from God for this insolent behavior. By diverting the interpretation of this complaint from one against the wife of Moses (as the biblical text seems to imply) to one on her behalf, the midrash produces strong opposition to celibate marriage.

The biblical story opens with the statement that Miriam and Aaron spoke against Moses regarding the Ethiopian woman (Tzipporah, according to the midrash[41]) that he had married:

---

formulations at the end, suggests strongly that both endings are later glosses. This suggestion is further supported by the enormous variations between the different manuscripts of Wayyiqra Rabba itself, often a sign of a belated addition. Second, there is nothing in the Palestinian version of the story that would prepare us in the slightest for the Rabbi's expression of concern and compassion. Third, the phrase "this poor woman" is a copy of the language of the Babylonian text and occurs previously in the Babylonian talmudic passage, from which it has almost certainly been imitated in our story, first in the Talmud and then secondarily in the Palestinian midrash. And indeed, the phrase does not occur anywhere else in Palestinian literature but does occur at least once more in the Babylonian Talmud (Hullin 7b).

40. Paul's famous declaration in 1 Corinthians 7 that husbands and wives should not deny each other, in spite of his clear valorization of celibacy, would be closely related to this understanding. Halakhically, such an obligation was equally addressed to wives, though the endemic androcentrism of the discourse addresses only men as to their obligations. Both husbands and wives were permitted to refuse sex at any given time, but not for an extended period.

41. The word "Ethiopian" is explained as a metaphor:

The Ethiopian woman: But was she indeed Ethiopian, she was Midianite, as it says "And the Priest of Midian had seven daughters" [Exod. 2:16]. So why does scripture say, "Ethiopian," but to teach us that just as the Ethiopian is unusual for his skin, so was Tzipporah unusual for her beauty more than all the other women. . . .

For he had married an Ethiopian woman: Why is it said again, hasn't he already said, "with regard to the Ethiopian woman," why does scripture say,

And Miriam and Aaron spoke against Moses [Num. 12:1]: This teaches that both of them spoke against him but Miriam initiated it, for Miriam was not accustomed to speaking in the presence of Aaron, except for an immediate need.

The midrashic text is a response to an anomaly in the biblical text, namely that while the verb has two subjects, one male and one female, the verb-form is feminine singular.[42] The midrash interprets this to mean that it was on Miriam's initiative that the slander or complaint against Moses took place. The midrash continues to explicate the story:

And Miriam and Aaron spoke with regard to the Ethiopian woman: And indeed, how did Miriam know that Moses had withdrawn from sexual intercourse?[43] She saw that Tzipporah no longer adorned herself with women's ornaments. She said to her, "What is the matter with you? Why do you not adorn yourself with women's ornaments?" She said, "Your brother does not care about the matter." And this is how Miriam knew. And she spoke to her brother [Aaron], and the two of them spoke against him.

Rabbi Nathan said Miriam was at the side of Tzipporah, at the time, when it says "And the youth ran . . . and said Eldad and Medad are prophesying in the camp" [Num. 11:28]. When Tzipporah heard, she

---

"for he had married an Ethiopian woman"? There are women who are comely in their beauty but not in their deeds, in their deeds but not in their beauty, as it says, "like a gold ring in the nose of a pig is a beautiful woman without wisdom" [Prov. 11:22]. But this one was comely in her beauty and in her deeds, therefore it says, "for he had married an Ethiopian woman."

Since it is impossible to suppose that Tzipporah fits the normal denotative meaning of "Ethiopian," the term is taken as a metaphor for distinctiveness, for being somehow unusual, a fairly common midrashic move. The midrash goes out of its way to read the attribution as positive, praising Tzipporah as both attractive and righteous, thus emphasizing all the more the injustice done to her by Moses's overzealous piety. As the Talmud remarks in another context, "Rabbi Yehoshua ben Levi said, 'Anyone whose wife is a fearer of Heaven and he does not sleep with her is called a sinner, as it says, And you shall know that your tent is at peace' [Job 5:25]" (Yevamot 62b).

42. To be sure, modern grammatical analysis of Hebrew does not recognize this as an anomaly, arguing that in Hebrew, as in other Semitic languages, when a verb appears before two coordinated subjects, it agrees with the first of them. However, as I have argued in my book (Boyarin 1990c), midrashic exegesis must be understood on the basis of the Rabbis' perceptions of Hebrew grammar and not ours, and the fact is that wherever this construction appears, it is treated by the midrash as having special meaning. Furthermore, the continuation of the story suggests strongly that the rabbinic reading that Miriam was the instigator of this event is not over-reading.

43. The literal translation would be from "procreation"; however, as this text and others indicate, this is a rabbinic term for sexual intercourse, whether or not it results in pregnancy and indeed whether or not procreation is its primary aim. The implications of this linguistic usage have been considered in Chapter 2 above.

said, "Woe to the wives of these!"[44] And this is how Miriam knew.
And she spoke to Aaron, and the two of them spoke against him.

In contrast to other early interpretative traditions that understand that
Miriam and Aaron were complaining *against* the wife of Moses, the
midrash understands it to be a complaint on her behalf. The midrashic
rewriting of the story is, as is usually the case at least in these early
midrashim, a response to a gap in the biblical text that demands interpretation. The story begins with Miriam complaining "with regard to the
Ethiopian woman," but in the elaboration, the complaint of Miriam and
Aaron is entirely different, "Did God only speak with Moses; He indeed
spoke with us as well?" Rather than being a charge having to do with
whom Moses had married, it seems to be a challenge to some power or
privilege of his. Moreover, God's defense of Moses cum punishment of
Miriam seemingly has nothing to do with his wife, being merely a statement of Moses's special holiness. There is accordingly an inner contradiction in the story: was the complaint because Moses had married
inappropriately or because Miriam was jealous of his status? The midrashic story fills this gap by connecting the two complaints as one; she
complained on behalf of the wife, arguing that he had behaved toward
her in a way that was arrogant and overbearing. Did she and her elder
brother not share his status, and yet they do not behave so toward their
spouses? The midrash, moreover, knows precisely what the complaint of
the wife was, and as plausible a resolution of the contradiction as this is, it
is not a straightforward account of the "meaning" of the biblical text. As
is typical for midrash, the interpretation seems to involve a synergy of two
factors: it both addresses a genuine interpretative difficulty and serves an
ideological investment.[45] Accordingly, the midrash doubly ventriloquizes
the voice of the woman and her complaint, first by making Miriam the
initiator of the action and the speaker here, and then also by reporting, in
her name, what she had heard from Tzipporah that had made her aware
of the wife's distress.[46] The text communicates two forms of the woman's

44. I.e., upon hearing that the two men were prophesying, she commiserated with
their wives, thinking that now the men would stop sleeping with them, as Moses had
stopped sleeping with her.

45. I am aware, of course, that my statement here of the hermeneutics of midrash
is highly oversimplified. It is dependent on my theory of midrash, as worked out in
Boyarin 1990c.

46. The use of the term "ventriloquy" indicates that one should *not* understand
that there is an *expression* here of women's subjectivity; there is, however, a *representa-*
tion of an imagined women's subjectivity, an effort at empathy with women and an

complaint against her husband. The first is more subtle in that only by indirection does it imply an indictment of Moses for not having intercourse with her, while in the second case, the grievance is sharp, direct, and clear: "Woe to the wives of these!" Woe to the wife of him who becomes overly holy, and owing to his holiness ignores the needs of his wife for sex. At the same time that Miriam is being condemned by the biblical text and by the midrash for her untoward accusation against Moses, the text ventriloquizes the voice of the woman whose husband devotes himself overly much to the study of Torah and refrains from intercourse.

The midrash goes on to emphasize the good intentions of Miriam, while still recognizing that the Torah narrates her punishment for this act:

> Behold, the matter is suitable for an argument from the mild case to the severe: Since Miriam did not complain to her brother for blame but for praise, and not to decrease procreation but to increase it and only in private, and thus was punished, all the more so one who speaks against his fellow for blame and not for praise, to decrease procreation and not to increase it, in public and not in private.

Many who commit the sin of slander do so in order to decrease procreation, either by preventing marriages from taking place or by promoting disharmony between husband and wife. Miriam did the opposite. Her intention was to promote the good by restoring harmony between Moses and Tzipporah, and the proof of this is that she made her charge in private. The midrash here goes out of its way to reduce the culpability of Miriam, in spite of the severe punishment she is given in the Torah narrative—temporary leprosy (following conventional, if inaccurate translations), precisely the expected punishment for slander in the rabbinic moral system. Her sin was only in being overly and inappropriately zealous for the performance of the commandment. By thus minimizing the disapproval of Miriam's speech against Moses and making its intentions entirely praiseworthy, the midrash is already expressing a negative attitude toward married celibacy, within the confines of a possible reading of the biblical text.

---

effort, moreover, with at least potential effect in actual marriage practices. (Compare Bloch 1991a, 2, who sees only the potential dangers here.) Women are often represented in rabbinic texts as subjects. Their subjectivity is, however, as here, only represented as an object of rabbinic discourse.

The midrash goes on to explain the rest of the story. Miriam and Aaron's complaint had to do with the way that Moses was holding himself above them—holier than thou—in his celibate behavior:

> *And they said, "Did God speak only to Moses?"*: Did He not speak with the Fathers, and they did not withdraw [from sex]? *Did the Holiness not speak also with us*, yet we did not withdraw?

To which comes God's reply to them:

> *If there will be for you a prophet*: Perhaps just as I speak with the prophets in dreams and visions, so I speak with Moses, therefore scripture tells us, "Not so is my servant Moses"—except for the ministering angels. Rabbi Yose says, even than the ministering angels.
> *Mouth to mouth do I speak with him*: Mouth to mouth I told him to withdraw from his wife.

At first blush this midrash seems to be an approbation of the holiness of celibacy and even of celibate marriage—a practice well known in certain early Christian circles (Brown 1988). After all, Moses is the highest model of what a human being can achieve in religious life. He chooses to be celibate at a certain point in his life and is very strongly approbated for this by God Himself. Seemingly, then, his celibacy would be an exemplum to the Rabbis themselves—and so, indeed, Finkelstein interprets it (1964, 80), as does David Biale (1989), arguing that the midrash is a support for the practice of extended marital separations.

In fact, I would claim, not only does this text not promote the ideal of celibacy or celibate marriage for the Rabbis, it constitutes a very strong polemic against such a practice or ideal. To see why, we shall need to read the text a little more closely. First, we must realize that the midrash is explicitly and formally *citing* the received tradition of Moses's celibacy. Note that it does not ask how *we* know that Moses had withdrawn from his wife after Sinai, only how Miriam came to know. The midrash thus conveys (and we know for a fact) that the motif of Moses's *mariage blanc* was current in earlier Jewish tradition. In Philo, for example, Moses is the very type of the highly regarded Therapeutae who renounce sex entirely (Fraade 1986, 264). My thesis is that the midrash cites this authoritative and widespread tradition here in order to counter it. By introducing this traditional theme precisely at this point in the midrashic text and not, for example, in the context of accounts of Moses's piety, the midrash has found a means of neutralizing and opposing the ideology of the tradition, without, however, denying its validity entirely—something the Rabbis apparently could not have accomplished given its widespread authority.

God's condemnation of Miriam and Aaron is explicitly put into terms that emphasize the exceptional nature of the relationship between Moses and God. Miriam and Aaron seem to be proposing that since they have the same status as Moses, having also spoken with God, either they should also refrain from sex or he should not. God's rebuke to them consists of a very strong statement that Moses is special—indeed, unique. There will be other prophets, just like Miriam and Aaron, but to them God will speak in dreams and visions. They, accordingly, are not required to refrain from sexual intercourse. Even the Patriarchs, Abraham, Isaac, and Jacob, were not expected or allowed to be celibate. Only Moses, with whom God spoke "mouth to mouth"—in itself, a highly erotic attribute—only he was required to withdraw from marital life. He is either only slightly below the angels or even more spiritual than they, and no other human being was ever like him. It would follow, of course, a fortiori, that mortals lesser than the Patriarchs, prophets, and Moses's siblings, whatever the degree of holiness to which they aspire, are not expected to be celibate. I read the midrashic text, then, as a form of opposition to the received tradition that Moses was a celibate husband. To neutralize the force of this authoritative motif, the midrash simultaneously cites it and contests it by marginalizing it as the practice expected of, and permitted to, only Moses in all of history. Thus the midrash manages both to remain faithful to a powerful received tradition and at the same time to counter it. When this point is combined with the vivid expression of empathy with the neglected wife of the "prophet" who opts for celibacy, we have a robust polemical statement against the sort of practice that the Babylonian Rabbis engaged in (or at any rate, say they engaged in) of leaving their wives for years on end without sexual companionship.[47]

Once more, comparing the Babylonian version of this tradition with the Palestinian text just read will reinforce this point. In the Babylonian Talmud, the story is cited thus:

Moses separated himself from his wife. What did he reason? He reasoned for himself by a syllogism (*Qal wehomer*). He said: If to Israel,

47. The dating of the midrash is contested. Paradoxically, I am among those who are inclined to regard it as earlier than the Babylonian Talmud, in which case it could hardly be a polemic against the practice that I am claiming was instituted by the

with whom the Shekina only spoke for a short time, and only for a set time, the Torah said, "For three days do not approach woman," I with whom the Shekina speaks at every moment and without a set time, a fortiori. And how do we know that God agreed with him, for it says, "Go tell them, return to your tents" and right after that, "But you stay here with me." And there are those who say [that we learn it] from "Mouth to mouth will I speak with him."

(Shabbat 67a)

This Babylonian retelling of the story is conspicuous for its absences and by its absences makes the presences of the Palestinian version all the more prominent. There is no representation here, whatsoever, of the feelings of the wife, indeed no recognition that she is, in any way, an interested party in the decision. Moreover, although the difference between Moses and the ordinary people is adduced here as well, the difference does not lead clearly to the understanding that for all others, renunciation of marital sex is excluded and regarded as arrogance and wrong, as it is in the midrash. One could easily read this text as a further authorization for the apparent Babylonian practice of long marital separations for the study of Torah, while the Palestinian version above strongly condemns the practice.

THE CASE OF THE MARRIED MONK

By cross-examining the talmudic texts, then, I have proffered a solution to the case of the married monk. A set of directly contradictory social demands was current within the culture; on the one hand, the highest of achievements was to devote oneself entirely to the study of Torah, and on the other hand, there was an absolute demand on everyone to marry and procreate. The Palestinians resolved this tension by following a common Hellenistic practice of marrying late after an extended period devoted to "philosophy"—for the Jews, Torah. The Babylonians, on the other hand, having a strong cultural model of the necessity of sexual activity for post-pubescent men, were prevented from such a pattern. They produced at some point, therefore, the impossible "solution" of men marrying young and then leaving their wives for extended periods of study, creating, as it

---

talmudic Rabbis; rather, it would have to be attacking other well-attested practices of *mariage blanc* among Jews and non-Jews at least as early as the first century. It becomes then a polemic against the Babylonian institution avant la lettre.

were, a class of "married monks." The romantic story of the marriage of the hegemonic symbol, Rabbi Akiva, is a text produced to institute a practical resolution of the social dilemma. The talmudic literature also represents strong (and often covert) opposition to the practice that this story attempts to institute.[48] These oppositional literary techniques take many of the forms of oppositional literature in other cultures as well, including ironic appropriation (Chambers 1991, 117). Even though we cannot know to what extent the practice of married monkship was ever "actually" implemented, the literary evidence can certainly be taken as evidence of socio-cultural struggle around the attempt (at least) to implement it. Literary analysis can be then a means to tentative exposition of cultural reality. Precisely through close (but contextualized) reading, the surface of the text manifests unresolved tensions and conflicts within the actual social structure. It is the failure of the narrative to totalize that is significant, not its success. We do not have to read the texts as documents that reflect social practice, as in the older historicism, nor as "texts" that are entirely self-enclosed and autonomous, as in the various formalistic practices of literary criticism, but as themselves practices of culture that can be pressured to reveal from within themselves the cultural work that they do.

My reading of the textual complex surrounding rabbinic marriage has suggested that a major goal of the hegemonic rabbinic discourse was the securing of a self-abnegating role for Jewish wives (at least those of a certain class)—a role in which their status or prestige was defined through the spiritual and intellectual achievements of their husbands. One extreme form of this development was the institution (ideal or real) of married monks, that is, of married Torah-students who spent years of study away from their wives. We have seen how opposition to the sexual deprivation imposed on women by this practice was registered within the rabbinic texts themselves. In the next chapter, we will see that there was internal opposition as well to the total confinement of women to sexual and procreative roles, however honored.

48. I would like to make clear the difference between my interpretative practice and that of structuralist readings of myth, which also see the myth as an attempt at resolution of tensions in the culture. In structuralism, the tensions are reconstructed at a level of deep structure, and the myth is read as a perfect resolution; the surface of the mythic text is, therefore, not significant. For an example of structuralist reading at its best, see Vernant (1990) on the Prometheus myth.

6

Studying Women

Resistance from Within the Male Discourse

In Late Antique society, gender stereotypes that assigned certain
virtues to each sex but not the other surely became obstacles to the
achievement of human wholeness, especially for people who sought
the broader and deeper forms of perfection envisaged by some philosophers, Jews and Christians. The question then becomes, were significant ways found within the culture to overcome these obstacles?

(Harrison 1992)

Several recent writers on the history of women's religion have made the
disturbing point that in ascetic religious formations, women paradoxically
achieve autonomy and power that they seem to have nowhere else in late
antiquity, or at all. This has been discussed in regard to the Therapeutae
by Ross Kraemer (1989) and for early Latin Christianity by Clark (1986,
180 and throughout; see also McNamara 1976). Virginity was considered
to make it possible for women to be "as men," or even for the distinction
of gender to be abolished entirely, and this abolition was a major goal
of sexual renunciation for women, as was freedom of another sort for
men (Harrison 1990b and forthcoming; Aspegren 1990; Meyer 1985;
Castelli 1986 and 1991; Clark 1986; Fiorenza 1983, 90; Warner 1976,
72). This tendency was not exclusively Christian, for in perhaps the only
case of a post-biblical Jewish woman who functioned as an independent
religious authority on the same level as men, the famous nineteenth century "Maid of Ludmir," precisely the same mechanism operates. Indeed, as
soon as she engaged in marriage, at the age of forty, at the urging of male
religious authorities—and a celibate marriage at that—her religious
power disappeared, *because she had revealed that she really was a woman,
and not a man in a woman's body* (Rapoport-Alpert 1988; David Biale
1991). There are modern religious groups, too, in which celibacy has been
the condition for achievement of full autonomy and political equality for
women, the obvious example of which is the Shakers (Kitch 1989).

Autonomy and power are bought for women at the cost of their sexuality, precisely as would be predicted by certain radical feminist theorists, who argue that sexuality itself (or at any rate, heterosexuality) is inevitably domination. On the other hand, rabbinic Judaism, as I hope to have shown till now, so strongly approved the married life, including the life of the sexual body, that there was virtually no escape from marriage within that culture—either for men or for women. Since marriage seems inevitably to have led to androcentric domination, the body was bought, it seems, at the price of autonomy, especially for women—a bleak picture indeed. In this chapter, I shall consider some intimations from within the rabbinic formation of the possibility of an escape from this implacable dilemma.[1]

Classical talmudic Judaism denies women access to the most valued practice of the culture, the study of Torah.[2] The significance of this exclusion has been discussed by many scholars, most recently by Peter Brown in his monumental *The Body and Society: Men, Women and Sexual*

---

1. For a similar (and very impressive) effort to find such a break in the Christian monolith, see Harrison 1990b and 1991. Harrison argues that for certain Christian thinkers, transcendence of gender went in both directions, with men transcending their maleness and assimilating female characteristics and women doing the opposite. But more common, it seems, was Philo's schema whereby perfection for both meant overcoming the feminine, a task even harder for women than for men (Genevieve Lloyd 1984, 26–27). In general, Harrison's splendid work should move us away from simple equations by which sexual renunciation is identified with contempt for the body, sexuality, and women. Even radical asceticism is not necessarily the product of such an ideology, and the fact that both men and women equally renounce sexuality in such religious groups is also not to be ignored.

2. This formulation already points up the paradox of my very inquiry here: the assumption that Judaism is "male" and can deny or impart to women some "privilege." When I presented this chapter at the University of California at Berkeley, a question was raised by Naomi Seidman as to the historical significance of this evidence from the point of view of feminist historiography. In brief, the question was, why should we assume that the learning of Torah was relevant to women? Is it not a reproduction of the same value system even to assume that study of Torah would have been attractive to women, that it is something that they would have wanted to be "let in on," given the androcentrism of that Torah's content? Plaskow 1990 is effectively asking this question also. Perhaps a feminist historiography must reconstruct entirely different models of Jewish piety in order to be meaningful at all. The question is challenging and legitimate, but rather than make any attempt to address that issue here, I prefer to present the analysis that I have made of the texts and leave the question of its significance for feminist practice for another essay (Boyarin 1993). The short answer is that for many women it seems to be important to have a vital connection with the historical, ancestral culture of their people, in this case the Jews, and that providing a place for feminist women (and male fellow travelers) to retain a positive sense of such identity seems to me consequential and empowering for such people.

Renunciation in Early Christianity (1988, 118 and especially 145). It has been much less recognized, however, that there are voices within the texts that oppose this exclusion. These voices can be placed, moreover, within a certain time frame and geographical subset of the rabbinic culture; the exclusion itself has a history. It is a measure of Brown's sophistication as a scholar that he warns:

> The reader must always bear in mind the composite nature of any over-all presentation of Judaism, drawn as it is largely from the Palestinian and Babylonian Talmud—that is, from writings of widely differing periods and regions. Such sources may serve to delineate certain general horizons and to emphasize certain options taken among the rabbis of Palestine and Babylonia in the course of the late antique period; but they can be used only with great caution.
>
> (Brown 1988, 35 n. 7)

But it must be emphasized that much more can be made of the talmudic texts on these issues than has been done until now. By careful, symptomatic reading of the Talmuds and cognate texts, the traces of more than one ideological strain can be teased out precisely on this vitally important issue. As in the case of the marriage of Rabbi Akiva in the preceding chapter, an underlying assumption upon which this chapter is based is that the amount of energy expended by a culture to suppress or marginalize an ideological voice serves as a reliable index to the effectiveness of that voice as posing a threat to the hegemonic practices of that culture (Macherey 1978).

My major contention is that there was a significant difference between the Babylonian and Palestinian Talmuds with regard to the empowering (or disempowering) of women to study Torah. Both in the Palestinian and in the Babylonian text the dominant discourse suppressed women's voices in the House of Study. These texts, however, provide evidence that in Palestine a dissident voice was tolerated, while in Babylonia this issue seems to have been so threatening that even a minority voice had to be entirely expunged. It must be emphasized, however, that this evidence alone is not self-interpreting, because the suppression of this voice in Babylonia could mean two opposite things: either that women never had access to the study of Torah there, or that women often studied Torah in Babylonia; if the latter is the case, it presumably produced the panicky reaction evident in the text. The historical effect of the Babylonian text, however, which was hegemonic for later European Jewish culture, was to suppress quite thoroughly the possibilities for women to study Torah until modern times. My hope is that the very dialogism and dispersal of authority within the talmudic texts (even though that authority is exclusively male) will provide not only evidence of the hegemonic discourse but also symptoms of dissident voices and realities within the society that impart to women the power of speech in Torah-learning.

Three texts will be read in search of the symptoms of the oppositional discourse in Palestinian culture and its suppression in Babylonia. Each belongs to an entirely different literary genre, but they all point in the same direction. In the first section, halakhic (ritual law) texts and their differing versions in the Palestinian and Babylonian Talmuds will be interpreted, and in the second section we will examine a clearly fictional narrative recounting the terrible end of a historical female scholar, the legendary Beruria.

HALAKHA

"A father should teach his daughter Torah"

The first ritual text is a passage in which, counter to the hegemonic view, a prominent rabbi, Ben-Azzai, holds that it is a religious obligation for a father to teach his daughter Torah. We are fortunate in having the legal-hermeneutic responses of two closely related cultures to this text, because both the Palestinian and Babylonian Talmuds have interpreted it. By looking at the differences between the techniques with which these two subcultures deal with Ben-Azzai's view, I believe we can learn something of the differential threat his view posed to the social practices of the two Jewish cultures. It should be emphasized that Ben-Azzai's statement, as we will immediately see, is itself ambivalent in the extreme (at best) from a feminist point of view. I do not cite it as evidence, therefore, at all. My evidence for cultural difference between Palestine and Babylonia comes rather from the way that the two Talmuds have reacted to this statement. The way that this text is nullified in the Babylonian Talmud is symptomatic of how great a threat even such an equivocal suggestion of empowerment was perceived to be in that culture. The Palestinian tradition, in contrast, seems much more sanguine about the possibility that there could be women who would be talmudic and Torah-scholars.

Interestingly enough, the context of Ben-Azzai's statement is the discussion in the Mishna of the ordeal of the "errant wife." The biblical text is found in Numbers 5:11–31. The text there deals with the case of a man who has become jealous of his wife, believing that she has had sexual relations with another. An elaborate ritual ordeal is prescribed, in which the woman drinks water into which this very passage of the Torah has been literally dissolved. If she is innocent, nothing happens, and she is rewarded liberally by God. If she is guilty, however, appalling physical consequences ensue (also from God) when she drinks of these bitter waters.

The Mishna, in accordance with its general practice, goes into great detail to prescribe the conditions under which the ritual is to be performed and to describe its effects. Immediately after indicating what happens to the guilty woman upon imbibing the water, the text says:

> If she had merit, her merit will mitigate [the punishment] for her.
>
> On this basis Ben-Azzai said, "A man is obligated to teach his daughter Torah, so that if she drinks [the bitter water], she will know—for merit mitigates."
>
> Rabbi Eliezer says, "Anyone who teaches his daughter Torah, teaches her lasciviousness."[3]
>
> (Mishna Sota, ch. 3, para. 4)

3. For this as the correct reading, see Epstein (1964, 536). The word which I have translated here as "lasciviousness," *tifluth*, means literally "childish things" or "foolishness," as we find in the midrash Bamidbar Rabba 4:20, where we are told of a child who speaks *tifluth* during prayer, to which his father answers, "What shall I do? He is a child and he plays!" However, it is a frequent euphemism for lasciviousness, as we can see clearly from the following text:

> *To bring Vashti the Queen before the King in her royal crown* [Esther 1:12]. Rabbi Aibo said: It is the atonement of Israel that when they eat and drink and are merry, they bless and sing the praises of God; when the nations of the world eat and drink they deal in matters of *tifluth*: One says Medean women are beautiful, and the other says, Persian women are beautiful. That fool (Ahashuerosh) said to them, "the vessel that I use is neither Medean nor Persian but Chaldean! Do you wish to see her?" They said, "Yes, on condition that she is naked" [Esther Rabba 3:13].

In this misogynistic context (actually one quite hostile to the King's misogyny, as noted above), it is quite clear that *tifluth* has the sense of lasciviousness; see also Tanhuma Exodus 28, which says that "all kisses are of *tifluth*, except for the kiss of parting, the kiss of honoring and the kiss of meeting." Finally, the very context of our Mishna supports this interpretation, for the continuation is Rabbi Yehoshua's claim that a woman "prefers one measure of food with *tifluth* to nine measures with sexual abstinence," i.e., a poor but lusty husband is preferable. Incidentally, the context of Rabbi Yehoshua's statement suggests that the term is not even being used pejoratively by him, but this needs further investigation. See also Epstein (1964, 670).

The two Talmuds have very different interpretations of this text. The Palestinian reading is that the merit that mitigates the punishment is the merit of having studied Torah; therefore, a father who wishes to protect his daughter should teach her Torah. The Babylonian Talmud, however, though not directly interpreting Ben-Azzai, manages to imply that according to him, all that the father is required to teach his daughter is the specific fact that merit mitigates.[4] Why such teaching should be important and why Ben-Azzai should phrase such a limited teaching as "teaching Torah" are left unanswered. Moreover, according to that reading, the merit that mitigates is *not the merit of knowing Torah*, but some other merit entirely. According to the Palestinian reading, the knowledge that the daughter should have of Torah is in no way restricted to issues having to do with the ritual of the errant wife, and it is the very merit of having studied Torah that stands in her favor. This view would lead to a practice in which women would have studied Torah no less than men, for in a situation in which merit is required, the more the better. Since the rabbinic discourse had enormous normative force in Jewish culture, such an interpretation would have had quite radical implications for the status of women in a society in which the study of Torah was the most valued of all practices. It leads to a construction of gender in which the roles of the sexes in symbolic life are not nearly as sharply differentiated as they have been in all traditional West Asian societies, including Judaism.

The Palestinian Reading of Ben-Azzai   The Palestinian Talmud comments directly on Ben-Azzai and seems to understand him in a straightforward way to mean that the merit of studying Torah is what will stand for the woman should she undergo the errancy test. I derive this conclusion from observing how the Talmud *contradicts* Ben-Azzai's position:

> *Palestinian Talmud:* R. El'azar Ben-Azariah's opinion contradicts Ben-Azzai, for it is taught that there was an incident in which R. Yohanan ben Broka and R. El'azar Hasma were on their way from Yavne to Lydda and they went to visit R. Yehoshua in Peki'in. He asked them what was innovated in the House of Study today? They answered: "We

4. In all candor it must be admitted that this is the simplest translation of the text as well, for it is most easily read as, "she will know *that* merit mitigates." However, as I claim in the text, this reading makes the statement practically incoherent, and the Hebrew can be read as I have translated it, which certainly seems to be the Palestinian understanding.

are all your disciples and we drink your water." He said to them: "For
all that, it is impossible that there was nothing new said in the House
of Study. Who gave the discourse today?"

"R. El'azar Ben-Azariah."

"And what was his text?"

"*Convoke the nation, the men, the women, and the children* [Deut.
31:12]."

"And what did he say about it?"

"Since the men come to study and the women to hear, for what do
the children come? Indeed to provide reward for those that carry
them."

Said R. Yehoshua: "The generation that has R. El'azar Ben-Azariah
in it is no orphan!"

Ben-Azzai's view is contradicted here by showing that a counterview has
been expressed. R. El'azar Ben-Azariah had stated that the only reason
that women are obligated to come to the grand convocation for reading
the Torah, which takes place once in seven years, is merely to hear the
Torah being read and not to study it as do their husbands. It is clear,
therefore, that his opinion is opposite to that of Ben-Azzai's, and no merit
accrues to women for the study of Torah. From this, I infer that Ben-
Azzai indeed was understood to mean that the merit that would protect
the wife is precisely the merit of having studied Torah. This is consistent
with rabbinic theological notions in general, whereby sinners are protected from punishment for their sins if they have studied much Torah.

This "normal" talmudic dialectical move of citing a counterview is
precisely the basis for my conclusion that for the Palestinian Talmud, the
possibility of women studying Torah, while perhaps unusual, was not out
of the question; by countering it in that way, the Palestinian Talmud is
accepting Ben-Azzai's statement into the universe of its discourse. As we
will see below, the Babylonian Talmud resists this move.[5] The normalcy

5. Cf. the reading of Simha Friedman (1983), whose reading is exactly the opposite, namely, that the Palestinian Talmud is *more* extreme in its rejection of Ben-Azzai,
because it cites another counter authority. To be sure, the Palestinian Talmud relates
a story indicating how extreme a misogynist R. Eliezer was, but that hardly constitutes
an argument for general approbation of his position, since in that story even his son is
astonished at his behavior (much as Imma Shalom is at his sexual practice, for which
see above), and R. Eliezer is typically regarded as a heterodox and extreme personality.
For this reason, Brown's repeated citation of exactly this figure (1988, 118 and 145) by
no means constitutes an adequate description of rabbinic culture as a whole. Friedman's article is important for its documentation of late medieval and modern rabbinic
authorities who ruled in favor of teaching Torah to women.

with which the Palestinian Talmud regards Ben-Azzai's position is also marked by the fact that in the parallel passage of the Mishna where R. El'azar Ben-Azariah is cited, that Talmud casually remarks that Ben-Azzai disagrees with *him*, in perfect parallelism to its observation here that Ben-Azariah disagrees with Ben-Azzai (Palestinian Talmud ad Hagiga 1:1). We see, therefore, that while the Palestinian Talmud does not clearly accept Ben-Azzai's position as normative, neither does it find it so shocking that is has to be suppressed. Indeed, it would be conceivable that someone who had only the Palestinian Talmud as a normative source might actually decide in favor of the view of Ben-Azzai. It should be remembered that according to the Talmud, the very reason that the Mishna cites rejected and minority opinions is to preserve them, that they might be available for future authorities who would see reasons to revive them. The view of Ben-Azzai has apparently been rejected or thrown into question by the citation of an authoritative counterview, but it has also been given a straightforward interpretation, namely, that the father should teach Torah to his daughter because the merit she accrues by studying would be a defense for her.

The Babylonian Interpretation of Ben-Azzai   This dialectical move was equally available to the Babylonian Rabbis, and indeed they have adopted this style in myriad other cases. But the move that the Babylonian Talmud does make here is much more radical in its rejection of Ben-Azzai, for it does not allow even the *meaning* of his statement to stand, not even as a rejected minority opinion. It thus erases his voice entirely.

The Talmud begins by discussing the issue of what merit it is that mitigates the woman's punishment, without reference to Ben-Azzai though in response to the initial statement that merit mitigates. The possibility, however, that it is the merit of the study of Torah is simply discarded out of hand:

> Mishna: If she had merit, her merit will mitigate [the punishment] for her.
>   Talmud: What sort of merit? Perhaps we will say, the merit of the study of Torah, but she is not commanded to do so![6] So it must mean

6. This does not mean that she is forbidden to study Torah. As far as I know, even the Babylonian Talmud nowhere states that women may not study Torah. Rather, it seems that this proscription was a medieval development, occasioned by taking Rabbi Eliezer's statement as halakhically normative and consistent with the entire diachronic pattern of gender ideology, for which see above Chapter 3 and below in this chapter.

the merit of [performing] commandments. The merit of commandments can hardly protect to such an extent, for we have learned, "So
did Rabbi Menahem the son of Yossi expound: *For a commandment is a
candle and the Torah is a light* [Proverbs 6 : 23]." Scripture compared the
commandment to a candle and the Torah to a light, to say to you, just
as a candle only protects for an hour, so does the commandment only
protect for an hour [i.e., while it is actually being performed], but as
light protects forever, so does the Torah protect forever. . . .

  Ravina said: Indeed it is the merit of Torah, and as for what you said
that she is not commanded to do so—indeed, she is not commanded,
but by the merit of her taking her sons to study Torah and Mishna and
waiting for her husband to come home from the study-house [she is
protected].[7]

The Talmud is quite clearly here setting out its hierarchy of values. In
spite of the fact that within the culture of the Rabbis, it is the study of
Torah that is the most highly valued of all practices, the Babylonian Talmud refuses to interpret the Mishna's point as being that the merit of
having studied will protect a wife in her moment of trial—refusing, as we
have seen, a conclusion that would have been perfectly consistent (as the
text itself remarks) with generally held opinion on the efficacy of Torah
in protecting sinners. Had the Rabbis not refused to take this simple path,
the entire tortuous effort to find an interpretation for the merit that mitigates would have been obviated. The upshot is that this Talmud is forced
ultimately into displacing the merit of the daughter from her own study of
Torah to merit accrued from supporting her husband and male children
in their study.[8]

Similarly, the midrash quoted in both the Babylonian and Palestinian Talmuds that
"Thou shalt teach thy sons—sons and not daughters" means only that one is not
obligated to teach daughters, not that it is forbidden (see Babylonian Talmud
Kiddushin 29b and Palestinian Talmud Berakhot 2 : 3 and 3 : 3 and Eruvin 10 : 1).

  7. For another possible interpretation of this last phrase, see below. It is this kind
of text that provides the evidence for Judith Plaskow's statement: "Women are objects
of the law but neither its creators nor agents. Halakhah concerning the religious sphere
assume a world in which women are 'enablers'. Women create the preconditions for
men and male children to worship and study Torah, but women cannot do these
things themselves without becoming less effective in their relational role" (Plaskow
1990, 63).

  8. It should be emphasized that the Babylonian Talmud *never* directly addresses
Ben-Azzai at all, and this is a major premise of my argument. One could argue, therefore, that what the Rabbis have done is, first, interpreted Ben-Azzai to mean that
there is merit for women in study of Torah, and then rejected his view; therefore, the
only element of the Mishna that is being interpreted to mean that women have no
merit in the study of Torah is the authoritative position (of the first speaker) that

The consequence of the Babylonian Talmud's approach is to render nearly incomprehensible Ben-Azzai's statement that a man should teach his daughter Torah against the eventuality that she may have to face the test. By the time the Talmud actually comes in its consecutive interpretation of the Mishna to the Ben-Azzai statement, it has nothing to say about it and simply skips over it. The Talmud begins by quoting the entire passage of the Mishna as a lemma for interpretation:

> *Mishna*: Ben-Azzai said, "A man is obligated to teach his daughter Torah, so that if she drinks [the bitter water], she will know—for merit mitigates."
> Rabbi Eliezer says, "Anyone who teaches his daughter Torah, teaches her lasciviousness."

The Babylonian Talmud thus cites both views of the Mishna, but at this point it says nothing at all about Ben-Azzai and skips right over to interpreting Rabbi Eliezer's claim that one who teaches his daughter teaches her sexual impropriety:

> *Talmud*: Does it indeed mean lasciviousness?! No, [he said that] it is *as if* he had taught her lasciviousness.

I will return to the Talmud's interpretation of the view of R. Eliezer, but for the moment what concerns me is the treatment of Ben-Azzai. That is to say, what we have here is a quotation of the two opposing views as a text for interpretation, but the Talmud's interpretative discourse sharply marginalizes Ben-Azzai by simply ignoring his statement entirely and beginning immediately to interpret R. Eliezer. Modern scholarship repeats the gesture of the Talmud, when Brown also "erases" Ben-Azzai's view:

> In Judaism, rabbis were remembered to have declared that women had no place in the intense and intimate atmosphere in which male students studied the Law: to teach Torah to one's daughter was tantamount to teaching her immorality.
> (Brown 1988, 118)

"merit mitigates." However, in discussing the view of the first speaker in the Mishna here that "merit mitigates," the Talmud, by dismissing entirely the interpretative possibility that it is the merit of Torah which stands for the woman, only emphasizes the more its total suppression of the dissident voice of Ben-Azzai. Even if one wishes to claim, therefore, that the Talmud, in interpreting the first speaker, is not making an explicit claim about the meaning of Ben-Azzai, such a claim is implied in the total silence that the Talmud maintains on Ben-Azzai as dissenting from this first speaker. Either they are ignoring his dissent or assimilating him to their interpretation of that first speaker; either way, his voice is effectively nullified.

The first bicolon is undoubtedly generally correct, the second only correct for a certain strain within the culture—hegemonic, to be sure, but not unchallenged by an internal oppositional discourse. The contemporary scholar, rather than criticizing the ideological imposition of the redactorial level of the text, thus inadvertently reiterates it and reinforces the Babylonian editor's silencing of Ben-Azzai's voice.[9]

Now, it is very important to note that even had the Talmud adopted the path of reading Ben-Azzai in accordance with the interpretation I have suggested, the talmudic Rabbis would *not* have been obligated to adopt his view. The alternative view of R. Eliezer is there for the taking, and there was, furthermore, ample support for such an antithetical position in other authoritative texts. The move of interpreting a passage and then rejecting its authority for religious law is, moreover, a very common one in the Talmuds, and it is the move we have seen actuated in the Palestinian Talmud's parallel text. But the Babylonians' dual moves of first interpreting the merit accruing to women from Torah as merit earned by their supporting the Torah study of males and then "ignoring" Ben-Azzai's statement have had the effect of causing the latter's point to be nearly forgotten. It seems, therefore, that our Babylonian text was at much greater pains to simply eliminate the possibility that women would be considered candidates for the study of Torah.

Some hint of the reason for this may be found in the Babylonian Talmud's interpretation of Rabbi Eliezer's view in the Mishna. The Palestinian Talmud's view of what Ben-Azzai has asserted—that the merit that protects is the merit of studying Torah—allows for quite a logical understanding of Rabbi Eliezer's apparently paradoxical view that women's study of Torah leads to sexual immorality. He agrees, according to this interpretation, that there *is* merit for women in the study of Torah, but he considers this an undesirable effect, because it would protect the woman from the effects of drinking the testing water. In other words,

---

9. I wish to emphasize Brown's modesty in his treatment of Judaism and his invitation to specialists to correct his work on this subject. A work that to my mind too uncritically reproduces the dominant ideology of the texts without examining the oppositional discourses within them is Archer 1983. This article is otherwise quite useful. I recently taught this material to a group of well-educated Orthodox Jewish women in Israel, who could not believe that I was quoting the Mishna correctly. It was inconceivable to them that any rabbinic authority had said that a father should teach his daughter Torah. They were sure that it said a father should *not* teach his daughter Torah. This anecdotal and single case is surely symptomatic of how thoroughly the counterview has been erased from the consciousness of modern Judaism.

Ben-Azzai and Rabbi Eliezer differ on the supreme value to be protected in this situation: Ben-Azzai clearly places paramount importance on protection of the daughter, while Rabbi Eliezer is most concerned with protection of the integrity of the Torah's test. If a woman knows that Torah protects and has acquired the knowledge of Torah that would constitute this protection, then a major obstacle has been removed from the way of her temptation into license, for she would no longer be afraid of the discovery of her sin and its punishment via the water ordeal.[10] On this interpretation, R. Eliezer is quite a straightforward and logical antithesis to Ben-Azzai. On the other hand, the Babylonian Talmud, since it has rejected the notion that women gain any merit from studying Torah, has to find an entirely different explanation for Rabbi Eliezer's claim that study leads to sexual sin:

> Said R. Abbahu: What is the reason for the statement of R. Eliezer? As it is written, *I am Wisdom, I dwelt with guile* [and knowledge will find intrigues][11] [Proverbs 8:12]. As soon as wisdom has entered a man [!], with it has entered guile.

Thus the interpretation of R. Eliezer promoted by the Babylonian Talmud[12] has the study of Torah as a *direct* cause of lasciviousness in women. Note that this is not an entirely unfamiliar move from other cultures as well. Often, when women take a public and active intellectual or political stand within patriarchal culture, they are stigmatized as sexually wanton and licentious (Jones 1990, 786). I would suggest that this move on the part of the culture is both a means of protecting male cultural cap-

10. This is the interpretation of R. Eliezer's view accepted by R. Israel Danzig. It is, moreover, consistent with the view of another Rabbi, R. Shimʿon, who says that it is impossible to argue that merit mitigates, because then one would have entirely vitiated the validity of the ordeal as a chastity test. Ben-Azzai is simply portrayed as more concerned with the fate of the girl than the certainty of the test. The fact that Ben-Azzai is the proverbial celibate of rabbinic literature, and that it is he who most insistently supports marriage (see last chapter), only adds to the complexity of the representation.

11. The word for "intrigues" in the biblical text, *mezimot*, is generally used in talmudic discourse to refer to sexual transgression. I believe that this association may be underlying R. Abbahu's citation of this verse in a context in which sexual license is the issue at hand.

12. Paradoxically, R. Abbahu himself is Palestinian, but that does not matter here, since I am arguing for the ideological positions manifested by the editors of the two Talmuds and it is in Babylonia that his view was preserved and transmitted while in the Palestinian text it is ignored.

ital and thus power from appropriation by women as well as a manifestation of a real anxiety that the men have about controlling the sexuality of "their" women and making sure that it is ever available. As just a single example of why this would work, we need only consider that because men had a virtual monopoly on Torah-study, the control of menstrual separation was in their hands, giving men tremendous power over the deployment of women's sexuality and reproductive powers. Let me explain this point. Even granted the existence of a practice of ritual menstrual separation from sex, this is not necessarily (or not only) an exercise of male power over women. Theoretically, in fact, it could function as a space of female autonomy or even of female power over men. But within the rabbinic community, since only they had the requisite knowledge, male authorities made all decisions as to the purity or impurity of a given woman, and even that control and power devolved to the men. For an explicit (and troubled) representation of the functioning of that power, see the story of Rabbi Shim'on ben El'azar in the next chapter. The fact that the Palestinian tradition seems to allow for at least the possibility of that power remaining in the hands of women provides a plausible (at least partial) explanation for the Babylonian efforts to deny that possibility.

It should be noted that there is not a single, ineluctable way to explain the difference between the Palestinian and Babylonian Talmuds. The Talmuds are complexly authored works, and any given passage does not necessarily reflect social practice or even theory of any more than the redactors of that particular passage. Moreover, even if we find consistent differences between the two Talmuds, we are not necessarily justified in assuming that the difference is geo-culturally based, because the Babylonian Talmud contains a large amount of textual material that is perhaps centuries later than the Palestinian Talmud. Indeed, in accordance with generally held scholarly opinion today, the materials that we have been considering in this discussion (anonymous commentary on the Mishna) are very possibly from the later strata of the Babylonian Talmud and perhaps even from a stratum of the Talmud that was added *after* the rabbinic period in the sixth to the eighth centuries.[13] We have seen, moreover, in Chapter 3, that there was an apparent chronological development within rabbinic Judaism toward an essentialization of women and a growing fear of their

13. David Kraemer 1990 provides a good introduction to the literary history of the Talmud.

sexuality in the early Middle Ages, so this difference between the Palestinian and Babylonian texts might well have as much to do with chronological as with geographical difference. It is possible that further research would help to sort out this issue; for the nonce, we have to leave it open. As we will see in the next section, however, this interpretation of a difference between the two texts, whatever its cause, is consistent with other indications within the Babylonian Talmud that for that community the notion of women studying Torah was not merely unusual but anathema.

Parturients and Menstruants May Study Torah

The Tosefta, a major Palestinian text of the ritual law (redacted slightly later than the Mishna), provides us with further strong support for the suggestion that there was a fundamental difference between Palestine and Babylonia with regard to the issue of women studying Torah. The Tosefta explicitly avers that "gonnorheics, menstruants and parturients are permitted to read the Torah, to study Mishna, midrash, religious law and aggada, but men who have had a seminal emission may not" (Tosefta Berakhot, ch. 2, para. 12). R. Eliezer Waldenberg, an important living rabbinical authority, observes that this text takes it as a matter of course that women are permitted to study all of these branches of Torah, and the only issue dealt with is whether they are permitted to do so in certain physiological situations (Waldenberg, ch. 3). The question raised by Waldenberg is how it came about that the later religious law forbids the study of Torah for women; his answer is that this Palestinian source follows Ben-Azzai's view, while the Babylonian Talmud follows R. Eliezer, and it is, of course, the Babylonian Talmud that is authoritative for later Judaism.

There is, indeed, near explicit evidence that the Babylonian Talmud differed with the Palestinians on this issue. The Palestinian Talmud (Shabbat 3:4) quotes this passage from the Tosefta in its original form. The Babylonian Talmud, on the other hand reads: "Gonnorheics and lepers and *those who have had intercourse with menstruants* are permitted to study Torah, but men who have had a seminal emission may not." (Babylonian Talmud Berakhot 22a). The Palestinian source has actually been rewritten in its passage to the Babylonian Talmud:[14] "Since the

---

14. I say explicitly "Babylonian Talmud," and not "Babylonia" to allow for the possibility that the shift took place in Babylonia at a later time than the time in which the text arrived there.

[Babylonian Talmud] holds like R. Eliezer that it is entirely forbidden for women to study Torah and not like Ben-Azzai, it omitted the menstruants from that law and included only the men" (Waldenberg). It is virtually certain that Waldenberg is justified in his claim, if for no other reason than that the Babylonian version of the text is incoherent and self-contradictory: those who have had intercourse have also had a seminal emission, so the text ends up saying at the same time that they are permitted and forbidden to study Torah.[15] The emendation of the *baraita*, which the Babylonian Talmud undertakes even at the cost of introducing a self-contradiction within it, is an index of how much concern the notion of women (menstruants!) studying Torah caused for the producers of the Talmud.

As we shall see below, it is this very text, the Tosefta, which also cites a woman as an authority in religious law. Menstruants can study Torah in Palestine. Thus we have once more evidence that in Palestine the notion that women might study Torah was not by any means unacceptable. Indeed, the very casualness with which the Tosefta reveals that women study Torah and with which the Palestinian Talmud cites such study (inadvertently—that is, by the way, as it were) constitutes an index of the acceptability of that notion there. It is a principle learned from my teacher, the late Saul Lieberman, doyen of critical talmudic studies in our century, that the presuppositions of a talmudic statement are a more reliable index to social reality than the manifest content of its statements. In this case, the Tosefta and Palestinian Talmud, by telling us that menstruants and parturients may study Torah, presuppose that women study and provide striking evidence for the plausibility of at least occasional study of Torah for women in that time and place. In the Babylonian Talmud, on the other hand, any voice dissenting from the stricture on the study of Torah for women was simply interpreted (in this case, edited) out of existence. Having proposed this context, we can begin to read the legend of Beruria, the female Torah-sage, as part of a significant cultural practice and historical development.

THE LEGEND OF BERURIA

If we do entertain the notion that Athenian citizen-wives had at least certain kinds of informal power, we must also be clear that it was

15. Compare Lieberman, *Tosefta Ki-fshuta*, ad loc.

socially necessary for men not to acknowledge it—to deal with it at
most indirectly through myths of Amazons and through their cultural
fantasies of rebellious wives in tragedy or comedy.

(Winkler 1989, 7)

Beruriah's learned status has often been used in apologetic arguments
that seek to minimize rabbinic misogyny. I assume rabbinic culture to
have been fundamentally sexist and even misogynist. The Beruriah
texts and their portrayal of women should be understood as a way of
nuancing that misogyny; it wasn't monolithic, but variegated. In some
eras, it was more severe, in some less. *In every age, there were likely to
be at least a few dissenters and non-conformists: rabbis who taught their
wives and daughters Torah, wives and daughters who naturally wanted to
display their knowledge to other women.* The Beruriah materials, which
span a thousand years, are a discourse on gender whose existence testifies to the possibility of imagining women in unfamiliar ways.

(Davis 1991; emphasis added)

Running through the talmudic and midrashic literature are narratives
about a very learned woman, generally called Beruria and often portrayed
as the wife of one of the greatest of the tannaitic sages, Rabbi Meir. In
this section of my text, I propose to read this narrative complex as just
such a "cultural fantasy" as Winkler has described—that is an acknowl-
edgment/denial of at least some access to Torah-study that women seem
to have had. Although we have no way of knowing whether or not such a
woman actually existed, the stories about her are certainly significant in
relaying some "reality" about the culture of the Talmuds.

The Palestinian text of ritual law, the Tosefta, the very text which had
taught us that women may study Torah, actually cites two cases in which
a learned woman made a point regarding ritual purity that was accepted
and approbated by the Rabbis. The first case involves a woman in the
guise of an anonymous daughter of R. Hanina:

An oven . . . which was plastered in purity and became impure—from
whence can it be purified? R. Halafta of Kefar Hananya said, "I asked
Shim'on ben Hananyah who asked the son of R. Hananya ben Tradyon,
and he said when they move it from its place. But his daughter said
when they disassemble its parts. *When this was told to R. Yehuda ben
Babba, he said, "his daughter said better than his son."*

(Tosefta Kelim Baba Qamma 4:17)

The second such story appears in the same text as about Beruria:

A *claustra*—R. Tarfon declares it impure, but the sages declare it pure.
And Beruria says, one removes it from this door and hangs it on another.

On the Sabbath these matters were related to R. Yehoshua. *He said, "Beruria said well."*

(Tosefta Kelim Baba Metzia 1:6)

These texts, whatever else they may be, are certainly highly marked representations of a learned woman. That is to say, they are an acknowledgment of the structural possibility within the culture that a woman could achieve such knowledge of Torah as to be authoritatively cited in an important question of ritual practice. As such, they can be read as part of the same social force represented by Ben-Azzai and the Tosefta cited in the previous section—a counter-hegemonic voice that recognizes the reality of *some* women's intellectual and spiritual accomplishment.[16]

In the Babylonian Talmud, the legend of Beruria the learned woman is also maintained. She is portrayed as having learned "three hundred ritual laws in one day from three hundred Rabbis" (Pesachim 62b). Moreover, she even teaches a moral lesson to her husband, the great Rabbi Meir, by besting him at midrashic reading of a verse:

16. Goodblatt argues two points with reference to these texts: one, that they do not constitute evidence for the identification of these two personalities (Goodblatt 1975, 77), and two, that they do not constitute evidence that this woman, or women, was learned (ibid., 83). He argues that this is the sort of knowledge that a daughter would have had by virtue of being part of a rabbinic household. On the first point, I am prepared to agree with the plausibility of his claim, but on the second, I disagree. Neither of these ritual situations is so common as to constitute the sort of matters that any member of a rabbinic household would have observed—indeed, both situations (certainly the first) are presented as unusual. Moreover, the first narrative contradicts Goodblatt's claim from within itself. If the daughter were simply reporting the practice in her household, why did her brother have a different suggestion? It is possible, of course, that the daughter obtained her knowledge not through formal instruction but simply through being present at learned discussions or lessons given by her father at home. This alone would form an avenue of resistance to the discourse of exclusion of women from study, and it is not the same as Goodblatt's claim that hers was merely "practical" knowledge of kitchen practice, which I find highly implausible for the reasons stated. There is even one version of this text (and quite an important one— R. Yehuda ben Kalonymos), in which it was her *father* that she bested here; that version, at any rate, would entirely forestall Goodblatt's claim that this was knowledge the girl had picked up from seeing the practice of her household. The story rather suggests in both cases that the woman (or girl) in question had an understanding of principles of religious law that she could apply to specific hypothetical situations, and the text in both cases strongly marks its approbation of her knowledge, a fact that will be of some importance below.

On the basis of these two traditions, it is less surprising that the Babylonians regarded these as two stories of the same woman (see also Davis 1991). In fact, I would suggest that the literary similarity of the two narratives suggests that they may be variants of the same basic story. It certainly seems from this text, moreover, that Beruria was a well-known figure in the Palestinian tradition as well.

There were two hooligans in the neighborhood of Rabbi Meir who were troubling him greatly. He would pray for them to die. His wife Beruria said to him: "What is your view? Is it because it says, 'Let the wicked be terminated from the earth' (Psalms 104:36)? Does it say 'wicked people'? 'Wicked deeds' is written! Moreover, interpret it according to the end of the verse, 'And there are no more evil-doers.' Now if the first half means that the wicked are dead, why do I have to pray that there will be no more evil-doers. Rather it means that since wicked deeds will exist no more, there will be no more evil-doers." He prayed for them, and they repented.

(Berakhot 10a)

In the light of such exceedingly positive contexts for Beruria and her learning at every turn, it is shocking to discover the following narrative of her end:

Once Beruria made fun of the rabbinic dictum, "Women are light-headed" [i.e., lewd]. He [her husband, R. Meir] said, "On your life! You will end up admitting that they are right." He commanded one of his students to tempt her into [sexual] transgression. The student importuned her for many days, until in the end she agreed. When the matter became known to her, she strangled herself, and R. Meir ran away because of the shame.

(Rashi ad Babylonian Talmud
Avoda Zara 18b)

In the Talmud itself, all we are told is that Rabbi Meir ran away to Babylonia, because of the "incident of Beruria." The Talmud tells no more. Our narrative is found only in the important medieval French commentator on the Talmud, Rabbi Shlomo Yitzhaki, the famous Rashi. The story recounts an ugly tale of entrapment and suicide. Rabbi Meir, to prove a point to his proud wife, has her seduced and disgraced (not so incidentally disgracing himself and a student of his in the bargain). This aberrant legend about the behavior of one of the greatest rabbis of the Talmud toward a wife presented otherwise as pious, wise, respected, and loved demands historicization and explanation, and to be sure, in both the traditional and scholarly literature, a great deal has been written about this text. Recently, a very powerful and moving feminist reading of this story has been written by Rachel Adler (1988, 28 ff.).[17] I am in

---

17. There is, however, one moment in Adler's text I wish to dispute directly, namely, her reading of the text of the Mishna Tractate Avot 5:16. Adler translates this text:

sympathy with the general thrust of her text and its reading practice ("Retelling it from the world in which we stand, we can see how character strains against context, how it shakes assumptions about what it means to be a woman, a Jew, a sexual being"), but I wish here to present another reading of the text, retelling it from the world in which we stand but attempting also to learn more from it about the world in which it was told. The main difference in principle between our readings is generated by Adler's declaration that, "I call it a story, though in fact it is many stories from many times and many texts" (28) and the consequent conflation of "Palestine in 200 B.C.E. [sic][18] or Babylonia in 500 C.E." (29). While Adler shows here a fine awareness of the distinctions between these historical moments, her intention seems to be to produce an account of the

---

> All love which is dependent on sexual desire, when the desire is gone, the love
> is gone. Love which is not dependent on sexual desire never ends. What is love
> dependent on sexual desire? The love of Amnon and Tamar. And love which is
> not dependent on sexual desire? The love of David and Jonathan.
>
> (Adler 1988, 32)

On this, Adler remarks: "If Amnon and Tamar and David and Jonathan represent the two ends of a continuum, the fact that one end is represented by an incestuous rape and the other by a relationship presumed to be nonsexual does suggest a dichotomy between sexual desire and true love."

I think that this is a misreading of this text, and one that has serious consequences for our understanding of the place of legitimate Eros in rabbinic culture. The Mishna's text does not read, "All love which is dependent on sexual desire," but "love which is dependent on something," that is, love that has an ulterior motive versus "love which is disinterested." The point of the comment is that love that grows out of the fulfillment of some particular need in the lover is not a true love and will last only as long as the need exists and the beloved is fulfilling it. See also Aspegren (1990, 45) for a similar idea in Aristotle. The story of Amnon and Tamar is, in fact, an apt illustration of this, for once Amnon had raped his sister, the Bible tells us that not only did he not love her any more but he hated her. The Mishna commentator, R. Israel Danzig, insightfully remarks that Amnon did not love Tamar at all but only himself, for it was only the pleasure of his body that he was seeking.

This text hardly represents the talmudic culture's generally positive appreciation of the power of sexual relations between husband and wife as an expression and enhancement of their love; there is even a rabbinic technical term for "the love caused by intercourse" (Babylonian Talmud Ketubbot 57a), a term that only functions in positively marked contexts, i.e., to indicate that only after a marriage has been consummated is there real commitment between the husband and the wife. After all, we also would hardly wish to claim the lust of the rapist as a model for a valorized erotic love. On the other hand, Adler's comments on the homosocial aspects of the institution of *havruta*, the practice of men studying in pairs, and the relationship of David and Jonathan as a model for it, are very important and suggestive of lines for further research. For the nonce, see Chapter 7.

18. In context, she certainly seems to mean Palestine in C.E. 200, the time of the historical Beruria, and "B.C.E." would be a misprint.

effect that the conflated stories of Beruria have had on women and men in hegemonic rabbinic culture since the early Middle Ages. My hope is that by paying attention precisely to the differences between the many stories from many times and many texts we will be able to generate a more nuanced and historicized understanding of the different readings of the signifier "woman" in different rabbinic cultures, opening up a space, perhaps, for new possibilities for the future. I will offer another reading of this text, taking it in the intertextual context of the legal discussion analyzed in the previous section of the chapter. This has suggested a difference precisely between the two historical terms of Palestine in 200 and Babylonia in 500.[19]

The end of Beruria's story, given to us only in the margins of the Babylonian talmudic text, as it were (but a very central margin indeed), is an extraordinary anomaly, not only in the presentation of her character throughout but also in the presentation of her husband's character. In Adler's reading, anomaly is the very meaning of this text. In an insightful comparison of this narrative with halakhic texts that portray unrealistic situations as test cases for legal theory, Adler writes:

> What do these surrealistic situations represent if not a passionate attempt to capture some elusive truth by smashing context? Imagining Beruriah must be regarded as just such an effort—a straining for a more encompassing context, an outrageous test case proposed as a challenge to all contextually reasonable assumptions: *What if there were a woman who was just like us?*
>
> (Adler 1988, 29)

The ambivalence of Beruria's story is then read by Adler as a single cultural unit representing ambivalence: "While it is threatening to imagine being ridiculed and exposed by a woman too learned and powerful to be controlled, it is also moving to imagine being loved and befriended by her. Thus the rabbis, in describing the domestic life of Beruriah and Meir, portray Beruriah as a feminine version of the ideal study partner" (32). The story of her downfall, then, is a solution to the negative pole of the ambivalence. Moreover, the very intimacy of the relationship with the

---

19. Goodblatt 1975 also argues for this historical difference, but in quite a different direction from the reading here proposed. Once again, I am deliberately fudging the question of chronological or geographical difference as determinative. Perhaps both were factors.

ideal study partner, when that partner is potentially a woman, makes it impossible for Beruria to fit in on Adler's reading. "Authority in rabbinic Judaism flowed through the medium of rabbinic relationships, and the rabbis could not imagine how to give Beruriah authority without including her in the web of rabbinic relationships—the web of teachers and students and study partners. And they could not imagine doing that without also imagining her sexuality as a source of havoc" (32).

We find excellent illustration of Adler's cultural thesis in a text that appears several times in the Palestinian corpus of rabbinic literature, but significantly perhaps, never in the Babylonian. Interestingly enough, and perhaps not coincidentally, the story involves, once more, Rabbi Meir:

> Rabbi Meir used to sit and teach on the Sabbath nights. A certain
> woman was there listening to him. Once his discourse was extended,
> and she waited until he had finished discoursing. She went home
> and found the candle already extinguished. Her husband said to her,
> "Where were you?" She said to him, "I was sitting and listening to the
> teacher." He said, "I swear that you will not enter here until you go and
> spit in the face of the teacher." She stayed away the first week, two,
> and a third. Her neighbor-women said to her, "Are you still angry with
> each other?! We will come with you to the teacher." When Rabbi Meir
> saw them, he saw by the Holy Spirit. He said to them, "Is there anyone
> among you who is learned in the magical curing of eyes?" Her neigh-
> bors said to her, "Now go and spit in his face and you will be permitted
> to your husband." When she sat before him, she withdrew from him.
> She said to him, "Rabbi, I am not learned in the magical curing of
> eyes." He said to her, "Spit in my face seven times and I will be cured."
> She spat in his face seven times. He said to her, "Go tell your husband,
> 'You said one time, I spat seven times!'" His disciples said to him,
> "Rabbi, are we permitted to dishonor thus the Torah?! Should you not
> have requested of one of us that we say an incantation?" He said to
> them, "Is it not enough for Meir to be like his Maker? For Rabbi
> Ishma'el has said, "Peace is so important that a name written in holi-
> ness can be erased in the water, in order to establish peace between a
> husband and a wife."
>
> (Wayyiqra Rabba 9:9; and see
> Palestinian Talmud Sota 1:4)

On the one hand, this story does confirm the structural anomaly to which Adler refers. The husband was clearly jealous of his wife's interest in Torah and the fact that as a result of that interest he was deprived of her company on the Sabbath eve. Indeed, he seems to have suspected her of being in love with Rabbi Meir, for otherwise why demand of her that she demonstrate contempt for that figure. This illustrates further the underlying eroticism of the study of Torah and why women were excluded from its precincts. Symbolically, they would have interrupted the pure erotic connection of the male students with their female lover, the Torah, and disturbed as well the homosocial mediation of that relationship, an aspect of the culture that will be explored in the next chapter. On the other hand, if this story is intended to serve as a cautionary tale against women studying Torah, it would be very curious indeed. The woman is the heroine of the story, her husband a dolt at best; in some versions the students wish to punish the husband severely. There is not the slightest suggestion of any impropriety in the woman's love for learning; indeed, the story is consistent with the general Palestinian assumption that some women do have a legitimate interest in the study of Torah. Finally, it is consistent as well with rabbinic notions that the function of the Sota ordeal was not to find out and punish guilty wives but to remove the jealousy of paranoid husbands, for this husband here is an analogue of the jealous husband of biblical times, and the spitting in the Rabbi's eye is an analogue of the ordeal. Just as Rabbi Meir was willing to have his eye spit in, in order that the stupid jealousy of the husband be obliterated, so God is willing to have his name obliterated in order to deal with the stupid jealousy of husbands. While it would be difficult to claim, of course, that this is anything like the "original" meaning of the biblical ordeal, it is fascinating and significant that this is how these Rabbis understood it, since it would be hard to imagine what apologetic purposes *they* would have had in turning its meaning in this fashion. It seems, therefore, that we must seek a more specific structural explanation for the story of Beruria's death than a generic, structural horror of women studying.

In contrast to Adler's reading of Beruria's story as a solution to an anomaly in the rabbinic culture in general, I propose to read it as an exemplum of a very specific and local principle, namely, R. Eliezer's statement that "anyone who teaches his daughter Torah, teaches her lasciviousness," as it was understood in the Babylonian Talmud.[20] Beruria

---

20. Compare the reading of Aliza Shenhar (1976), who argues that the story is an attempt to exemplify R. Meir's great zeal to prove the truth of rabbinic dicta, in this case, that "women are light-headed." That is, on her reading, the text is prepared to defame the wife in order to present a positive [!] picture of the husband. It would be, however, a strange storyteller who would imagine that this story of entrapment is a positive story of the rabbi. I think that my reading, namely, that the storyteller is

is, after all, the very paradigm case of a daughter learned in Torah. If R. Eliezer's dictum is true, in the way that the Babylonian Talmud understood it—namely that there is an intrinsic connection between the woman studying Torah and sexual immorality—then Beruria's fall into license is a structural necessity. Any other denouement to her biography would constitute a refutation of R. Eliezer. Another way of putting this would be to say that the same cultural forces in the Babylonian rabbinic community that did not even permit Ben-Azzai's voice to be retained as minority opinion could not tolerate the exceptional case of even one woman learned in the Torah. The horror of her end, the extraordinary lengths to which the text goes, even defaming one of its greatest heroes to achieve its purpose, is once again a symptom of the extraordinary threat that the learned woman represented to the *Babylonian* (and later European) rabbinic culture, a power that threatened to upset the whole apple cart of gender relations and social organization and that had to be suppressed, therefore, by extraordinary means. The best context for this legend is, in my reading, the discussion of ritual law that we have read above, and the differential between the Palestinian and Babylonian texts is reproduced in the differential of the readings of Beruria in these two traditions—in both she is atypical, but only in one does she become a scandal.

In the rest of this section, I wish to deepen and extend this reading of

---

prepared to defame both husband and wife in order to preserve the force of R. Eliezer's opinion, is much more plausible. Cynthia Ozick has gotten much closer to this reading in her suggestion that, "To punish her for her impudence, a rabbinic storyteller, bent on mischief toward intellectual women, reinvented Beruriah as a seductress. She comes down to us, then, twice notorious: first as a kind of bluestocking, again as a licentious woman. There is no doubt that we are meant to see a connection between the two" (Ozick 1979, 44). I wonder, however, why Ozick makes it worse and turns Beruria into the seducer, rather than the seduced, indeed the seduced after much resistance. See also Schwarzbaum (1983, 69–70), who argues that the story is a realization of an international folk topos of the best of women seduced. This element is surely present in the story, but by no means enough to explain it entirely and certainly not enough to account for its presence here. See Boyarin 1990a. None of the interpreters that I have seen, except Adler, has pointed out the parallels between the stories of the two sisters (see below), but she reads them differently: "It is no coincidence that Rashi juxtaposes his story to the story of Meir's adventure in Rome. The two stories share several motifs. In both, Meir conducts a chastity test. In both, female sexuality brings shame and causes Meir to leave home. In both, women are assumed to be solely responsible for sexual behavior, even when pressured, deceived, or entrapped by men" (1988, 103). I believe that my analysis of the *contrastive* structure between the two tales, and the way that the earlier one clones itself in mirror image, as it were, to produce the later one only strengthens the points that Adler wishes to make about how the story represents women.

the text of Beruria's end as being generated specifically in the intertextual web of the Babylonian talmudic tradition. Although the story of Beruria's seduction and suicide is extant only in Rashi's authoritative eleventh-century French commentary on the Babylonian Talmud, I think I can show how it was generated there and why it is not a fluke in Rashi. The story I will tell of the production of this text will strengthen the connection between it and its hypogram, the saying of R. Eliezer. Beruria had, according to the Talmud, a double, in fact a sister. In the wake of their father's martyrdom for rebellious teaching of the Torah, the Romans condemned Beruria's sister to a life of prostitution in Rome. Beruria sent Rabbi Meir to Rome to rescue her. The Babylonian Talmud relates:

> He took a *tarqeva* of coins and went, saying that if she has not done anything forbidden, there will be a miracle; while if she has done forbidden things, there will be none. He went disguised as a cavalry officer and said to her: Be with me. She said to him: But I am menstruating. He said to her: I am burning with passion. She answered: There are many here much lovelier than I. He said [to himself]: I understand from this that she has done nothing forbidden; anyone who comes, she says the same thing.
>
> (Avoda Zara 18b)

R. Meir, the miracle worker, performs his miracle (an allusion to the miracle performed for the innocent wife), and the sister of Beruria is saved. As a result of this activity, however, R. Meir ends up having to run away to Babylonia. But according to another tradition, the Talmud tells us, he ran away not because of this but because of the "story of Beruria." That is all that the Talmud itself tells of the story of Beruria. But we know from the Talmud something more of the story of this other daughter of R. Hanina. The Talmud asks what she did to deserve such a fate and answers that she would not have suffered had she not brought it on herself in some way: "R. Yohanan said: Once his daughter was walking in front of Roman nobles. They said, 'how lovely are the steps of this maiden!' She began to be very careful of her steps." As usual in rabbinic discourse, "the punishment fits the crime." She wished to attract Roman men; now that is her "profession." We can begin to construct the picture: this daughter embodied in her behavior precisely the rabbinic dictum that women are light-minded and lascivious. To be sure, she had a terrible experience, but by strength of character, she passed the test of R. Meir, and by miracles was saved from her fate. Presumably, she lived happily ever after.

Her sister Beruria's story is the exact structural opposite. Beruria began as the very antithesis of the light-minded and lascivious girl; indeed, she was interested from girlhood in the Torah and in wisdom. She is represented over and over as the embodiment of morality. When the time comes, she is also tested by R. Meir, but unlike her sister, she fails the test. The consequence of her exemplary life is ignominious suicide. Her story, only tantalizingly hinted at in the Talmud, and told only in its margins, is generated by simply reversing the polarity of every element in the sister's story that *is* told in the text of the Talmud itself. One sister becomes the exemplum of the proper behavior of a woman, because she had not studied Torah in accordance with Rabbi Eliezer and thus was not led into lewdness. The other sister dies a wanton, because she violated the taboo, submitted to temptation, and learned Torah.

My theory is that Beruria's story is generated as the dark double of the story of her sister, out of the matrix of the Babylonian understanding of R. Eliezer—namely, that there is an essential nexus between a woman studying Torah and the breakdown of the structure of monogamy, that a wife like Beruria could not possibly end up beloved and befriended by her husband, and that a husband like R. Meir who would love and befriend such a woman, must himself end up an exile. Taken together, the story of the two sisters forms one exemplum, one paradigm case that illustrates R. Eliezer's dictum as it was understood and experienced in the Babylonian Talmud's cultural field, a demonstration that there is an intrinsic and necessary connection between a scholarly woman and uncontrolled sexuality.[21] This point-for-point homology between the two narratives can be laid out as a series of structural oppositions.

---

21. Laurie Davis has read the connection between the two sisters in a slightly different fashion. She emphasizes (following Goodblatt 1975) that it is *only* in our talmudic passage that the two women are identified as sisters. Disconnecting Beruria from the family of Rabbi Hananya ben Tradyon, she suggests that the daughter of the story here, before she is awarded Beruria as a sister, is identical to the learned daughter of the Tosefta. Then:

> Moreover, the life of the unnamed daughter is a mirror image of what Beruriah's life would become. These are parallel stories of righteous, morally upright, Torah-studying females who are "supplied" with a sexual crime that contradicts all other stories about their character. The parallel aspect of their lives can only be discerned after Rashi's story of Beruriah's seduction and death in the eleventh century.
>
> (Davis 1991)

I would grant that this reading is as plausible as my suggestion but does not materially change the overall picture I am drawing. Rather than a structure of binary oppositions, we would have a doubling of the two women in each other.

The Sister	· Beruria
behaves light-mindedly (−)	studies Torah (+)
sent to brothel (−)	marries scholar (+)
passes R. Meir's test (+)	fails R. Meir's test (−)
rescued by miracle (+)	commits suicide (−)

The paradoxes of these oppositions and the reversal of the usual expectations of reward and punishment mark all the more strongly the significance of this narrative as an exemplum of the danger of teaching a
daughter Torah. But I again emphasize that this explanation for the story
is intelligible only on the Babylonian Talmud's interpretation of the
Mishna. This story is not told, nor does it fit in with the Palestinian interpretation in which Ben-Azzai holds that there is real merit for women
in studying Torah. Moreover, even R. Eliezer's view according to the
Palestinian reading is that there *is* merit for women in studying Torah,
and that this merit would protect them from punishment for adultery,
thus removing the very deterrent that the Bitter Waters is meant by the
Torah to be. This interpretation implies no *necessary and essential* causal
relation between a woman studying Torah and sexual license, and indeed,
in the Palestinian texts there is no hint of censure of Beruria for studying
Torah or her father for teaching her Torah. She is certainly an anomaly
in Palestine as well, but her halakhic opinion was cited as authoritative
and there are no stories condemnatory of her.

Another rabbinic authority, slightly later than Rashi, has quite a different understanding of what the "incident of Beruria" is. In his tradition,
it is not the "incident" of Beruria but the "*precedent*" of Beruria, and the
"real story" is that R. Meir was exiled because he did not listen to his wife
on a point of ritual law![22] Furthermore, according to this same authority,
it was not her brother that she bested in knowledge and acumen (see
above, n. 16) but her father, the great scholar R. Hanina himself, which

22. Namely the requirement that one study out loud. See Babylonian Talmud
Eruvin 53b–54a, where Beruria rebukes (or kicks) a disciple who was not studying out
loud. Davis is absolutely correct in her reading that that passage, along with several
others she cites, brooks no anxiety or defensiveness over the fact that it is a woman
rebuking a man and citing chapter and verse to do so. Adler's notion that these are
texts of gender reversal imposes notions of gender on the texts that are not presup-
posed by them. It nevertheless remains the case that nearly all of the stories about
Beruria (including the ones in which she is given an unambiguous positive valence
and could be any Rabbi, like this one) all portray her as besting a man at some
halakhic/midrashic task.

establishes her even more firmly as an actual halakhic authority (Kalony-mos 1963, 31–34). According to R. Yehuda ben Kalonymos's traditions, then, the story of Beruria is a decisive refutation of R. Eliezer's dictum. I would read these antithetical productions of Beruria's end as evidence that the conflict over women studying Torah continued into the eleventh and twelfth centuries in Ashkenaz, too. Indeed, seen in this light, the per-sistent legends that Rashi's daughter was a medieval "Beruria" (moreover, without any evil end) become highly charged as well.

The legend of Beruria is precisely the sort of ambivalent, troubled acknowledgment/denial of women's autonomy and intellectual achieve-ment as the Greek plays that Winkler refers to or the legends of Amazons, although—and this is important—it is not until the grotesque end to the story is supplied in the medieval commentary that the denial that the Babylonian Talmud achieves in regard to the other texts considered is consummated in respect to Beruria as well. Davis (1991) astutely notes that in another text of the Gaonic (post-talmudic) period, Beruria is neu-tralized in another way—by being turned into the ideal Jewish wife and mother (Midrash Mishle 31:10). Her motherhood is never mentioned in the talmudic texts themselves. This provides, then, a less violent and there-fore perhaps more insidious mode of eliminating the threat of the daugh-ter who studied Torah. Indeed, this Beruria ends up more like Rachel! Notice that all of this evidence is consistent with the hypothesis—and it is only a hypothesis—that a change took place in Jewish gender ideology in the early Middle Ages, a change that resulted in a much more essen-tialized notion of women as dangerous and threatening.

It is difficult to find any historical context for the daughter who stud-ied Torah, precisely because, as we have seen, the energy expended to suppress even this limited autonomy was great. However, the material dis-cussed by Bernadette Brooten (1982) provides some help. Brooten shows that in approximately a dozen synagogue inscriptions from the talmudic period, women are mentioned as having the title of "Head of the Syna-gogue." This evidence has traditionally been dismissed by scholars too willing to take at face value the talmudic statements of the forced igno-rance of women in Torah. Brooten argues, plausibly in my view, that the evidence should a priori be taken seriously, and if the inscriptions refer to women with the title "Head of the Synagogue," it means that the women performed the task as well, and, moreover, that such a position implied learning (Brooten 1982, 5–37, esp. 30–31).

The relevance of Brooten's work has recently been a subject of discussion. Shaye Cohen, a historian who accepts her reading of the evidence, has nevertheless argued (1980, 27–28) that since the inscriptions come from the non-rabbinic communities of Crete, Thrace, Italy, and North Africa, they are not relevant for the history of that form of Judaism that achieved historical hegemony—talmudic Judaism. In contrast, Judith Plaskow contends that precisely the evidence for non-rabbinic forms of ancient Judaism "leads us to question rabbinic authority as the sole arbiter of authentic Judaism"; Plaskow argues that "texts may reflect the tensions within patriarchal culture, seeking to maintain a particular view of the world against social, political or religious change" (Plaskow 1990, 45). I do not intend to enter here into the theological questions involved, but it certainly seems relevant to me to emphasize that the readings done here bring those tensions home, as it were, locating them within the talmudic texts and thus the rabbinic discourse and power structure themselves. They certainly help to answer the questions that Brooten raises: "Could Jewish women actually have been scholars? Could they have had some say about the reading of the bible in the synagogue?" (Brooten 1982, 55).

The geographical irrelevance of the inscriptional data for rabbinic Judaism is disappointing, however, in another respect, as it does not help us evaluate the presented evidence for greater anxiety about learned women in the rabbinic community of Babylonia than Palestine. Does this represent more or less Torah-study by Babylonian women than their Palestinian sisters? But there is, perhaps, one piece of tantalizing evidence for the first possibility (i.e., that women studied *more* in Babylonia). In the very talmudic text that interprets the Mishna in Sota by claiming that the study of Torah does not give a woman any merit, the conclusion is that a woman's merit comes from "her taking her sons to study Torah and Mishna." But this passage could, as well, be translated "from *teaching* her sons Torah and Mishna"—in fact, this is the literal, grammatical reading of the phrase. In order to teach, they obviously must have learned.[23] This would strongly suggest that the Babylonians' energetic denial of any merit for women in the study of Torah and, indeed, the erasure in the Babylonian Talmud of the Palestinian remarks on women studying are more a "wishful" prescriptive determination than a reflection of actual social conditions. We could then interpret the evident threat of the texts that

23. That is, we have here causative forms of the verbs for "reading Bible" and "studying Mishna." This significant point was made to me by Milan Sprecher.

denote women studying as owing to the fact that women did study in that culture and it is this which explains the greater anxiety of the Babylonian Rabbis. In either case, the suggestion remains valid that the increasing ambivalence about women studying Torah, as reflected both in halakhic proscriptions and in the changes in the traditions about Beruria, provides a parallel for the introduction of gynecophobic expressions into rabbinic Judaism in the same period, which I have discussed in Chapter 3 above.

Within a literary, cultural tradition, there are always forces contending for hegemony. This is at least as true in the heterogeneous texts of the Talmuds produced over hundreds of years and in two separated geographical areas as it is in Shakespeare, where also cultural studies finds both patriarchal hegemony and forces contending against it. The Babylonian tradition with Rashi as its definitive interpreter achieved hegemony in medieval and post-medieval Jewish culture. Within the ancient Jewish texts, however, there is also vivid dissent from the exclusion of women from the study of Torah. The texts we have read here precisely in the differing ways that they suppress this dissent provide symptoms of a cultural difference between Palestine and Babylonia, suggesting that while in Babylonia (at any rate, late in the rabbinic period) it was unthinkable and perhaps terrifying that a woman might study Torah, in Palestine it was merely uncustomary and noteworthy.[24] I would claim much more than Brown for the possibilities of learning cultural history from the talmudic texts. We must very carefully tease out from these texts the different strands of discourse and counter-discourse which they preserve and suppress and sometimes preserve *by* suppressing—complicating our reading of ancient ideology and not simplifying it.

Just as in the case of Rachel discussed in the last chapter, Beruria remains a paradigm for traditional Jewish women until this day. As evidence for the effectiveness of the story of Beruria in forming practice, I need only remark that as recently as in our century, her (Palestinian) story has been cited as a precedent for the empowering of women to study Torah and that argument rejected by other rabbis who cited the legend of her death as counter-precedent (Waldenberg ad loc). The story of Beruria

24. I am not forgetting, of course, R. Eliezer's misogyny, which is also Palestinian, of course. It is not my intention to reify either of these cultures into one monolithic position, and certainly not to claim that the Palestinian culture was anything like egalitarian, but only to surmise that dissent on this issue was more tolerated there than in the other culture.

is thus historical in just the same way as the story of Rachel considered in the last chapter, and as such, we have the possibility even to rewrite future history by reading the story differently.[25]

On my hypothesis, the main motivating force for the confinement of women to the sexual and procreative role in rabbinic culture was fear that were they not so confined, that vitally important role would not be fulfilled—that what concerned the Rabbis was not so much the contamination by a fearful and defiling force so much as the loss of control of a very valued resource. In addition to this, as we have amply seen in the last two chapters, the Torah-study situation was structured as a male homosocial community, the life of which was conducted around an erotic attachment to the female Torah. The Torah and the wife are structural allomorphs and separated realms in the culture—both normatively to be highly valued but also to be kept separate. In the next chapter we will see that neither of these two poles was quite settled in the culture; both were indeed highly troubled sites of meaning.

25. It may be fairly charged that to a certain extent I am bursting through an open door here, as in many (if not most) Orthodox circles today it has been fully accepted that women study Torah. Indeed, I heard a sociologist describe this as the greatest social change that modern Orthodoxy has undergone, namely that this is the first generation in Jewish history in which young women sitting around a Sabbath table are likely to be as learned as the men in Talmud. In Stern College, the Orthodox college for women of Yeshiva University, women may now study Talmud for several years, and the same is true of Bar-Ilan, the Orthodox university in Israel, an institution that is otherwise hardly progressive. I would hope that my historical/literary analysis would further underpin this turn in the culture, which seems to me exemplary for the way that even a very traditional culture can reform itself in a healthy way and retain its integrity.

7

(Re)producing Men
Constructing the Rabbinic Male Body

Said Rabbi Yohanan, "Rabbi Ishma'el the son of Yose's member was like a wineskin of nine *kav;* Rabbi El'azar the son of Rabbi Shim'on's member was like a wineskin of seven *kav.*" Rav Papa said, "Rabbi Yohanan's member was like a wineskin of three *kav.*" *And there are those who say: like a wineskin of five kav. Rav Papa himself had a member which was like the baskets of Hipparenum.*

(Babylonian Talmud
Baba Metsia 84a)[1]

A learned discussion of traditions comparing the size of the penis of our hero with that of others of the Holy Rabbis is not something we expect to find in the Talmud.[2] In this chapter, we will be reading an extended narrative text that is entirely focused on the construction of maleness, and an anxious construction it is. Enormous phalli, particularly on clerics, inevitably remind one of Rabelais,[3] suggesting that our text is part of the grotesque tradition, associated so strongly by Bakhtin with cultural issues centering on procreation (Bakhtin 1984)—and indeed, investigation of the text shows that the thematics of the material body, the body

1. This passage, as well as all of the text here, is translated from the best manuscript of this section of the Talmud, Hamburg 19.

2. It is so unexpected that nearly all commentators quite "interpret" it out of existence. The Aramaic word *'evreh* means exactly "member" and can refer, just as in English, to various parts of the body. Accordingly, some interpreters claim that the reference here is to the innards, while others say it is to arms or legs. However, as in English, the word when unqualified otherwise commonly means *membrum virile*. As we shall see, this interpretation is the one strongly suggested by the context. As a hedge, however, let me say that even should my interpretation of this word be less certain than I think it to be, my argument in this chapter would not be appreciably weakened, because there is enough left in the text to support the overall reading.

3. Apparently not so inevitably, since an anonymous reader remarked that he or she found nothing of the grotesque in this text at all!

of reproduction, is its major emphasis.[4] All that we have read in this book until now of rabbinic Judaism strongly supports the commonplace that reproduction was a site of central, vital significance in the rabbinic culture, with genealogy serving as a crucial source of meaning. In Bakhtin's account, the grotesque body is the very triumph of life over death:

> It is the people's growing and ever-victorious body that is "at home" in the cosmos. It is the cosmos' own flesh and blood, possessing the same elemental force but better organized. The body is the last and best word of the cosmos, its leading force. Therefore it has nothing to fear. Death holds no terror for it. The death of the individual is only one moment in the triumphant life of the people and of mankind, a moment indispensable for their renewal and improvement.
>
> (341)

In this chapter I wish to focus on the cultural dynamics of a talmudic text in which the thematics of the grotesque are obsessively present, as in Rabelais. The biography of the holy Rabbi El'azar the son of Shim'on in the Babylonian Talmud (Baba Metsia 83b–85a) is surely one of the strangest of "hagiographies" in the literature. With only the slightest gestures toward plot-level consistency, the text consists of a series of incidents whose dominant feature is that they nearly all deal with the body of the subject, and the text is further interrupted by stories about the bodies of other Rabbis. I propose that this is a text about male bodies, sexuality, and reproduction and, moreover, that it is a text that manifests enormous anxiety about the reproduction of men in the rabbinic culture. On the one hand, the text brilliantly corroborates Bakhtin's reading of the grotesque as powerfully, centrally involved with the reproductive body and thus with reproduction, but on the other hand, this text will show not the body that has nothing to fear but the body in terror and anxiety.

---

4. Previous scholarly work on this text has generally focused on determining the so-called "kernel of [historical] truth" that the text is alleged to preserve. Other work has challenged the kernel-of-truth model. Shamma Friedman (1985 and 1989), Meir (1988), and Yassif (1990, 114–19) all challenge the dominant historical interpretations. All of these studies advance our understanding of the redaction of these texts and of their formal literary properties. Although none attempts to deal with them as culturally significant documents, the work they do is a necessary prelude to the present analysis, for according to the dominant paradigm in *Science of Judaism* research (the nineteenth-century paradigm still prevalent in Jewish studies, though receding in the last decade), the stories were not understood as literary documents at all but *mirabile dictu* as more or less accurate historical chronicles. Friedman's studies challenge the historical-research paradigm particularly directly.

The fabula of the narrative runs as follows:

Rabbi El'azar the son of Shim'on is appointed to catch Jewish thieves for the Roman government. Rabbi Yehoshua the Bald meets him and calls him by the insulting epithet "Vinegar, son of Wine," implying that he is a most unworthy son of a great father. He defends his actions somewhat disingenuously. When, however, a certain laundry man refers to him by the same designation, he becomes furious and has the man arrested. After calming down, he feels regretful and goes to have the man released but does not succeed. Standing under the crucified laundry man, he begins to cry, whereupon a passing Jew sees him and says that he should not be concerned, for the crucified one and his son had both had intercourse with a married woman on the Day of Atonement, thus committing several capital crimes. The Rabbi rejoices and placing his hands on his guts, says, "Be joyful, my guts. If you are so accurate when you have no certain information, imagine how accurate you are when you are certain. I am certain that neither rot nor worms will ever prevail over you." In spite of this expression of self-assurance, the text tells us, the Rabbi was still not certain, so he actually tests the claim that his guts are impervious during his lifetime, by having several basketsful of fat removed from his stomach with their blood vessels and placed in the sun to see if they rot (which they don't). After some significant "digressions," which I will be treating at length later on, the story continues by telling us that the Rabbi, still unsure of himself, takes upon himself a penance that results in illness such that every morning sixty felt mats soaked with blood and pus are removed from beneath his body. His wife, fearing the other Rabbis' reprobation of her husband, prevents him from attending the House of Study, until finally, disgusted by his ascetic behavior, she leaves him. He then returns to the rabbinic community, where his first activity is to permit sex for sixty doubtful menstruants, leading to the birth of sixty male children who are named after him. His wife returns to him (though we are never told when, how, or why) and upon his death, he tells her that the other Rabbis are still angry with him and will mistreat his corpse, which should be left in the attic, where it does not rot for twenty years or so. Finally, one day a worm is seen exiting from the ear of the corpse. The Rabbi's father communicates from beyond the grave that he would like his son buried beside him, and after some further misadventures his desire is fulfilled, and the corpse is buried. We have then some codas to the story which, as we shall see, powerfully amplify its meaning.

Neither this brief summary of the plot nor my extended reading below can encompass the unencompassable body of this fat text. A complete translation is presented at the end of the discussion.

POLITICS AND THE GROTESQUE

At first glance, the text seems readable as a sort of social-political satire, an attack on certain Rabbis who were grotesquely fat in body and by implication undisciplined and gluttonous and who allowed themselves to be recruited by the Roman authorities to betray their fellow Jews:

> They brought Rabbi Elʿazar the son of Rabbi Shimʿon, and he began to catch thieves [and turn them over to the Romans]. He met Rabbi Yehoshua, the Bald, who said to him, "Vinegar son of Wine: How long will you persist in sending the people of our God to death?!" He [Elʿazar] said to him, "I am removing thorns from the vineyard." He [Yehoshua] said to him, "Let the Owner of the vineyard come and remove the thorns." One day a certain laundry man[5] met him [Elʿazar], and called him, "Vinegar son of Wine." He said, "Since he is so brazen, one can assume that he is wicked." He [Elʿazar] said, "Seize him." They seized him. After he [Elʿazar] settled down, he went in to release him, but he could not. He [Elʿazar] applied to him [the laundry man] the verse, "One who guards his mouth and his tongue, guards himself from troubles" (Proverbs 21:23).[6] They hung him [the laundry man]. He [Elʿazar] stood under the hanged man and cried. Someone said to him, "Be not troubled; he and his son both had intercourse with an engaged girl on *Yom Kippur*." In that minute, he placed his hands on his guts, and said, "Be joyful, O my guts, be joyful! If it is thus when you are doubtful, when you are certain even more so. I am confident that rot and worms cannot prevail over you." But even so, he was not calmed. They gave him a sleeping potion and took him into a marble room and ripped

---

5. The clever laundry man, who often opposes the Rabbis and sometimes bests them, is a topos of talmudic legend. For a similar confrontation in Greek literature, one could cite the confrontation of Kleon by the "sausage maker" in Aristophanes's *Knights* 877–80, cited in Winkler (1989, 54).

6. Although on the surface the Rabbi is certainly applying the verse to the condemned man, who if he had not been so brazen would not have gotten into trouble, on another (ironic?) level the verse is applicable to Rabbi Elʿazar himself. He is certainly already experiencing a great deal of remorse at this point and will have considerable troubles later on in the story as a result of his not "guarding his mouth and tongue"— his failure to keep silent and avoid condemning the laundry man to the Romans. According to one venerable manuscript (the Florence MS), the text reads that "he applied to *himself* the verse," thus openly activating this hermeneutic possibility.

open his stomach and were taking out baskets of fat and placing it in the July sun and it did not stink. *But no fat stinks. It does if it has red blood vessels in it, and this even though it had red blood vessels in it, did not stink.* He applied to himself the verse, "even my flesh will remain preserved" (Psalms 16:8–9).

The rabbi is recruited by the Roman authorities as a sort of collaborator, who turns over Jewish tax evaders to the Roman authorities. This behavior is roundly condemned by the narrative. Rabbi Elʿazar is called "Vinegar, son of Wine" (i.e., Wicked One Son of a Saint; see below) and asked, "How long will you persist in sending the people of our God to death?" It is a gross oversimplification of the text, however, to read it in such political terms. Indeed, the text keeps undermining such a reading. True, the rabbi is referred to as "Vinegar, son of Wine," thus seemingly supporting a reading of the text in political terms. But the successful test of his flesh and the strong testimony regarding the sinfulness of the laundry man (who several times over deserved the death penalty) undermine this reading. Moreover, at a later point in the text he is referred to as a saint (precisely when his own child is portrayed as a sinner!). We need more complex cultural models to understand such a self-contradictory text. Bakhtin provides the models. He has discussed similar ambivalences in the European grotesque tradition:

> The soul of the people as a whole cannot coexist with the private, limited, greedy body. There is the same complex and contradictory character in the bodily images related to the banquet; the fat belly, the gaping mouth, the giant phallus, and the popular positive image of the "satisfied man." The fat belly of the demons of fertility and of the heroic popular gluttons (for instance, Gargantua in folklore) are transformed into the paunch of the insatiable simonist abbot. The image, split between these two extremes, leads a complex and contradictory life.
>
> (292)

It is precisely this complex and contradictory association of the grotesque body with exploitation on the one hand and with such positive images as fertility and fecundity, on the other hand, which will provide an important clue to a richer reading of our text.

The text clearly manifests several of the elements of the grotesque that Bakhtin has identified. As Bakhtin has shown, the grotesque body is the uncontained body. The topoi of exaggerated size, detachable organs, the

emphasis on the orifices, and stories of dismemberment are all representations of the body as interacting with the world, not self-enclosed as the
classical body:

> All these convexities and orifices have a common characteristic; it is
> within them that the confines between bodies and between the body
> and the world are overcome: there is an interchange and an interorien-
> tation. This is why the main events in the life of the grotesque body,
> the acts of the bodily drama, take place in this sphere. Eating, drinking,
> defecation and other elimination (sweating, blowing of the nose,
> sneezing), as well as copulation, pregnancy, dismemberment, swallow-
> ing up by another body—all these acts are performed on the confines
> of the body and the outer world, or on the confines of the old and new
> body. In all of these events the beginning and end of life are closely
> linked and interwoven.
>
> (Bakhtin 1984, 317)

Not surprisingly, the grotesque cultural tradition manifests remarkable
ambivalence on this aspect of the body. The opposing principles of corporeal fecundity and corporeal degradation in illness and death are one of
the sources of that ambivalence, and they are powerfully animated in the
talmudic story. Images of decay, dismemberment, and bodily mortification pervade the story.

The rabbi performs a bizarre purity test on himself. In order to
demonstrate that his actions with regard to the Jew that he sent to his
death were righteous ones, he attempts to prove (to himself) that his
body is indeed a classical, impermeable one. He begins by making the
claim that since he is so certain that he is righteous, he is equally sure
that his body will be impervious to the depredations of worms after his
death. That is, he experiences himself as a classical body, pristine and
closed off from the outside world. Ironically, the test that the rabbi
devises in order to prove his self-image is precisely one that undermines
it. He has the integrity of his body violated even in his lifetime in
the bizarre operation of removing basketsful of fat from his stomach
and having them placed in the sun to see if they will, indeed, be im-
mune from rotting. We have, then, a fantastically sardonic moment of
the very apotheosis of the grotesque being claimed as a proof for the
classic!

As Bakhtin has already pointed out, the image of the body part grown
out of all proportion is "actually a picture of dismemberment, of separate
areas of the body enlarged to gigantic dimensions" (328). The rabbi is

clearly grotesquely obese if several basketsful of fat could be removed from his body, and his activity is portrayed as a grotesque violation of the integrity of the body of the Jewish people. The association of the grotesqueness of body and of behavior is underlined by being doubled in another rabbinic figure, Rabbi Ishma'el the son of Rabbi Yose, who performs similar services for the Roman government and is also marked as an inferior son to a superior father:

> To Rabbi Ishma'el the son of Yose there also occurred a similar situation. Eliahu (the Prophet Elijah) met him and said to him, "How long will you persist in sending the people of our God to death?!" He said to him, "What can I do; it is the king's order?" He said to him, "Your father ran away to Asia-Minor; you run away to Lydia."
>
> When Rabbi Ishma'el the son of Yose and Rabbi El'azar the son of Rabbi Shim'on used to meet each other, an ox could walk between them and not touch them.

These rabbis truly are proto-Gargantuas if when they stand together their stomachs form an arch so big that an ox can walk under it. It is exciting to see how the talmudic text bears out Bakhtin's remarkable insight by combining in one moment the monstrous belly that "hides the normal members of the body" and the actual dismemberment of that monstrous organ. Indeed, the image of what is done to the body of the rabbi is almost comparable to giving birth, to a kind of lunatic Caesarean section. This association makes perfect sense in the logic of the grotesque body, because it is precisely in the association of fertility and death that the grotesque draws its power (Bakhtin 1984, 238), and in the next episode of the narrative is explicitly thematized.

REPRODUCTION AND THE
GROTESQUE BODY

The theme of reproduction begins explicitly to obtrude in the sequel to the anecdote about the two fat rabbis and thus connects the theme of grotesque obesity with the theme of fecundity:

> A certain matron said to them, "Your children are not yours." They said, "Theirs are bigger than ours." "If that is the case, even more so!" *There are those who say that thus they said to her: "As the man, so is his virility." And there are those who say that thus did they say to her: "Love compresses the flesh."*

The Roman matron who sees the two obese rabbis cannot believe that they could possibly perform sexually, so she challenges the legitimacy of their children. A brief, highly comic linguistic farce ensues. They answer her cryptically, "Theirs are bigger than ours," apparently understanding the matron to have meant that since they have such enormous penises, they could not have intercourse and replying that their wives have even bigger vaginas.[7] The matron, misunderstanding their answer and thinking that they are referring to their wives' abdomens, retorts, "If your wives are even fatter, then all the more so that you could not have intercourse." At this point the fat rabbis finally understand the matron's concern and answer—according to one tradition, that the size of a man's genitals is in keeping with the size of the rest of his body, and according to the other, that desire overcomes obesity.

It is at this moment of anxiety about paternity in the text that the account of the gargantuan phalli of the rabbis is mustered. Beginning from this incident, the text produces a phenomenal series of stories that all have anxiety over gender and reproduction as a major motif. The most obvious sign of this thematic concern is the fact that when Rabbi El'azar returns to the House of Study, his first activity is to permit marital sex for sixty women who have had a flux of blood that may or may not be menstrual. According to rabbinic practice, when a woman has a discharge, if it is certainly menstrual blood, then she and her husband are forbidden to have sex until after the period and a purification ritual. However, if it is doubtful as to whether the discharge is menstrual or not, a stain is shown to a rabbi who makes a judgment based on his expertise.[8] In our story, Rabbi El'azar was shown sixty of such stains and judged them all to be non-menstrual, thus permitting intercourse for these wives. All of the sixty children born of the intercourse permitted by R. El'azar were named after him, signifying him as in some sense their parent. My claim for the significance of this narrative moment in signaling the thematic emphasis of the text is occasioned by its very gratuitousness. We could have had the rabbi performing any feat of halakhic (rabbinic law) ingenuity in

7. I owe this interpretation to David Satran, and to my student Christine Hayes I owe the brilliant suggestion that the matron meant one thing and the two rabbis another.

8. This practice has, of course, disturbing aspects with regard to gender and power over women's bodies and sexualities. In a forthcoming research project, this issue will be dealt with fully, dv.

order to prove the great loss to Torah of the years that he was away from the House of Study, but the halakhic feat that he happens to perform is precisely one concerned with sexuality and reproduction. The choice of this particular halakhic matter as the example of Rabbi El'azar's great ability is a strong symptom, then, of what our text is "about":[9]

> One day he went to the study-house. They brought before him sixty kinds of blood, and he declared all of them pure. The Rabbis murmured about him, saying, Is it possible that there is not even one doubtful case among those? He said, "If I am right, let all of the children be boys, and if not, let there be one girl among them." All of them were boys. They were all named after Rabbi El'azar. Our Rabbi said, "How much procreation did that wicked woman prevent from Israel!"

The guilt for the prevention of this procreation is displaced from the rabbis themselves who, by their undue stringency in applying their laws, prevented wives from having intercourse with their husbands and projected onto the wife of Rabbi El'azar, whose only guilt was in protecting her husband from maltreatment by those selfsame Rabbis. Moreover, the "credit," as it were, for the procreation that took place is claimed by the Rabbis for themselves in the naming of the children after the rabbi.[10] This reading suggests a source for the tremendous tension manifested in our text around the male reproductive body: anxiety about the role of the rabbinic community in the reproduction and genealogy of Israel, and first and foremost about their own genealogies, their own continuation through replication in their offspring.

Another particularly strong and disturbing connection between the grotesque body of Rabbi El'azar and the female reproductive body is evident in the description of his illness: "In the evening, they used to fold under him sixty felt mats, and in the morning they would find under him

---

9. I.e., what its cultural business is. Note that in the parallel text of the Palestinian tradition, the story is nearly the same, but all the themes having to do with sex and procreation are absent. For a comparison of the two texts, see Boyarin 1991. Even a theme such as the loss of strength from studying Torah, which does occur in the Palestinian text, has none of the sexual and gender-related overtones that it has in the Babylonian one. See Mandelbaum (1962, 194 ff.). That text is accordingly "about" something else.

10. Of course, I am referring here to the narrator or author of our story and not to the Rabbis in the diegesis. Compare also *The Fathers According to Rabbi Nathan*, Version A, para. 12: "Moreover, how many thousands there were in Israel named Aaron! For had it not been for Aaron these children would not have come into the world [because he reconciled their quarreling parents]" (Goldin 1955, 64).

sixty vessels full of blood and pus." The text signals by a formal device the gender-related issue at stake here. These sixty vessels of the blood of dying cannot be separated from the exactly sixty issues of feminine blood that were brought before the rabbi in the segment discussed above. Our text of the grotesque body, then, not surprisingly turns on explicit thematic issues having to do with sexuality, gender, and reproduction. The Bakhtinian concept of the grotesque body and its complex and ambivalent connection with death and birth thus provides a conceptual model for reading as a complex textual system passages that are often taken as a series of individual textual moments.[11]

VINEGAR, SON OF WINE:
THE PROBLEM OF REPRODUCIBILITY

The epithet awarded to Rabbi El'azar ben Shim'on, "Vinegar, the son of Wine," can now be read not as a political evaluation but as an expression of the problematic of reproducibility which is the concern of the text.[12] Rabbi Shim'on, the father of our hero, was one of the holiest and most ascetic of all the Rabbis, a man who was famous for his entire devotion to the study of Torah alone, as well as for his implacable opposition to the Romans. His son, as signified by both his obesity and his willingness to serve as errand boy to the Romans, is not "Wine," as would be hoped for, but "Vinegar," a decidedly inferior product. Exactly the same applies to Rabbi Ishma'el the son of Rabbi Yose, again an ignoble son of a noble father. With great (dramatic) irony, it is these two men who are challenged by the Roman matron insisting, "Your children are not yours." Their obesity prevents them, she suggests, from being able to have intercourse with their wives. They answer her, however, in convincing manner that indeed they are the fathers of their children, so as to prevent

---

11. This should not be mistaken for either a New Critical or a structuralist claim for totalizable meaning in the narrative, but rather for a claim that the text deals with one large thematic moment. Other thematic moments may also be present in the same text.

12. Once more, the theme already occurs in the Palestinian "source-text." My claim is not, therefore, of an absolute conflict between Palestinian and Babylonian ideologies, but of the further development of internal conflict in the relatively Hellenism-free Babylonian branch of the culture. It is interesting to note that one of the justifications for celibacy in Shaker philosophy was that children often enough turn out badly (Kitch 1989, 52).

their children from being mocked. The matron misreads the signification of their bodies, thinking that their grossness and grotesqueness in body signify an interruption of genealogical connection between them and their children. But we, the readers, know that the pertinent genealogical signification is not the physical one between these men and their children, but the spiritual one between these men and their fathers. The fathers were wine; the children are vinegar.

The text, then, seems to bear out the suggestion that its issue is a rabbinic anxiety about their own "continuity through replication." The mistakenness of the Matron's taunt that the children of the two fat rabbis are not theirs only underlines through its ironies the truth that they are not truly sons of their fathers. The theme is unmistakably taken up, once more, in the remarkable sequel to our story on the next page of the Talmud:

> Rabbi happened to come to the town of Rabbi El'azar the son of Rabbi Shim'on [after the latter's death]. He asked, "Does that righteous man have a son?" They answered, "He has a son, and any prostitute who is hired for two [coins], would pay eight for him." He [Rabbi] came and ordained him and gave him over to Rabbi Shim'on, the son of Issi, the son of Lakonia, the brother of his mother [to teach him Torah].

The son of Rabbi El'azar, he who had once been dubbed "Vinegar, son of Wine," is again presented as an unworthy son to his father. The problematic of continuity through procreation is intensely signified in this brief incident. On the one hand, we have an unbeautiful father, who has a son whose body is so beautiful that whores are willing to pay four times their normal fee in order to sleep with *him*. On the other hand, he is presented again as the highly unrighteous son of a (suddenly saintly) father. Thus, we find the comfort of belief in survival through reproduction is twice challenged in the same figure; he neither looks like his father nor follows in his footsteps. The story also suggests a response to this tragic despair; namely, reproduction through education.[13]

This story is immediately doubled by an even more remarkable one:

> Rabbi happened to come to the town of Rabbi Tarfon. He asked, "Does that righteous man have a son?" [for Rabbi Tarfon] had lost his children.

---

13. I am not insensible that there may be another dimension here as well, namely, the relationship of brothers-in-law to each other, a theme we will find adumbrated below and which needs further amplification.

They said to him, "He has no son, but he has the son of a daughter,
and any prostitute who is hired for four, hires him for eight." He said
to him, "If you return [to Torah], I will give you my daughter." He
returned.

This is a recapitulation of several of the themes we have seen so far.
Rabbi Tarfon has no living sons, and moreover, his [only?] grandson is as
far from Torah as could be. Rabbi takes him under his wing through a displaced erotic relationship, a situation which we will be meeting again and
interpreting later on.[14] I read here the extraordinary tension that the rabbinic culture seems to feel between the desire on the one hand to pass on
the mantle of Torah from father to son and the anxiety that, in a profound sense, *people do not reproduce each other, and reproduction is not the
answer to death.*

Once again, after Rabbi El'azar's death, his body is put to the test of
impermeability. The text produces another very intense image of a grotesque birth out of the flesh of a feminized male (dying) body. This association makes perfect sense in the logic of the grotesque body, because it
is precisely in the association of fertility and death that the grotesque
draws its power (Bakhtin 1984, 238). Moreover, obesity itself is an issue
of gender, being associated with the maternal grotesque body:[15]

> When he was dying, he said to his wife, "I know that the rabbis are
> furious with me and will not take proper care of me. Let me lie in the
> attic and do not be afraid of me." Rabbi Shmuel the son of Rabbi
> Nahman said, "Rabbi Yohanan's mother told me that the wife of Rabbi
> El'azar the son of Rabbi Shim'on told her that 'not less than eighteen
> and not more than twenty-two [years] that he was in the attic, every
> day I went up and looked at his hair, when a hair was pulled out, blood
> would flow. One day I saw a worm coming out of his ear. I became very
> upset, and I had a dream in which he said to me that it is nothing, for
> one day he had heard a rabbinical student being slandered and had not
> protested as he should have.'"

---

14. The cultural analysis in Sedgwick 1985 is certainly relevant here and will be
developed in another place in my work. See also the remarks of R. Howard Bloch on a
very different group of scholarly men: "More than just a men's club, this exclusion [of
women] imagines at its outer limit the possibility of a nearly womanless parthenogene-
sis working, not only to structure the scholarly community, but to guarantee its dynas-
tic continuity as well" (Bloch 1991b, 81). These remarks could be applied *en bloch* to
the rabbinic community as well.

15. In the classical world, fat men were considered effeminate. See the fascinating
discussion of Nicole Loraux (1990, 31–33). See also Paglia (1990, 91) and Traub
(1989, 461–64).

Again here, we have exactly the same situation of the very zenith of the grotesque in precisely the place where the text is claiming to represent the classical. The theme of the Saint's body which does not rot after death is a topos of classical hagiography.[16] But, the grotesqueness of its handling in this text, and particularly the grotesque denouement with the worm coming out of the Rabbi's ear, suggest not a hagiography but a satire or parody on hagiographies. Although the text reduces the force of the image by moralizing it, its power "to upset" does not really disappear. If a worm is seen coming out of the ear of a corpse, the suggestion is certain that the cavity is, in fact, full of worms. In order to better understand this moment, we have to remember that until the modern period, the corpse was understood to produce the very worms that devoured it. The corpse is said "to beget" the worms, that is to give birth to them. A more powerful icon, then, of death in life and life in death, of the imbrication of death in the production of life, is hard to imagine.[17] This talmudic grotesque can hardly be said to represent the "last best word of the cosmos."

I have my doubts about Rabelais as well. Certainly the image of an infant so gigantic that he suffocates his mother in being born no more supports these rhapsodic remarks about "triumphant life" than does a corpse being consumed by the worms that it has "begotten." Indeed, where Bakhtin talks about "birth-giving death" (392), I think often we must think of "death-bringing birth."[18] Indeed, I would suggest that it is the very question of reproduction as providing the kind of "triumphant life of the people," the conquering of death that Bakhtin conjures, that is the source of the inner tension of our discourse. For Bakhtin's Rabelais, it is clear that his children will not only repeat the father [sic] and render

16. For the association of hagiography and the classical, see Brown 1983. Recently it was reported in the Israeli press that a group of French Jews buried in Paris in the mid-nineteenth century were reinterred in a mass grave in Jerusalem because their remains had been disturbed. One was found to have had his corpse preserved intact, and was given, therefore, a separate grave since this "miraculous" preservation proved his holiness. A more relevant comparison, perhaps, to a satiric reflection of this topos is of course the story of Father Zosima in *The Brothers Karamazov*. Another possible cultural source for this theme is a motif of Hellenistic romances regarding the preservation of a dead lover, which would make it a sort of early "A Rose for Emily." See Hadas (1953, 151).

17. Compare the birth of Pantagruel, as discussed in Bakhtin (1984, 328).

18. These images fit more with Paglia's conception of fecundity as being terrifying, of liquid, female nature gone wild (Paglia 1990). Where I part company with her is at two crucial and related points; one, her assumption that such images are somehow natural and not cultural in origin, and two, her enthusiastic acceptance of the values implied by the imagery of classical male and grotesque female.

him immortal,[19] but "the father's new flowering in the son does not take place on the same level but on a higher degree of mankind's development. When life is reborn, it does not repeat itself, it is perfected" (Bakhtin 1984, 406 ff.). This utopian desire is, it seems, the exact contrary of the Talmud's fear that the "father's new flowering" will be a sour one, a Vinegar, son of Wine. Reproduction, then, so far from continuing one's existence into the future, only emphasizes the dissolution that death brings. The reproductive principle was not, it seems, sufficient for this culture to provide a conviction that "death hath no dominion."

Our text, however, rejecting almost entirely the utopian character of reproduction so emphasized by Bakhtin, attempts to provide its own utopian solution, substitution of the phallic mouth for the phallic penis. This substitution has been brilliantly documented and analyzed by Howard Eilberg-Schwartz (1990b, 229–34). Our text shows it to be, however, the product not so much of discomfort with the body and genealogical reproduction as of despair at the failure of that ideal. The Rabbis are in a strong sense the inheritors of the priestly role in Israel. This transfer of authority is dramatized in the Talmud (Yoma 76b), where all of the people who were following the High Priest upon his departure from the Holy of Holies on the Day of Atonement turned and followed Shemaia and Avtalyon, semi-legendary founding figures of the rabbinic movement, when the latter appeared.[20] Note that the very activity in which Rabbi Elʿazar engages, the distinction between menstrual blood and blood that does not cause impurity, is a priestly task *par excellence*. Concerns with procreation and genealogy are critical in the Priestly culture of the Bible, and a sexually damaged priest was even disqualified from serving at the altar and blessing the people.[21] The signifier of biological filiation has a strong anchoring in the values of the culture. As such, the rabbinic mantle should have passed from father to son, as does the crown of priesthood. But it doesn't, at least not in any straightforward way. On the one hand, the Rabbis have created a sort of meritocracy to replace the religious aristocracy that the Bible ordains. Filiation is no longer from father

19. According to Elisheva Rosen, there is reason to trace Bakhtin's optimistic reading of the grotesque back to Victor Hugo (Rosen 1990, 129).

20. The issue is made even sharper there by the fact that these two Rabbis are not only not hereditary priests but converts! I am grateful to Joshua Levinson for reminding me of this source.

21. For an excellent discussion of this matter from a comparative anthropology perspective, see Eilberg-Schwartz (1990b, 141–76).

to son but from teacher to disciple.[22] But the desire that genetic replicability be homologous with pedagogical replicability persists. For a powerful signifier within the story of this desire and its failure, we need look no further than the following moment:

> As for Torah, what did he mean? When Rabban Shim'on the son of Gamliel and Rabbi Yehoshua the Bald used to sit on benches, Rabbi El'azar the son of Rabbi Shim'on and our Rabbi used to sit in front of them on the ground and ask and answer. And the rabbis said, "We are drinking their water, and they sit on the ground!?" They built them benches and put them upon them. Rabban Shim'on ben Gamliel said, "I have one chick among you and you wish to cause him to be lost from me!"[23] They moved Rabbi down again. Rabbi Yehoshua ben Korha said, "Shall he who has a father live, and he who has none shall die?!" They took Rabbi El'azar down as well. He became upset. He said, "They think we are equals. When they put him up, they put me up; when they put him down, they put me down." Until that day, when Rabbi would say something, Rabbi El'azar the son of Rabbi Shim'on used to say, "There is a tradition which supports you." From that day onward, when Rabbi said, "This is my answer," Rabbi El'azar the son of Rabbi Shim'on said, "This is what you will answer; you have surrounded us with vain words, answers that are empty." Rabbi became upset. He came and told his father. He said, "Don't feel bad. He is a lion the son of a lion, and you are a lion the son of a fox."

22. See Eilberg-Schwartz (1990b, 206–16 and 229–34). Of course, the rabbinic interpretation of biblical "father" and "son" as "master" and "disciple" is common. See, for example, Sifre Deut. 34 (p. 61), 182 (p. 224), 305 (p. 327), and 335 (p. 385). The New Testament polemicizes against the Pharisees for turning their followers against their biological parents. Becoming a "disciple of the sages" often meant accepting a rabbinic father in place of one's biological father. See the story of R. Eliezer b. Hyrcanus in *The Fathers According to Rabbi Nathan*, par. 6 (Goldin 1955, 43), and parallels. However, this meritocracy is not simple, for the institution of the patriarchate, an institution of both temporal and religious power and prestige, is precisely a hereditary office. The issue of this institution and its hereditary nature is raised in our text in the story of Rabbi El'azar and Rabbi as children, cited immediately below in the text.

But finally, it is Rabbi, not Rabbi El'azar, who carries the mantle not only of political power for his time but of central cultural prestige for the talmudic Judaism of the narrator's time as well. However, the institution of the patriarchate and its hereditary nature were a source of political and cultural conflict all through the early stages of the rabbinic period. The political dimensions of this cultural conflict are, of course, very significant but beyond the scope of the present work. For the passing of rabbinic offices from fathers to sons, and the tension of this hereditary principle with that of Torah meritocracy, see Alon (1977, 436–57), Moshe Beer 1976, summarized in Moses Beer 1980, and Gafni 1986. I am grateful to Steven Fraade for these references.

23. He was Rabbi's father. Apparently, the concern is that by singling him out as talented, the Evil Eye would be attracted to him.

Rabban Shim'on ben Gamliel, the patriarch, has power to take care of his son in this world—"Rabban Shim'on ben Gamliel said, 'I have one chick among you and you wish to cause him to be lost from me!'"—but he cannot guarantee that his son will be superior in learning to the sons of his inferiors in power. On the other hand, the injustice of the power that the father has in this world to promote his inferior son is given a utopian solution in the text when the other Shim'on, who had no power while alive (indeed was considered as if nonexistent then: "Shall he who has a father live, and he who has none shall die?!") can take care of his son from the next world: "Some say that his father appeared to the rabbis in a dream and said, '*I have one chick that is with you, and you do not want to bring it to me.*'" The text thematizes, by repeating the exact phrase, the conflict that was aroused by the desire that merit and prestige should pass in a homologous way from father to son, only emphasizing the more that they do not in the real world.

The text ends with the comforting conclusion, "Said Rabbi Parnak in the name of Rabbi Yohanan, 'Anyone who is a disciple of the wise and his son is a disciple of the wise and his grandson is a disciple of the wise, the Torah will not cease from his progeny forever.'" According to this apothegm, the very relationship of replication through discipleship is paradoxically and precisely what guarantees that one's physical progeny will be a replication of one. The very bravado of this statement, however, reveals more anxiety and the strength of desire for this to be so, than any confidence that it is indeed the case.[24]

THE HOPLITE WHO LOST HIS SPEAR

The text includes as well another episode—generally read as unrelated—that reinforces its concern with maleness and reproduction. This sub-text makes practically explicit the near-obsessive anxiety about relations between men, on the one hand, and their reproducibility, on the other:

24. It is, indeed, quite ironic that the one figure in our narrative who *does* seem to have transferred his qualities to his son is the laundry man, of whom it is said, "that he and his son had intercourse with a betrothed girl on Yom Kippur!" This point strengthens, moreover, my argument against the political historical readings of the text as a critique of collaboration. The laundry man transgressed genealogical rules, marriage rules, and the sacred calendar, a stunningly thorough vindication of Rabbi El'azar against Rabbi Yehoshua ben Korha who used the same epithet that the demonstrably wicked laundry man employed in his attack on Rabbi El'azar. Rabbi El'azar is presented as physically "Oriental" and anti-classical but as politically a Roman "collaborator"—and he is ultimately justified in both respects!

Said Rabbi Yohanan, "I have survived from the beautiful of Jerusalem."
One who wishes to see the beauty of Rabbi Yohanan should bring a
brand new silver cup and fill it with the red seeds of the pomegranate
and place around its rim a garland of red roses, and let him place it at
the place where the sun meets the shade, and that vision is the beauty
of Rabbi Yohanan. *Is that true?! But haven't we been taught by our
master that, "The beauty of Rabbi Kahana is like the beauty of Rabbi
Abbahu. The beauty of Rabbi Abbahu is like the beauty of our father
Jacob. The beauty of our father Jacob is like the beauty of Adam," and
that of Rabbi Yohanan is not mentioned. Rabbi Yohanan did not have
splendor of face.* Rabbi Yohanan used to go and sit at the gate of the
ritual bath. He said, "When the daughters of Israel come out from the
bath, they will look at me in order that they will have children as
beautiful as I am." The Rabbis said to him, "Are you not afraid of the
Evil Eye?" He replied, "I am of the seed of Joseph, our father, of whom
it is said, 'A fruitful son is Joseph, a fruitful son by the spring'" [Gen.
49:22], and Rabbi Abbahu said (of this verse), "Do not read it, 'by the
spring' but 'safe from the Eye.'" Rabbi Yosef the son of Rabbi Hanina
learned it from here, "'And they will multiply like fish in the midst of
the Land' [Gen. 48:16], just as the fish of the sea, the water covers
them and the Eye does not prevail over them, so also the seed of
Joseph, the Eye does not prevail over it."

On one level, all we have here is a topos of folk literature that an embryo
is affected by appearances that the mother has seen either during pregnancy or at the time of conception.[25] As such, it would not be a particularly remarkable story. However, according to talmudic morality, thinking
of another person while having intercourse with one's spouse is accounted
as a kind of virtual adultery. The theme of the importance of the sexual
partners having no images of another person at the time of intercourse is
emphasized again and again in rabbinic literature. It even carries over
into halakhic prescriptions for the act of love, e.g., that sexual intercourse
should be practiced at an hour when no voices will be heard from the
street. Violation of this principle is represented as resulting in children of
a sort of mixed genealogy who are not lovely.[26] Furthermore, we find:
"Our Rabbis have said: When a woman has intercourse with her husband,
and her mind is on another man that she saw on the way—there is no

25. "Both the Hippokratics and Soranos recommend preparations prior to intercourse: the prospective mother's sense of sober well-being concentrates her thoughts
upon her man and causes her child to look like him, themes that extend far beyond medical circles" (Hanson 1990, 315–16. See also Huet 1983 and G. E. R. Lloyd 1983, 174).
26. See, e.g., Babylonian Talmud Nedarim 20b.

adultery greater than this" (Buber 1964). An exception is made in our case. In fact, I believe that this is a correct reading of the challenge the Rabbis make to Rabbi Yohanan, i.e., that they are really challenging him on these moral grounds:

> "Are you not afraid of the Evil Eye?" He replied, "I am of the seed of Joseph, our father, of whom it is said, 'A fertile son is Joseph, a fertile son by the spring'" [Gen. 49:22], and Rabbi Abbahu said [of this verse], "Do not read it, 'by the spring' but 'out of reach of the Eye.'"[27]

Ostensibly, the challenge that the Rabbis made to Rabbi Yohanan is some-thing like, are you not afraid that by calling attention to your beauty, you will be attracting the Evil Eye? And the Rabbi's reply is made to mean merely, I am of the seed of Joseph who are proof from the Evil Eye. However, I am convinced that there is another meaning lurking within Rabbi Yohanan's words, which the Talmud has either willingly or unwit-tingly obscured. The whole verse that Rabbi Yohanan quotes is, "A fertile son (or young man) is Joseph, a fertile young man by the spring; the daughters walked on the wall." The last word can, however, be taken as a verb meaning "to look." The verse, so read, becomes an exact authoriza-tion for Rabbi Yohanan's practice, "a fertile young man is Joseph, he is a fertile young man alongside the ritual bath [= the spring]; the daughters walked to look at him." It is as if, therefore, what Rabbi Yohanan is proposing is that spiritually he would become the father of all of these children, transferring his qualities to them, through the thoughts of their mothers at the moment of intercourse with their physical fathers.[28] If my reconstruction of Rabbi Yohanan's midrash is correct, then, the original challenge must have been, "Isn't it immoral for you to be sitting near the ritual bath and introducing yourself into the thoughts of these women as they sleep with their husbands?" But Rabbi Yohanan's answer would be: "I am exceptional because of my beauty and have a precedent for my actions. Joseph, my ancestor!, also behaved thus." This reading is doubled by Rabbi Yohanan's very claim to be of the seed of Joseph as well, for he certainly could not have meant that literally he was a physical descen-dant of Joseph, the tribes of Joseph having been long exiled from the

27. The words for "spring" and "eye" are homonyms in the Hebrew, and the prepo-sition "by" can also mean "above, out of the reach of."

28. It is even possible that this is the original sense of Rabbi Abbahu's midrashic comment as well, for "going up from the spring" would be a very natural way in Hebrew to refer to returning from the ritual bath.

Land and lost. He meant, on my reading: "I am of the spiritual seed of Joseph; just as he was beautiful of form and spirit and sat by the ritual bath and produced spiritual progeny, so also I." The beauty of Joseph and his ardent sexual purity were, of course, both topoi of the culture and would have been easily recognized in Rabbi Yohanan's claim. Rabbi Yohanan thus embodies the ideology of the classic.[29]

The story of Rabbi Yohanan and Resh Lakish continues the theme of gender, sex, and reproduction. The former is extraordinarily beautiful, nearly androgynous, beardless and so sexually attractive to the masculine Resh Lakish that the latter is willing to perform prodigious athletic feats to get to him. Moreover, compared to the other Rabbis, he had the smallest penis as well, in the Hellenistic world a signifier of male beauty.[30] Lest we miss the message, the narrator segues immediately into the story of Resh Lakish's misidentification of Rabbi Yohanan as a woman:

> One day, Rabbi Yohanan was bathing in the Jordan. Resh Lakish saw him and thought he was a woman. He crossed the Jordan after him by placing his lance in the Jordan and vaulting to the other side. When Rabbi Yohanan saw Rabbi Shimʿon the son of Lakish [= Resh Lakish], he said to him, "Your strength for Torah!" He replied, "Your beauty for women!" He said to him, "If you repent, I will give you my sister who is more beautiful than I am."

As in the Greek *Paideia,* still enormously influential in late antiquity (Jaeger 1961), Rabbi Yohanan does manage to produce Resh Lakish as a spiritual copy of him, just as he wished to produce infants who would be physical copies of him. Just as he is effeminate or androgynous, he feminizes Resh Lakish also, and by doing so, reproduces him as a "great man":

29. Lest there be any misunderstanding, let me make it explicit that "Rabbi Yohanan" here means the character Rabbi Yohanan in this particular text. Thus, no claim is being made that the historical Rabbi Yohanan was more or less influenced by Greek culture than any other Rabbi but only that here he, as the representative *par excellence* of Palestinian rabbinism for the Babylonians, is a signifier of a certain cultural moment and cultural struggle. In other Babylonian stories about him, he is represented as grotesque in his person as well.

30. "The Greek aesthetic prefers discreet genitals, small in size" (Lissarrague 1990, 56 and texts cited there). For classical male beauty as being androgynous, see Paglia (1990, 99 ff.). In particular, for the small penis as a standard of male beauty, see Paglia (ibid., 114–15). In truth, I am not certain that, given the size of a *kav,* Rabbi Yohanan's penis is actually represented as small, but there can be no doubt that the contrast of nine and seven versus three suggests just that. In any case, we should not misunderstand that the Rabbis considered themselves eunuched. Rabbi Yohanan does, after all, have a penis, one of at least normal size.

He agreed. He wanted to cross back [vault back on his lance!] to take his clothes but he couldn't. He taught him Mishna and Talmud and made him into a great man.

The feminizing virtue of Torah is strongly represented in this story. As soon as Resh Lakish even agrees to study Torah, he can no longer vault back over the river on his spear! "His strength has been sapped as that of a woman."[31] What we have here is, in fact, an almost exact reversal of the pattern of Greek pederasty, in which an older man, marked as such by his beard,[32] takes an adolescent under his wing and in an erotic relationship educates him and prepares him for full participation in civic life. At the end, the young man is a *hoplite*, a spear-bearer. Here, however, it is the beardless, androgynous one who takes the virile *hoplite* under *his* wing, educates him and makes him a "great man," sapping, however, his physical prowess and disempowering his "spear" in the process. To be sure, within the Jewish moral economy, the homoerotic implications *must* be displaced from a relationship between Resh Lakish and Rabbi Yohanan to his sister, a displacement that the text makes explicit. Rabbi Yohanan's almost androgynous quality is once more underlined in the text further on when in the discussion of why he is not mentioned in a list of beautiful Rabbis, it is remarked that the others had splendor of face, but "Rabbi Yohanan did not have splendor of face":

Is that true?! But haven't we been taught by our master that, "The beauty of Rabbi Kahana is like the beauty of Rabbi Abbahu. The beauty of Rabbi Abbahu is like the beauty of our father Jacob. The beauty of our father Jacob is like the beauty of Adam," and that of Rabbi Yohanan is not mentioned. *Rabbi Yohanan did not have splendor of face.*

The Talmud raises an objection to the citation of Rabbi Yohanan as the very embodiment of beauty because there is a tradition that lists beautiful Rabbis and does not mention him. The answer is that Rabbi Yohanan, although beautiful, was left out of this list, because he did not possess "splendor of face." This phrase refers to the biblical verse in which we

31. The Talmud in Sanhedrin 26b explicitly refers to the Torah as "sapping the strength of a man," and "his strength was sapped as that of a woman" is a common phrase in the talmudic literature.

32. Foucault (1986b, 199) remarks on the appearance of the beard as the sign that the relationship between the man and boy must end and that now the young man ought to become the subject and not the object of pedagogy (and pederasty). See also Frontisi-Ducroux and Lissarrague (1990, 217) and Gleason (1990, 405 n. 63).

find the injunction to "give splendor to the face of an elder" (Leviticus 19:32), which is interpreted in midrash to mean that one must grow a beard. What was lacking, then, in Rabbi Yohanan's beauty was a beard, the lack of which was precisely what defined his beauty for Resh Lakish, his effeminate appearance! The text seems then to contradict itself, asserting that the lack of the beard is a marker of beauty and at the same time that it is a defect in beauty. This text manifests, therefore, an ambivalence or anxiety about the value of virility; on the one hand, the signs of virility are what produce beauty in the male, and at the same time, it is the very lack of those signs that produce the male as beautiful.[33] This ambivalence about the effeminate body of Rabbi Yohanan is thus the double of the ambivalence about the grotesquely masculine bodies of the fat rabbis. The ideal male seems to be feminized in this culture, but since that very ideality is openly marked as effeminate, the text—and presumably the culture—seems hopelessly ambivalent about male identity.

I would claim that contestation of the significance of physical virility, substituting replication through teaching for replication through reproduction, is an attempt (doomed to failure, as it happens) to reduce this anxiety. The production of spiritual children, those who will follow in the moral and religious ways of the parent, is claimed by our text as more important than the production of biological children—not, I hasten to add, because of a hierarchical privileging of "spirit"[34] over body, but rather because of a profound skepticism about replication of the qualities of the parent in the child. Spiritual excellence is claimed as superior to physical prowess. Reversing the Hellenic pattern, the masculine figure joins the "effeminate" one, and while losing his physical virility, becomes nevertheless, or accordingly, a "great man."[35] The narrative seems, therefore, to be challenging the cult of physical virility and male beauty, substituting

33. See Gleason (1990, 400–401) for the sources of one pole of the ambivalence.

34. In fact, one of the main points of this entire project is to argue against such dualism in rabbinic culture.

35. Jonah Fränkel already remarked this reversal of expectations (Fränkel 1981, 73–77). Fränkel's reading of the story of Rabbi Yohanan and Resh Lakish is of great interest, but it entirely removes that story from its literary context as part of a larger narrative text, apparently assuming that it was attached here secondarily and by mere association. However, as Shamma Friedman (1985, 79–80 nn. 49, 50) has already shown, there is no doubt that the present editor carefully wove these two sources into a single narrative text, and it is that text that I am reading here. This does not invalidate Fränkel's reading as far as it goes, and indeed his work is a necessary supplement to the interpretation I am giving here.

for it a spiritual reproduction through the oral dissemination of Torah. However, it would be very difficult to claim that our text substitutes for these values anything clear or unambivalent:

> Once they [Rabbi Yohanan and his pupil/child Resh Lakish] were dis-
> puting in the study-house: "The sword and the lance and the dagger,
> from whence can they become impure?" Rabbi Yohanan said, "From
> the time they are forged in the fire." Resh Lakish said, "From the time
> they are polished in the water." Rabbi Yohanan said, "A brigand is an
> expert in brigandry." He said to him, "What have you profited me?
> There they called me Rabbi and here they call me Rabbi!" He became
> angry, and Resh Lakish became ill. His sister came to him and cried
> before him. She said, "Look at me!" He did not pay attention to her.
> "Look at the orphans!" He said to her, "Leave your orphans, I will give
> life" [Jeremiah 49:11]. "For the sake of my widowhood!" He said, "Place
> your widows' trust in me" [loc. cit.]. Resh Lakish died, and Rabbi
> Yohanan was greatly mournful over him. The Rabbis said, "What can
> we do to set his mind at ease? Let us bring Rabbi El'azar the son of
> Padat whose traditions are brilliant, and put him before him [Rabbi
> Yohanan]." They brought Rabbi El'azar the son of Padat and put him
> before him. Every point that he would make, he said, "There is a tradi-
> tion which supports you." He said, "Do I need this one?! The son of
> Lakish used to raise twenty-four objections to every point that I made,
> and I used to supply twenty-four refutations, until the matter became
> completely clear, and all you can say is that there is a tradition which
> supports me?! Don't I already know that I say good things?" He used to
> go and cry out at the gates, "Son of Lakish, where are you?" until he
> became mad. The Rabbis prayed for him and he died.

Even pedagogical filiation is not left unproblematic by our narrative; the eventual treatment of the student by the teacher and its tragic result are an eloquent exposure of trouble in paradigm. The level of anxiety in the text reaches new heights here. Indeed, the concept of spiritual filiation replacing biological one is given a very bitterly ironic reading, when Rabbi Yohanan replies to his sister that she needn't be concerned about the death of her husband (whom her brother is killing with his curse),[36] because God is the "father of orphans." We are left, therefore, with a highly inconclusive evaluation: the text seems able neither to comfort-

---

36. It is fascinating to note that in another place in the Talmud (Baba Metsia 60a) we also have a story of brothers-in-law in which the curse of one kills the other, but reversed. There, the husband kills his wife's brother, whom she has tried to protect, also over an insult (a major one) concerning the study of Torah.

ably inhabit nor to reject the importance of biological filiation as a signifier of value. Indeed, the text is not at all sure about the educability (or malleability) of human nature. Both Rabbi Yohanan, with his assertion that Resh Lakish is still, as it were, a brigand and the latter's answer that "There they called me Rabbi, and here they call me Rabbi" seem to express great reservation about whether anything at all has changed. So while the raising of spiritual progeny is produced by our text, on my reading, as a solution to a deep-seated problem in the culture, it was itself perhaps no less of a problem for the culture than the problem of procreation which it was supposed to solve. Having downplayed out of a certain despair the consequence of genetic filiation, the culture seems still very uncertain about the reliability of filiation through pedagogy as well.[37] The result is the very anxious and conflicted text we have before us. In a culture in which the body is the very center of the sense of being human, the problem of the body—male and female—remains unsolved.

APPENDIX: THE TALE OF RABBI EL'AZAR THE SON OF RABBI SHIM'ON (BABYLONIAN TALMUD BABA METSIA 83b–85a)

Rabbi El'azar the son of Rabbi Shim'on found a certain officer of the king who used to catch thieves. He asked him, "How do you prevail over them? Aren't they compared to animals, as it is written 'at night tramp all the animals of the forest' [Psalms 104:20]?" *There are those who say that he said it to him from the following verse: "He will ambush from a hiding place like a lion in a thicket"* [Psalms 10:9]. Said he to him, "Perhaps you are taking the innocent and leaving the guilty." He said to him, "How shall I do it?" He said to him, "Come I will teach you how to do it. Go in the first four hours of the morning to the wine-bar. If you see someone drinking wine and falling asleep, ask of him what his profession is. If he is a rabbinical student, he has arisen early for study. If he is a day-laborer, he has arisen early to his labor. If he worked at night, [find out] perhaps it is metal smelting [a silent form of work], and if not, then he is a thief and seize him." The rumor reached the king's house, and he said, "Let him who read the proclamation be the one to execute it." They brought Rabbi

---

37. I am indebted for this last comment to David Resnick.

El'azar the son of Rabbi Shim'on, and he began to catch thieves. He met Rabbi Yehoshua, the Bald, who said to him, "Vinegar, son of Wine: How long will you persist in sending the people of our God to death?!" He said to him, "I am removing thorns from the vineyard." He said to him, "Let the Owner of the vineyard come and remove the thorns." One day a certain laundry man met him, and called him "Vinegar, son of Wine." He said, "Since he is so brazen, one can assume that he is wicked." He said, "Seize him." They seized him. After he had settled down, he went in to release him, but he could not. He applied to him the verse "One who guards his mouth and his tongue, guards himself from troubles" [Proverbs 21:23]. They hung him. He stood under the hanged man and cried. Someone said to him, "Be not troubled; he and his son both had intercourse with an engaged girl on *Yom Kippur*." In that minute, he placed his hands on his guts, and said, "Be joyful, O my guts, be joyful! If it is thus when you are doubtful, when you are certain even more so. I am confident that rot and worms cannot prevail over you." But even so, he was not calmed. They gave him a sleeping potion and took him into a marble room and ripped open his stomach and were taking out baskets of fat and placing it in the July sun and it did not stink. *But no fat stinks. It does if it has red blood vessels in it, and this even though it had red blood vessels in it, did not stink.* He applied to himself the verse, "even my flesh will remain preserved" [Psalms 16:8–9].

To Rabbi Ishma'el the son of Yose there also occurred a similar situation. Eliahu (the Prophet Elijah) met him and said to him, "How long will you persist in sending the people of our God to death?!" He said to him, "What can I do; it is the king's order?" He said to him, "Your father ran away to Asia-Minor; you run away to Lydia."

When Rabbi Ishma'el the son of Yose and Rabbi El'azar the son of Rabbi Shim'on used to meet each other, an ox could walk between them and not touch them. A certain matron said to them, "Your children are not yours." They said, "Theirs are bigger than ours." "If that is the case, even more so!" *There are those who say that thus they said to her: "As the man, so is his virility." And there are those who say that thus did they say to her: "Love compresses the flesh." And why did they answer her at all? Does it not say, "Do not answer a fool according to his foolishness"? In order not to produce slander on their children, that they are bastards.*

Said Rabbi Yohanan, "Rabbi Ishma'el the son of Yose's member was like a wineskin of nine *kav*; Rabbi El'azar the son of Rabbi Shim'on's member was like a wineskin of seven *kav*." Rav Papa said, "Rabbi Yohanan's member was like a wineskin of three *kav*." *And there are those who say: like a wineskin of five kav. Rav Papa himself had a member which was like the baskets of Hipparenum.*[38]

Said Rabbi Yohanan, "I have survived from the beautiful of Jerusalem." One who wishes to see the beauty of Rabbi Yohanan should bring a brand new silver cup and fill it with the red seeds of the pomegranate and place around its rim a garland of red roses, and let him place it at the place where the sun meets the shade, and that vision is the beauty of Rabbi Yohanan. *Is that true?! But haven't we been taught by our master that, "The beauty of Rabbi Kahana is like the beauty of Rabbi Abbahu. The beauty of Rabbi Abbahu is like the beauty of our father Jacob. The beauty of our father Jacob is like the beauty of Adam," and that of Rabbi Yohanan is not mentioned. Rabbi Yohanan did not have splendor of face.* Rabbi Yohanan used to go and sit at the gate of the ritual bath. He said, "When the daughters of Israel come out from the bath, they will look at me in order that they will have children as beautiful as I am." The Rabbis said to him, "Are you not afraid of the Evil Eye?" He replied, "I am of the seed of Joseph, our father, of whom it is said, 'A fruitful son is Joseph, a fruitful son by the spring'" [Gen. 49:22], and Rabbi Abbahu said [of this verse], "Do not read it, 'by the spring' but 'safe from the Eye.'" Rabbi Yosef the son of Rabbi Hanina learned it from here, "'And they will multiply like fish in the midst of the Land' [Gen. 48:16], just as the fish of the sea, the water covers them and the Eye does not prevail over them, so also the seed of Joseph, the Eye does not prevail over it."

One day, Rabbi Yohanan was bathing in the Jordan. Resh Lakish saw him and thought he was a woman. He crossed the Jordan after him by placing his lance in the Jordan and vaulting to the other side. When Rabbi Yohanan saw Rabbi Shim'on the son of Lakish [Resh Lakish], he said to him, "Your strength for Torah!" He replied, "Your beauty for women!" He said to him, "If you repent, I will give you my sister who is more beautiful than I am." He agreed. He wanted to cross back to take his clothes but he couldn't. He taught him Mishna and Talmud and made him into a great man. Once they were disputing in the study-house: "The sword and the lance and the dagger, from whence can they become

---

38. Rav Papa is also a legendary fat rabbi, as is known from several other Babylonian talmudic intertexts.

impure?" Rabbi Yohanan said, "From the time they are forged in the fire." Resh Lakish said, "From the time they are polished in the water." Rabbi Yohanan said, "A brigand is an expert in brigandry." He said to him, "What have you profited me? There they called me Rabbi and here they call me Rabbi!" He became angry, and Resh Lakish became ill. His sister came to him and cried before him. She said, "Look at me!" He did not pay attention to her. "Look at the orphans!" He said to her, "Leave your orphans, I will give life" [Jer. 49:11]. "For the sake of my widowhood!" He said, "Place your widows' trust in me" [loc. cit.]. Resh Lakish died, and Rabbi Yohanan was greatly mournful over him. The Rabbis said, "What can we do to set his mind at ease? Let us bring Rabbi El'azar the son of Padat whose traditions are brilliant, and put him before him [Rabbi Yohanan]." They brought Rabbi El'azar the son of Padat and put him before him. Every point that he would make, he said, "There is a tradition which supports you." He said, "Do I need this one?! The son of Lakish used to raise twenty-four objections to every point that I made, and I used to supply twenty-four refutations, until the matter became completely clear, and all you can say is that there is a tradition which supports me?! Don't I already know that I say good things?" He used to go and cry out at the gates, "Son of Lakish, where are you?" until he became mad. The Rabbis prayed for him and he died.

And even so, Rabbi El'azar the son of Shim'on did not trust himself, perhaps God forbid, such an incident would befall him again. He accepted painful disease upon himself. In the evening, they used to fold under him sixty felt mats, and in the morning they would find under him sixty vessels full of blood and pus. His wife made him sixty kinds of relishes and he ate them. His wife would not let him go to the study-house, in order that the Rabbis would not reject him. In the evening, he said, "My brothers and companions [i.e., his pains], come!" In the morning, he said, "My brothers and companions, depart!" One day his wife heard him saying this. She said, "You bring them upon you. You have decimated the inheritance of my father's house." She rebelled and went to her family home. Sixty sailors came up from the sea and came to him carrying sixty purses and they made him sixty relishes, and he ate them. One day she said to her daughter, "Go see what your father is doing." He said to her, "Ours is greater than yours." He applied to himself the verse, "From afar she will bring her bread" [Proverbs 31:14].

One day he went to the study-house. They brought before him sixty kinds of blood, and he declared all of them pure. The Rabbis murmured about him, saying, "Is it possible that there is not even one doubtful case among those?" He said, "If I am right, let all of the children be boys, and if not, let there be one girl among them." All of them were boys. They were all named after Rabbi El'azar. Our Rabbi said, "How much procreation did that wicked woman prevent from Israel!"

When he was dying, he said to his wife, "I know that the Rabbis are furious with me and will not take proper care of me. Let me lie in the attic and do not be afraid of me." Rabbi Shmuel the son of Rabbi Nahman said, "Rabbi Yohanan's mother told me that the wife of Rabbi El'azar the son of Rabbi Shim'on told her that 'not less than eighteen and not more than twenty-two [years] that he was in the attic, every day I went up and looked at his hair, when a hair was pulled out, blood would flow.[39] One day I saw a worm coming out of his ear. I became very upset, and I had a dream in which he said to me that it is nothing, for one day he had heard a rabbinical student being slandered and had not protested as he should have.'" When a pair would come for judgment, they would stand at the door. One would say his piece and then the other would say his piece. A voice would come out of the attic and say, "I find for the plaintiff and not for the defendant." One day his wife was arguing with her neighbor. She said to her, "May you be like your husband, who is not buried." *Some say that his father appeared to the Rabbis in a dream and said, "I have one chick that is with you, and you do not want to bring it to me."* The Rabbis went to take care of his burial, but the townspeople did not let them, because all of the time that Rabbi El'azar was lying in the attic, no wild animal came to their town. One day, it was the eve of Yom Kippur, and the people of the town were worried and they went to the grave of his father. They found a snake which was surrounding the opening of the tomb. They said, "Snake, snake, open your mouth and the son will come in unto his father."[40] The snake opened for them. Our Rabbi sent to her to propose to her. She said, "A vessel which has been used for the holy, shall it be used for the profane?!" *There they say, "In the place where the master hangs his battle-ax, shall the shepherd hang his stick?!"*[41] He sent to her, "Indeed in Torah he was greater than me, but was he greater than me in deeds?" She sent to him, "As for Torah, I know nothing; you have told me, but as for deeds, I know, for he took upon himself suffering."

---

39. For hair that grows after death, see Satran (1989, 119).
40. Snakes protecting saints' tombs are a common feature of rabbinic legend.
41. The sexual imagery of both these proverbs is quite stark.

As for Torah, what did he mean? When Rabban Shim'on the son of Gamliel and Rabbi Yehoshua the Bald used to sit on benches, Rabbi El'azar the son of Rabbi Shim'on and our Rabbi used to sit in front of them on the ground and ask and answer. And the Rabbis said, "We are drinking their water,[42] and they sit on the ground!?" They built them benches and put them upon them. Rabban Shim'on ben Gamliel said, "I have one chick among you and you wish to cause him to be lost from me!"[43] They moved Rabbi down again. Rabbi Yehoshua ben Korha said, "Shall he who has a father live, and he who has none shall die?!" They took Rabbi El'azar down as well. He became upset. He said, "They think we are equals. When they put him up, they put me up; when they put him down, they put me down." Until that day, when Rabbi would say something, Rabbi El'azar the son of Rabbi Shim'on used to say, "There is a tradition which supports you." From that day onward, when Rabbi said, "This is my answer," Rabbi El'azar the son of Rabbi Shim'on said, "This is what you will answer; you have surrounded us with vain words, answers that are empty." Rabbi became upset. He came and told his father. He said, "Don't feel bad. He is a lion the son of a lion, and you are a lion the son of a fox." . . .[44]

Rabbi happened to come to the town of Rabbi El'azar the son of Rabbi Shim'on [after the latter's death]. He asked, "Does that righteous man have a son?" They answered, "He has a son, and any prostitute who is hired for two [coins], would pay eight for him." He brought him and ordained him "Rabbi" and gave him over to Rabbi Shim'on, the son of Issi, the son of Lakonia, the brother of his mother [to teach him Torah]. He taught him and spread a mantle over his head. Every day he would say, "I wish to return to my town." He said to him, "They call you 'sage,' and place a golden crown on your head, and call you 'Rabbi' and you say, 'I wish to return to my town'?!" He said to him, "Here is my oath that I leave that be." When he became great, he went and studied in the Yeshiva of Rabbi Shemaia. He heard his voice and said, "This one's voice is similar to the voice of Rabbi El'azar the son of Shim'on." They said to

42. A common figure for learning Torah from someone.
43. I.e., by distinguishing them as extremely talented children, you are attracting the Evil Eye to them.
44. There follow here stories about the sufferings that Rabbi took upon himself in order to "compete" for holiness with Rabbi El'azar, stories I will treat in another research project on mutilation and mortification of the flesh in Jewish culture.

him, "He is his son." He applied to him the verse, "The fruit of the righteous is a tree of life; and he that wins souls is wise" [Proverbs 11:30]. "The fruit of the righteous is a tree of life": this is Rabbi Yose the son of Rabbi El'azar the son of Rabbi Shim'on, and "he that wins souls is wise": this is Rabbi Shim'on, the son of Issi, the son of Lakonia.

When he died, they brought him to the burial cave of his father. A snake surrounded the cave of his father. They said, "Snake, open the door and the son will enter to be with his father." It did not open for them. The people thought that it was because [the father] was greater than the son. A voice came from heaven saying that it was because [the father] suffered in a cave,[45] and the son did not suffer in a cave.

Rabbi happened to come to the town of Rabbi Tarfon. He asked, "Does that righteous man have a son?" [for Rabbi Tarfon] had lost his children. They said to him, "He has no son, but he has the son of a daughter, and any prostitute who is hired for four, hires him for eight." He said to him, "If you return [to Torah], I will give you my daughter." He returned. *There are those who say that he married her and divorced her, and those who say that he did not marry her at all, in order that people would not say that he returned for that.* And Rabbi, why did he go to such lengths? For Rabbi Yehuda said that Rav said *and there are those who say it in the name of Rabbi Hiyya the son of Abba in the name of Rabbi Yohanan and those who say it in the name of Rabbi Shmuel the son of Nahmani in the name of Rabbi Yonathan,* "Anyone who teaches the son of his friend Torah, will be privileged to sit in the Yeshiva on High . . ." Said Rabbi Parnak in the name of Rabbi Yohanan, "Anyone who is a disciple of the wise and his son is a disciple of the wise and his grandson is a disciple of the wise, the Torah will not cease from his progeny forever."

45. When hiding from the Romans for thirteen years for the crime of studying Torah.

Concluding Forward
Talmudic Study as Cultural Critique

> In short, genealogy as resistance involves using history to give voice
> to the marginal and submerged voices which lie "a little beneath
> history"—the voices of the mad, the delinquent, the abnormal, the
> disempowered. It locates many discontinuous and regional struggles
> against power both in the past and present. These voices are the
> sources of resistance, the creative subjects of history.
>
> (Sawicki 1991, 28)

In my introduction I outlined several cultural goals for this book. The
three to which I would like to return in this conclusion are (1) the notion
of cultural dialectics, (2) generous critique, and (3) the desire to
change—in some small way—the world. I would like to suggest (or perhaps hope against hope) that if the book achieves anything of its third
ambition, it will be owing to the success of the first two as modalities of
cultural criticism.

My assumption is that we cannot change the actual past. We can only
change the present and the future, in part by changing our understanding
of the past. Unless the past is experienced merely as a burden to be
thrown off (which indeed it might be by many), then constructing a
monolithically negative perception of the past and cultivating anger at it
seem to be counterproductive and disempowering for change. Finding
only misogyny in the past reproduces misogyny; finding only a lack of
female power, autonomy, and creativity reifies female passivity and vic-
timhood. In contrast to this, recovery of those forces in the past that
opposed the dominant androcentrism can help put us on a trajectory of
empowerment for transformation. Jana Sawicki has made a similar point
in a different context, arguing that some feminist scholars portray the
power of reproductive technologies over women's bodies as such that "our
only options appear to be either total rejection of them or collaboration
in our own domination" (Sawicki 1991, 14). Instead of this, Sawicki

227

suggests a strategy of paying "constant attention to the ruptures, discontinuities and cracks in the systems of power," such that, "multiple strategies
for resisting their dangerous implications" can be developed without
either collaborating in domination or totally rejecting the past. Since I
do not wish to collaborate in domination and certainly do not wish to
reject Judaism, the latter type of research can be a powerfully redemptive
tool. Precisely and paradoxically: where the culture did not work then,
that is where we can make it work for us now. That is the strategy of the
current project.

There are two lines of inquiry to be pursued. The first delves for evidence of women's power, autonomy, and creativity that the dominant
discourse wishes to suppress but cannot entirely expunge. This line of
research has been very fruitful for study of ancient Greece, the biblical
period, and the Hellenistic period.[1] The second line of inquiry, however,
promises to be more fruitful for the Talmud, namely the search for male
opposition, *within the Talmud itself,* however rudimentary, to the dominant, androcentric discourse.

Perhaps the critic who has had the greatest effect on forming the
explicitly feminist aspects of my critical practice is Mieke Bal, most obviously, though not exclusively, owing to her work on the Hebrew Bible
(Bal 1987, 1988a, and 1988b). The theoretical factor in her work that
has made it most productive for me is the explicit way it engages the
assumed monolithic character of patriarchy and shows that the very assumption of that monolith serves the interests of those who wish to
retain gender hierarchy today, and even more important that it is an artifact of particular masculist[2] readings of biblical texts. In a recent essay, Bal
has articulated the intended cultural function of her work concisely and
persuasively:

1. This has been realized generally by many feminist critics and historians who
have begun searching in the Bible and in other ancient literature and cultural remains
for whatever evidence might be found or reread for women's creativity and cultural
power. Some feminist scholars have been pursuing this line of research with regard
to late-antique Judaism, notably Bernadette Brooten, Ross Kraemer, and Amy-Jill
Levine. This kind of work can be and has to be pursued for the Talmud as well,
although, to be sure, with regard to the talmudic literature and period the evidence
will be sparse indeed.

2. This term is in some ways problematic and in other ways very useful. It is problematic in that it parallels *feminist,* but feminism is not a project of female domination
over males, while masculism has historically been a project of male domination over
females. On the other hand, it is a useful term in that it clearly marks out the "universal" and the realm of "common knowledge" as inscribed by male interests.

In other words, these translations seemed to endorse too smoothly the notion that patriarchy is a monolithic, transhistorical social form. As a consequence, they suggest that patriarchy is unavoidable; they blame ancient Judaism for our being saddled with it; they even obscure the "otherness within," that is the pluralities of modern society in relation, precisely, to patriarchy. Specifically, modern translations of the ancient text are comparable to Western narratives about Eastern behavior, of which Geertz's account is an example. In both cases, our source of knowledge is a narrative, which by definition imperialistically filters the utterances of the other.

(1990, 734)

There are two important points being made in this brief quotation. The first point is that there is the same obligation to the ancient text and people that there is to the "Eastern" people, to avoid as much as possible an imperialist filtering of the utterances of the other. In the past decade a trenchant critique of "Orientalism" in anthropology has been leveled, beginning with Edward Said's paradigm-making work—Orientalism being the descriptive reification of the "Other" (Said 1979). It is vitally important that the same critique of Orientalism now be transferred to the study of our own past. When we are describing an ancient culture, it is important to maintain the same ethical standards that anthropologists have been working so hard to develop in their work with living cultures—that is, to avoid assuming a position of cultural superiority from which to judge or blame the "Other."[3] Yet when that ancient culture is powerfully (and painfully) effective in producing aspects of our current social practice, an important part of our descriptive work must be to criticize the culture. To pretend to an objectivity in describing biblical or talmudic gender practices, for example, is, in effect, to further bolster the effects that those practices still have (Boyarin 1990d). Cultural critique involves then, in my view, precisely the ability to contextually and historically understand practices of the past "Other"—who is ourselves—in such a way that that culture can serve us well in constructing our own social practices, providing the richness of belonging to the past without constricting us in forming more liberatory and egalitarian practices in the present. By generous critique, I mean, then, a mode of analysis that is not apologetic and yet maximizes our understanding of the needs and drives

---

3. After writing this paragraph I discovered that Page duBois has made nearly the same point in almost the same language (duBois 1988, 25–26).

that motivated a certain group of people to make the cultural "decisions" they made. My goals are both redemptive and cultural-critical, and in some ways the talmudic culture that I hope to partly describe is both my own and not my own. It is thus imperative for me to do two things: to facilitate a feminist critique of the rabbinic formation, but also to ex-culpate that same formation from charges of a founding misogyny that would render it irredeemable. Once again, I would like to reiterate the point I made in the introduction, that while I am obviously invested in the results of my readings and that while expectations inevitably affect results, the project will have been successful only to the extent that the readings of the texts carry conviction for others as at least a possible, or plausible, way to make sense of them—and this is, of course, something I cannot, by myself, judge.

The second postulate I derive from Bal is that a practice of cultural studies that seeks to make a difference in the present must be able to see and describe difference in the past. If the past culture is portrayed as a monolith, then its claims to a natural trans-historical status seem strongly buttressed. Accordingly, cultures that base themselves on the interpreta-tion of the Bible have sought to reduce or eliminate (rather, suppress) the textual evidence for difference within the biblical text itself, in the inter-ests of precisely that naturalization of dominance and gender asymmetry. This is true of Hellenistic Judaism, of much of Christianity, and of Ju-daism from the Middle Ages and until the modern period. It is, however, considerably less true of rabbinic Judaism, where the heterogeneity of the biblical text is represented in the canonized dialogue and dialectic of mid-rash. When Bal's compelling point that the reduction of internal "other-ness" serves the interests of the monolithic male-dominant system is taken seriously, then we can see that even explicitly feminist research that can-not see difference within the texts and the culture is self-defeating. Ac-cordingly, it is vitally important that trained talmudists turn to cultural criticism and that cultural critics interested in making effective use of tal-mudic materials take the trouble to learn the specific discursive practices that mark off this particular kind of textuality.

CULTURAL DIALECTIC
AND THE MIND-BODY SPLIT

Rabbinic Judaism is a particular Jewish formation of late antiquity. Although this is the type of Judaism that became the historical ancestor of virtually all later groups that call themselves Jewish, in the early centuries of our era it was just one form of Judaism. Various types of Hellenistic Judaism, apocalyptic groups such as the one at Qumran, and early Christianity were all competing with the Judaism of the Rabbis and their followers for hegemony, and the discourse of the body was the major arena of contention. For most Jews of late antiquity (as well as for most non-Jews), the human being was conceived of as a spirit housed, clothed, or even trapped and imprisoned in flesh, while for the Rabbis, resisting this notion, the human being was a body animated by a spirit. This definition is what lies at the bottom of such diverse and distinctive rabbinic practices as the insistence on sex and procreation as obligations, the practice of midrashic reading as opposed to allegory, and the focus on the corporate identity of Israel as a particular ethnic unit. My claim in this book is that each of these formations presents cultural ethico-social problems that the other solves (from my political perspective) more successfully. Thus, if Hellenistic Judaisms (including, in my view, Paulinism) provide an attractive model of human equality and freedom—"There is no Jew or Greek, no male or female"—they do so at the cost of a severe devaluation of sexuality, procreation, and ethnicity. And if rabbinic Judaism provides a positive orientation to sexual pleasure and ethnic difference, it does so at the cost of determined stratifications of society. A dialectical reading practice puts these two formations into a relation of mutual thesis-antithesis, thus exposing the cultural problems that each answered but the other did not. Let us look at two examples of such cultural dialectics.

The Body and Difference

> Plotinus, the philosopher of our times, seemed ashamed of being in the body. As a result of this state of mind he could never bear to talk about his race or his parents or his native country.
>
> (Porphyry, *Life of Plotinus*)

Porphyry exposes with rare incandescence the intimate connection between the individual's corporeality and her "race," filiation, and place, as well as the neo-platonic revulsion from both corporeality and particular identity. This interpretation also furnishes us a key to understanding the resistance of the Rabbis to platonism. As loyal a Jew as Philo was, he could not entirely escape the consequences of his allegorizing in a devaluing of the physical practices and genealogy of Israel. Where physical history and physical ritual exist only to point to spiritual meanings, the possibility of transcending both is always there. As Ronald Williamson has put it:

> It seems that for Philo, alongside traditional, orthodox Judaism, there was a philosophical outlook on life, involving the recognition of the purely spiritual nature of the Transcendent, in which one day, Philo believed, all mankind would share. In *that* Judaism the idealized Augustus, Julia Augusta and Petronius—among, no doubt, many others—had already participated.
>
> (Williamson 1989, 13)

For Philo, such a spiritualized and philosophical Judaism, one in which a faith is substituted for works, remains only a theoretical possibility,[4] whereas for Paul, it becomes the actuality of a new religious formation that tends strongly to disembody Judaism.[5] If the body of language is its

---

4. According to H. A. Wolfson, Philo allowed for the possibility of uncircumcised "spiritual" proselytes (1947, 369). Borgen (1980, 87) seems to think that such uncircumcised proselytes could have been fully accepted as Jews by Philo, a proposition I find unconvincing. Nor am I convinced by Borgen's reading of the Talmud at Shabbat 51a, to the effect that for Hillel circumcision was not a prerequisite for conversion. The arguments of Neil McEleney (1974) are not convincing, since they involve faulty readings of talmudic texts, as I will show, Deo volente, in my forthcoming work on Paul. Shaye Cohen's comprehensive work on conversion in late-antique Judaism will clear up many of these doubtful issues.

5. In a recent letter to me, John Miles has made the following important comments:

> The faith-vs.-works dispute which you present as Christianity-vs.-Judaism has a long history, starting well before the Reformation, as a dispute *within* Christianity. A pagan who converted even to the Pauline form of Christianity was enjoined to follow a strikingly different ethical code and to abstain from a host of usages that were incompatible with monotheism. The result did not put him in continuity with Judah as a tribal, genetic community, but it was works, nonetheless, not just faith. It is, in fact, the survival of this much of the concrete Jewish program that makes Christianity indigestible for Gnosticism. The sentence to which I allude continues "whereas for Paul it becomes the actuality of a new religious formation which disembodies Judaism entire." Christianity looks disembodied by comparison with Rabbinic Judaism, but by comparison with Gnosticism it looks pretty corporeal.
>
> (Miles 1991)

The attentive reader will note that I have modified the quoted sentence in partial response to Miles's wise cautions. Note that I am *not* claiming that there is a fundamental incompatibility between a literalist reading and Christianity. Even as radical an allegorist as Origen is ambivalent as to the literal meaning of the Gospels and the sacraments, often distinguishing between the letter of the Law which kills and the letter of the Gospel which gives life (Caspary 1979, 50–55). However, as Caspary points out in the same place, at other moments Origen proclaims that the letter of the Gospel also kills.

meaning and essence, and the body of the person is his or her "self," then the history of Israel and the practices of that Israel are the physical history and practices of the body Israel. This resistance to dualism in language, body, and peoplehood is both the distinction of rabbinic Judaism and its limitation, while the universalizing possibility of post-Pauline Christianity, with its spiritualizing dualism, was also obtained at an enormous price.

Paul's allegorical reading of the rite of circumcision is an almost perfect emblem of this difference. In one stroke, by interpreting circumcision as referring to a spiritual and not corporeal reality, Paul made it possible for Judaism to become a world religion. It is not that the rite was difficult for adult Gentiles to perform—that would hardly have stopped devotees in the ancient world—but rather that it symbolized the genetic, the genealogical moment of Judaism as the religion of a particular tribe of people. This is so both in the very fact of the physicality of the rite, of its grounding in the practice of the tribe and in the way it marks the male members of that tribe (in both senses), but even more so, by being a marker on the organ of generation, it represents the genealogical claim for concrete historical memory as constitutive of Israel.[6] By substituting a spiritual interpretation for a physical ritual, Paul was saying that the genealogical Israel, "according to the Flesh" is not the ultimate Israel; there is an "Israel in the spirit." The practices of the particular Jewish People are not what the Bible speaks of, but faith, the allegorical meaning of those practices. It was Paul's genius to transcend "Israel in the flesh." On this reading, the "victory" to which Mopsik refers was a *necessary* one: "a split opened two millennia ago by the ideological victory over one part of the inhabited world of the Christian conception of carnal relation—and of carnal filiation—as separate from spiritual life and devalued in relation to it" (Mopsik 1989, 49).

As Jewish culture, both in Palestine and in the diaspora, came into contact with other cultures in the Hellenistic and Roman periods, it was faced with the issue of how the biblical religion fit in a world in which Jews live among other peoples. The dualism of Hellenized Judaism provides one answer to this question by allegorizing such signifiers as "Israel," "history," and the practices of Judaism. Thus, Philo interprets these signifiers as having meanings of universal applicability. The Bible, its

6. See the brilliant interpretation of circumcision in Eilberg-Schwartz (1990b, 141–77; and 1991).

prescriptions, and the history it relates are universal in that they teach everyone important truths. Paul went Philo one step further and concluded that that being the case, there is no need to continue the corporeal meaning of the concrete history and practices, and he then proceeded directly to the spiritual signified and thus created Gentile Christianity as a direct offshoot of Hellenistic Judaism.[7]

This solution had the cultural advantage of making the message of the Bible available to the entire world, and indeed Christianity was to become, of course, the dominant religious formation of the Western world, but it deracinated both the specificity of the Jewish historical and cultural experience, and, by implication (and in practice) that of all other peoples of the world. The Rabbis can be read, then, as a necessary critique of Paul (or, if I am wrong in my reading of Paul, of other, slightly later, Christian thinkers who certainly held such views), for if the Pauline move has within it the possibility of breaking out of the tribal allegiances and commitments to one's own family, it also contains the seeds of an imperialist and colonizing missionary practice. The very emphasis on a universalism, expressed as concern for all of the families of the world, turns rapidly (if not necessarily) into a doctrine that they must all

---

7. Once again, I realize that this is a controversial interpretation of Paul's doctrine. I think it was truly a matter of near total indifference to Paul whether Jews kept the Law or not. I will defend this interpretation in my work in progress, tentatively entitled *A Radical Jew: Paul and the Politics of Identity*. See for the nonce Sanders 1977 and 1983 and Segal 1990. Dunn seems to me also particularly accurate in identifying Paul's issue as the distinctiveness or "nationalism" of the Jews:

> Most persistent of all is the argument regarding the relation of faith and the law. How is (the initial expression of) faith to be correlated with "works of the law"? The implication of . . . [Galatians] 2:16a, especially in its context as referring back to the issue of food laws at Antioch (2:11–14), is that Jewish Christians thought works of the law (like observance of the dietary laws) were quite compatible with faith in Christ and still a necessary (covenantal!) obligation for Jewish believers in Messiah Jesus. But Paul drives that distinction (faith in Christ and works of law) into an outright antithesis (2:16b–c; 3:2, 5, 10–12): to regard the law (covenantal nomism) as the outworking of faith is retrogressive, a stepping back from the freedom of the children of God into immature childhood and slavery (3:23–4:11; 4:21–31). The outworking of faith has to be conceived in different terms from works of the law (circumcision etc.): that is, in terms of the Spirit as against works of the flesh (5:16–26; 6:7–9), a focusing on physical features which would include a nationalistic evaluation of circumcision (3:3; 4:21–31; 6:12–13). This outworking may be conceived in terms of the law, but not the law focused in such Jewish distinctives as circumcision, but focused rather in love of neighbor (5:6, 13–14) as exemplified by Christ (6:1–4).
>
> (Dunn 1991, 129)

become part of our family of the spirit, with all of the horrifying practices against Jews and other Others that Christian Europe produced (Shell 1991). From the retrospective position of a world that has, at the end of the second Christian millennium, become thoroughly interdependent, each one of the options leaves something to be desired. To the extent that, on the one hand, the insistence on corporeal genealogy and practice of tribal rites and customs produces an ethnocentric discourse, a discourse of separation and exclusiveness, then, on the other hand, the allegorization, the disembodiment of those very practices produces the discourse of conversion, colonialism, the White Man's Burden—Universal Brotherhood in "the body . . ." of Christ (Shell 1991).

The Rabbis insisted on the corporeality of human essence and on the centrality of physical filiation and concrete historical memory as supreme values. Consistent with their rejection of dualism in anthropology, they also rejected dualist theories of language. They thus insisted on a literal interpretation of scripture, its histories and practices. Wild as midrash may seem to us sometimes in its reconstruction of events, it is always hypothetically concrete events that it reconstructs. The Rabbis could resist being allegorized out of existence, thus maintaining the possibility of cultural specificity, at the cost, however, of an ethnocentrism that has had its unfortunate effects in history, particularly as Jews have recovered political power in the world. The disembodied universalism of Hellenistic Judaism (and ultimately of Christianity) has had its own unfortunate effects in history, as it led to such practices as forced conversion and worse. The notion of cultural dialectic allows us to put both of these formations into a situation in which they criticize each other and perhaps will help us find more adequate solutions to the problems of cultural particularity in a context of human solidarity.[8]

A similar dialectical structure can be discovered with respect to the issue of gender.

Gender Trouble and the First Century

The human body is always normatively given as already divided anatomically into two kinds, which we call sexes.[9] If human beings are defined as

8. In my work on Paul in progress, I take up these issues in much greater detail.

9. This is an admittedly positivistic notion that I cannot seem to shake. Reading Judith Butler has, to be sure, gone a way toward shaking it (Butler 1990, 25–26, 92–106, and especially 110). See also Wittig (1992, 1–8).

being their bodies, as I claim was the case for rabbinic Judaism, then sex ineluctably becomes a (if not the) central category for social practice. This has its promises as well as its problems. On the "positive" side of the ledger, sexuality was affirmed in rabbinic Judaism as an enduring aspect of the personality and as a God-given benefice to humanity both for their pleasure and well-being and for the propagation of the species, itself understood as an unmitigated good. Moreover, I claim that this affirmation largely precluded a gynecophobic abhorrence of women as "the flesh," which developed in the context of Hellenistic, dualist Judaisms. But on the negative side, this construction defined sex roles absolutely and rigidly. Women were daughters, wives, and mothers, nearly exclusively. Although the activities of study of Torah and prayer were not opposed to procreation as spirit to flesh, and although, to the best of my knowledge, there were no representations of procreation in which the male contribution was spirit and the female, matter,[10] there can be no doubt that the "upper body" was more valued than the "lower" in the culture, and upper-body activities were nearly entirely a male preserve (Eilberg-Schwartz 1991). Moreover, such women as had intellectual ability were nearly always denied access to the satisfactions afforded by intellectual life—although, as we have seen, there were some counter-voices to this exclusionary practice. Hellenistic Judaisms (including once more several forms of Christianity) reversed this socio-cultural situation. The body, sex, and procreation were seriously devalued with respect to "the spirit"—with, I would claim, some serious deformations of life—but on the other hand, women were granted access to precisely those unbodied pursuits that were defined as the province of the spirit. In particular, by choosing celibacy, women could achieve in those formations a high degree of intellectual, spiritual satisfaction and expression, at the cost of their sexuality and maternity, a cost often (but not always) figured as becoming male or sexless (Meyer 1985; Harrison 1990a and 1990b; Aspegren 1990; Castelli 1991). As Clement of Alexandria expressed it, "As then there is sameness [with men and women] with respect to the soul, she will attain to the same virtue; but as there is difference with respect to the peculiar construction of the body, she is destined for child-bearing and house-keeping" (Clement 1989b, 420; quoted in Ford 1989, 20). The implication is clear; no soul, no sameness.

---

10. One of my current research projects is to answer just such questions more definitively.

Recent gender theory has provided us with extraordinarily subtle analyses of the ways that the mind-body split is inextricably bound up with the Western discourse of gender. The work of Judith Butler is of particular importance. She argues that the critique of dualism is in fact at the heart of the founding text of modern feminist theory, Simone de Beauvoir's *The Second Sex:*

> Although Beauvoir is often understood to be calling for the right of women, in effect, to become existential subjects and hence, for inclusion within the terms of an abstract universality, her position also implies a fundamental critique of the very disembodiment of the abstract masculine epistemological subject. That subject is abstract to the extent that it disavows its socially marked embodiment and, further, projects that disavowed and disparaged embodiment on to the feminine sphere, effectively renaming the body as female. This association of the body with the female works along magical relations of reciprocity whereby the female sex becomes restricted to its body, and the male body, fully disavowed, becomes, paradoxically, the incorporeal instrument of an ostensibly radical freedom. Beauvoir's analysis implicitly poses the question: Through what act of negation and disavowal does the masculine pose as a disembodied universality and the feminine get constructed as a disavowed corporeality?
>
> (Butler 1990, 12)

What Butler has shown here is that the Western discourse of gender cannot be separated from Western metaphysics in general, a point also made definitively by Genevieve Lloyd (1984, 7 and, on de Beauvoir, 99). Thus, Philo says, "To begin with, the helper is a created one, for it says 'Let us make a helper for him': and in the next place, is subsequent to him who is to be helped, for He had formed the mind before and is about to form its helper." It is quite clear that "Man = Adam" is interpreted by Philo as "mind," while "Woman = Eve" is "body," the helper of mind. We can see quite clearly the origins of the act of negation and disavowal that Butler speaks of and its necessary complicity with a platonic dualist anthropology, adopted by Plato from earlier Greek thought (Lloyd 1984, 6), which identifies the human being as his or her (universal) mind and not his or her gendered, socially marked body. Lloyd has shown how this dualism became rewritten historically so that the universal mind came to be identified as male, while the gendered body became female (26). This dichotomy or opposition inscribes the opposition man ∼ woman in a whole series of culturally charged binary oppositions, already in Pythagoras, although the actual list has changed (3). Thus, man is to woman as:

substance:	accident
form:	matter
univocity:	division and difference
soul:	body
meaning:	language
signified:	signifier
natural:	artificial
essential:	ornamental[11]

It is quite obvious that in all of these pairs of opposed terms, the first is the privileged one in our post-platonic culture and the second marked as "supplement." Many feminist analyses of gender seem to be as bound up in that metaphysics as the discursive practices that they seek to displace.[12] Butler demonstrates the operations of the very same platonic metaphysics within the writings of an important radical feminist theorist, Monique Wittig:

> Hence, Wittig calls for the destruction of "sex" so that women can assume the status of a universal subject. On the way toward that destruction, "women" must assume both a particular and a universal point of view. As a subject who can realize concrete universality through freedom, Wittig's lesbian confirms rather than contests the normative promise of humanist ideals premised on the metaphysics of substance. In this respect, Wittig is distinguished from Irigaray, not only in terms of the now familiar oppositions between essentialism and materialism, but in terms of the adherence to a metaphysics of substance that confirms the normative model of humanism as the framework for feminism. Where it seems that Wittig has subscribed to a radical project of lesbian emancipation and enforced a distinction between "lesbian" and "woman," she does this through the defense of the pregendered "person," characterized as freedom. This move not only confirms the presocial status of human freedom, but subscribes to

11. Cf. also Bynum (1986, 257): "*Male* and *female* were contrasted and asymmetrically valued as intellect/body, active/passive, rational/irrational, reason/emotion, self-control/lust, judgment/mercy, and order/disorder."

12. See also the inscription of this dualism in the following statement: "For them [the Shakers], celibacy implied communal familial and economic systems, unified social classes, and, most important to this discussion, *equality along with genuine, spiritual (rather than false, physical) unity of males and females*" (Kitch 1989, 3, emphasis added). I am convinced and moved by Kitch's demonstration of the genuine feminist commitments of the Shakers, Koreshantists, and Sanctificationists, though the opposition between "genuine, spiritual" and "false, physical" seems to me no solution. My "old Adam," it seems, is not expunged.

that metaphysics of substance that is responsible for the production
and naturalization of the category of sex itself.

(Butler 1990, 20)

The consequence of Butler's incisive analysis is that Wittig ends up being
almost entirely a reflection of the patristic ideology of freedom as pregendered and non-gender as male. Wittig's lesbian is another version of
the woman of Hellenistic Judaism (e.g., Philo's Therapeutrides) or early
Christianity who through celibacy is made male and thus free (Wittig
1980)—though to be sure with the enormous difference that sexual pleasure is not denied Wittig's lesbian. Metaphysically speaking, nothing has
changed. Thecla and Perpetua are not women, and Wittig's lesbian is not
a woman.[13] What, however, of a human being born with a vagina, who
happens not to be a lesbian or a nun? Is she condemned to be a woman?[14]
Is being a woman always to be understood as a condemnation? The
female body is still the devalued and secondary term. Moreover, according to certain thinkers, *all* sexual activity involves domination, so that
the "destruction of sex" as a taxonomy of human bodies is not sufficient
to produce parity; there must also be an actual destruction of sexuality
itself. Andrea Dworkin poses this plight directly (if, I suspect, inadvertently) when she cites *The Gospel to the Egyptians* and writes, "it would
be in keeping with the spirit of this book to take Christ as my guide and
say with him: 'When ye trample upon the garment of shame; when the
Two become One, and Male with Female neither male nor female'"
(Dworkin 1974, 173). Dworkin is citing this passage in support of an
early vision of gender equality, little realizing, it would seem, that the
"garment of shame" to be trampled on is the body—male or female
(Macdonald 1987). Without bodies, we are indeed all equal.

I have cited these passages from Judith Butler at such length because I
think they show how current is the precise quandary of gender that the
dialectic between Hellenistic Judaism and Rabbinic Judaism sets up for
us.[15] We dwell in exactly the same tension. If we speak of a pregendered

13. Note that throughout his work, Philo explicitly contrasts "women" with "vir-
gins" (Sly 1990). Wittig also explicitly joins lesbians and nuns: "One might consider
that every woman, married or not, has a period of forced sexual service. . . . Some lesbians and nuns escape" (1992, 7).

14. Diana Fuss makes a related point when she writes, "One implication of this
ideality is that Wittig's theory is unable to account for heterosexual feminists except
to see them as victims of false consciousness" (Fuss 1989, 44).

15. The same dialectic is internal to Christianity as well, as I will suggest in a
forthcoming article, entitled "Paul and the Genealogy of Gender," *Representations* 41.

person, a universal subject—necessarily, it seems, disembodied—then we are implicitly valorizing the very metaphysics that causes all of the gender trouble in the first place, and in the bargain, problematizing (hetero)sexuality beyond retrieval. If, on the other hand, we insist on the corporeality and always already sexed quality of the human being, then it appears that we trap the human race in the (necessarily?) hierarchical category of gender.[16] Is there any way to think ourselves out of this trap? It seems to me that any solution that seeks to transcend gender is doomed to failure, while those that seek to transfigure its hierarchical structure are much more likely candidates for a transformation of actual human lives lived.

GENEROUS CRITIQUE: DE-ORIENTALIZING CULTURAL HISTORY

The "payoff" of this research from the critical point of view seems to me the discovery that even the androcentrism of the rabbinic social forma-tion was not entirely successful or monolithic. (I suspect that this is true for virtually any culture.) In two central chapters, I have argued that there were significant oppositional practices to the hegemony of the dominant discourse preserved in the canonical texts. One of these involves the suggestion that at least at the margins of social practice, and maybe even in more central practice, there were important ways in which women were autonomous or participated in highly valued cultural activi-ties, such as studying Torah. Since such participation would have been threatening to the dominant male ideology, there was a determined attempt to suppress its memory, as we have seen in the story of Beruria, the female talmudist discussed in Chapter 6 of this book. This brings my

16. I say "necessarily?" because empirically it seems that no society has yet been found in which gender is not a hierarchical category. I am holding out some hope here that that empirical fact is factitious, that is, contingent on specific historical, material conditions. The fact, then, for instance, that rabbinic Judaism, as I am arguing, does not found its gender practices on a *theory* of essential difference between female and male may hold out more hope for change in a changed material world than we realize. Once again, the question of whether hierarchy is a necessary or merely contingent consequence of "intercourse" remains (for me) open. I certainly hope that it is the lat-ter. See also Kitch (1989, 23–73) and especially her comment, "In fact, women's exclusion from cultural prestige systems is a direct result of reproductive/sexual rela-tionships to men" (32).

analysis in line with the methods of the late John Winkler, who in his work on classical Greece has constructed a somewhat less bleak situation for women than the male texts would have us believe:

> The more we learn about comparable gender-segregated, pre-industrial societies, particularly in the Mediterranean area, the more it seems that most of men's observations and moral judgments about women and sex and so forth have minimal descriptive validity and are best understood as coffeehouse talk, addressed to men themselves. Women, we should emphasize, in all their separate groupings by age, neighborhood, and class, may differ widely from each other and from community to community in the degree to which they obey, resist, or even notice the existence of such palaver as men indulge in when going through their bonding rituals. To know when any such male law-givers—medical, moral, or marital, whether smart or stupid—are (to put it bluntly) bluffing or spinning fantasies or justifying their 'druthers is so hard that most historians of ideas—Foucault, for all that he is exceptional is no exception here—never try.
>
> (Winkler 1989, 6)

The interests of the masculist hegemony were not served by preserving records of female autonomy. Discovery of such female autonomy, or rather, its re-construction, constitutes a point of resistance to the dominant, present hegemonies as well, in this case the ones of many segments of rabbinic orthodoxy (not all) that still wish to exclude women from full cultural participation.

Furthermore, the very discordant or antithetical memories were produced and preserved in the androcentric, male-authored texts. They represent, therefore, a voice of male struggle (however nascent and inadequate from our perspective) against the ideology of gender asymmetry, "a breaking of [cultural] context," to use Rachel Adler's evocative terms (Adler 1988). It is this very rudimentary oppositional practice in the early culture that gives us the power now to redeem and reclaim a usable past. In the other of these two chapters on opposition to dominant gender discourse (Chapter 5), I have tried to show that there was significant male opposition to the institution of extended marital separations, a practice that erases recognition of female subjectivity and desire almost entirely, and that this opposition was grounded in an empathetic thinking beyond male cultural power or even rigid gender-based hierarchy. The opposition did not succeed in dislodging the hierarchy, nor realistically did it even truly imagine an alternative, but it did suggest internal sub-versions.[17] I am not arguing that there is no problem for us with talmudic gender practice, because there was a Beruria, and therefore we see that women could study Torah, or because we can show that an aggadic passage stood in opposition to a practice that we find disturbing, or that a single voice in the Talmud recognized women's parity with men in the expression of sexual desire. Undoubtedly, women did not often study Torah in the talmudic period, a situation that manifests a set of role definitions reinforcing gender asymmetry and hierarchy. Many husbands then, and even more later, did indeed leave their wives for years on end to pursue intellectual and religious aims, and women were trained to be modest and silent about their sexuality. The exceptions, as it were, only prove the rule. But, and this is the crux of my argument, on the margins of that dominant and hegemonic discourse, there was something else happening. There were some women who were breaking the mold, and also some men who were uncomfortable, who even opposed the dominant ideology. Those perhaps marginal men and women can become for us prototypes in a reformation of traditional Jewish gender practices that nevertheless finds itself rooted firmly in the talmudic text and tradition. Once more, the dominant hegemony seeks to strike such cracks and fissures, to erase the sub-versions from the cultural record, but it is unsuccessful, leaving us a place to creep back into.[18] I would suggest that the same is true of any ancient culture that is powerfully formative of our own.

Reading texts as only misogynistic thus can in itself be a misogynistic gesture; conversely, seeking to recover "feminist," that is resistant or even oppositional, voices in ancient texts can be an act of appropriation of those ancient texts for political change. This does not imply in any way a denial of the patriarchy (if not misogyny) of the hegemonic practices of the culture. The texts when read in the way that I am proposing to read them do not only reflect a dissident proto-feminist voice within Classical Judaism; they constitute and institute such a voice. This is manifestly the case with reference to the Talmud, which is regarded as an authoritative source for social practice by many Jewish collectives up to this day.

Women in rabbinic culture are imagined as enablers of men, providing for their sexual and procreative needs, as I concluded in Chapter 3.

17. I owe this brilliant coinage to Chana Kronfeld.
18. The wonderful image of cultural change as a "creeping back" into history is Mieke Bal's.

Abomination of women, fear of sexuality and of the body, on the other hand, are only minor themes in this cultural formation, when they are studied in their textual and cultural contexts. Their promotion to a central and major role is an artifact of later readings of the culture that suppress the rabbinic dissensus, as I have also argued. If the sexuality of women, however, is not represented in general as fearful or abominable by the texts of the men of rabbinic culture, neither are women empowered by that culture. The cultural reward of this analysis is not, then, in the discovery or recovery of a golden age in the past, still less in the awarding of relative values to different forms of late-antique culture. Indeed, I would claim that all such attempts are both doomed to failure and inevitably triumphalistic in effect, whether they are attempts to find feminist Paradise in paganism before the coming of the Jews, in Jesus or in Paul vis-à-vis the Jews (see von Kellenbach 1990 for extensive documentation), or in Jewish culture in comparison to Christian. Nonetheless, even if we have not succeeded in discovering cultural formations in the past that did empower women equally with men, the very fact that we can show that the different androcentric formations functioned in entirely different fashions at different times and places provides a kind of demystifying historicization, showing that each was contingent and specific and that all are equally unsettled from the position of trans-historical natural status. If my argument is persuasive that rabbinic Jewish culture did not base its gender asymmetry on an instinctive, atavistic fear of women's bodies or sexuality, then we must look *in general* somewhere else for the origins of androcentrism in all and any cultures.[19] This suggests at least to me that the question of the near universality of gender asymmetry in culture will need to be answered by materialist and historical models and not grounded in universal trans-historical structures in the human psyche. The historicist project, I believe, holds out much more hope for change.

By material conditions, I mean here the conditions of human reproduction and child-rearing within hunter-gatherer and later agrarian societies. Certain psychoanalytic discourses have tended to naturalize misogyny by locating its sources in an eternal psychic drama of infancy. What I am suggesting, then, is that by disabling that (perhaps obsolete

19. Note that this does not preclude the possibility that within a given cultural formation, or even within many such formations, men are socialized into a fearful attitude toward the female body; my argument is only that such fear is culturally specific and not species-bound.

even among psychoanalytic theorists) approach to male dominance, one
that derives it from a primitive and universal male fear of the female
body, we denaturalize male domination and come to understand it as a
historically derived condition, a condition that could change in history as
well (Bloch 1991a, 1). Our very psyches are formed in historical, socio-
cultural conditions through the discursive practices in which we are socialized (including ideation—ideas are thus material facts as well).[20] We
take as natural and universal certain psychic inclinations, which can be
shown to be culture-specific.[21] Psychoanalysis may have produced, indeed seems to have produced, an account of the formation of the psyche
in our culture; its claims to transcultural adequacy, however, are not
ineluctable.[22] Although in this book I have not made any case or argument for the specific material determinants of male dominance in
ancient Judaism, I believe that I have shown that the sort of psychoanalytic explanation that locates male dominance systems in allegedly universal fears of female power going back to earliest childhood are invalid
for this culture—and thus for all, because such theories only derive their
explanatory power from the very claim to universal applicability. Other
cross-cultural studies also support this questioning of the location of male

20. This sentence was inspired by remarks made by Carol Delaney at Stanford
University, when I presented this text to a cultural studies colloquium there. Of
course, she is not responsible for the actual form that her inspiration took here.

21. Camille Paglia's work (1990) is an excellent example of how this error is per-
petuated in a context that is not explicitly psychoanalytic; she insists on generalizing
that which is found in our Western (broadly understood) cultural formation to all of
humanity by assuming that it is an essential, psychic reality.

22. I have been properly chastized (as the book goes to press) by Ruth Stein, who
writes in a letter of November 25, 1991:

> I agree that the claim that cultural and historical phenomena can be explained
> wholly or even mostly by psychoanalytic tools is foolish. Nevertheless, I find
> that in such areas as literary theory, cultural theory, etc. one very often talks of
> psychoanalysis in a very loose, undiscerning, and not updated way, and when-
> ever I read such general(izing) statements about psychoanalysis, I automatically
> hear myself asking "*which* psychoanalysis?"

Stein is undoubtedly correct. I am *not* attempting here to discredit psychoanalysis,
a practice that has benefited me beyond description, but only to challenge a certain
model of explanation for male domination once very current in psychoanalytic circles
and still, I think unfortunately, alive, to wit, that men universally fear, reject, loathe
women's bodies because of the experiences of early childhood. I am convinced that
such loathing is not a psychic universal but a cultural production, and to the extent
that psychoanalytic thinkers no longer hold such views, my descriptive terms need
modifying.

dominance deep in the universal male psyche (duBois 1988; see also Gottlieb 1989). I simply do not see in the talmudic texts a culture of men afraid of female power or of female sexuality, but I do see a culture in which men dominated women to ensure that male corporeal needs for sex and progeny would be met efficiently. Again, I am not arguing that misogyny was not present within the rabbinic culture, but only that it does not seem to have been a key symbol (Ortner 1973), as it seems to have been in some Hellenistic formations. A consequence of my discussion in this book, then, is that certain arrangements of gender asymmetry in culture may not be as intractable to determined desire for change as might at first appear to be the case in light of their apparent ubiquitousness. Material conditions gave them rise, and changing material situations can create the conditions for dislodging them. I hope to have shown here in some small way how one culture might find within itself the resources with which to preserve itself and continue its vitality while making also the necessary changes. And this, to me, is the task of a redemptive and consciousness-raising cultural critique.

Bibliography

Adler, Rachel
  1988   The Virgin in the Brothel and Other Anomalies: Character and
          Context in the Legend of Beruriah. *Tikkun* 3.
Alexandre, Monique
  1988   *Le Commencement du Livre Genèse I-V: La Version Grecque de la
          Septante et sa Réception*. Ed. P. Nautin. Christianisme Antique.
          Paris: Beauchesne Editeur.
Alon, Gedalyahu
  1977   *Jews, Judaism and the Classical World: Studies in Jewish History in the
          Times of the Second Temple and Talmud*. Trans. Israel Abrahams.
          Jerusalem: Magnes Press.
Anderson, Gary
  1989   Celibacy or Consummation in the Garden? Reflections on Early
          Jewish and Christian Interpretations of the Garden of Eden. *Harvard
          Theological Review* 82:121–48.
Archer, Léonie J.
  1983   "The Role of Jewish Women in the Religion, Ritual and Cult of
          Graeco-Roman Palestine." In *Images of Women in Antiquity*, ed.
          Averil Cameron and Amélie Kuhrt, 273–88. Detroit: Wayne State
          University Press.
Aschkenasy, Nehama
  1986   *Eve's Journey: Feminine Images in Hebraic Literary Tradition*.
          Philadelphia: University of Pennsylvania Press.
Aspegren, Kerstin
  1990   *The Male Woman: A Feminine Ideal in the Early Church*. Ed. Reneé
          Kieffer. Uppsala Women's Studies: Women in Religion. Stockholm:
          Almqvist & Wiksell International.
Astel, Ann W.
  1990   *The Song of Songs in the Middle Ages*. Ithaca, N.Y.: Cornell
          University Press.
Augustine
          Tractatus adversus Judaeos.
Bakhtin, Mikhail
  1984   *Rabelais and His World*. Trans. Hélène Iswolsky. Bloomington:
          Indiana University Press.
Bal, Mieke
  1987   *Lethal Love*. Indiana Studies in Biblical Literature. Bloomington:
          Indiana University Press.

1988a   *Death and Dissymmetry*. Chicago: University of Chicago Press.

1988b   *Murder and Difference: Gender, Genre, and Scholarship on Sisera's Death*. Indiana Studies in Biblical Literature. Bloomington: Indiana University Press.

1990   The Point of Narratology. *Poetics Today* 11:727–54.

1991   Lots of Writing. *Semeia* 54:77–102.

Beer, Moses

1980   The Hereditary Principle in Jewish Leadership. *Immanuel* 10:57–61.

Beer, Moshe

1976   The Sons of Moses in Rabbinic Lore. *Bar-Ilan: University Yearbook of Judaic Studies and the Humanities* 13:149–57.

Biale, David

1986   Eros and Enlightenment: Love Against Marriage in the East-European Jewish Enlightenment. *Polin* 1:49–67.

1989   From Intercourse to Discourse: Control of Sexuality in Rabbinic Literature. Paper Presented at Center for Hermeneutical Studies Colloquium 60, Berkeley.

1991   Ejaculatory Prayer: The Displacement of Sexuality in Chasidism. *Tikkun* 6:21–28.

1992   *Eros and the Jews: From Biblical Israel to Contemporary America*. New York: Basic Books.

Biale, Rachel

1984   *Women and Jewish Law: An Exploration of Women's Issues in Halakhic Sources*. New York: Schocken Books.

Bialik, Haim Nahman

1951   *Sefer ha'aggadah* [Hebrew]. Tel-Aviv: D'vir.

Bloch, R. Howard

1987   Medieval Misogyny. *Representations* 20:1–25.

1991a   *Medieval Misogyny and the Invention of Western Romantic Love*. Chicago: University of Chicago Press.

1991b   "Mieux Vaut Jamais Que Tard": Romance, Philology, and Old French Letters. *Representations* 36:64–86.

Borgen, Peder

1965   *Bread from Heaven*. Leiden: E. J. Brill.

1980   "Observations on the Theme 'Paul and Philo': Paul's Preaching of Circumcision in Galatia (Gal. 5:11) and Debates on Circumcision in Philo." In *The Pauline Literature and Theology,* ed. Sigfred Pedersen, 85–102. Teologiske Studier. Århus: Forlaget Aros.

Bowersock, G. W.

1990   *Hellenism in Late Antiquity*. Jerome Lectures, no. 18. Ann Arbor: University of Michigan Press.

Boyarin, Daniel

1987   Two Introductions to the Midrash on Song of Songs. *Tarbiz* 56:479–501.

1989   Language Inscribed by History on the Bodies of Living Beings: Midrash and Martyrdom. *Representations* 25:139–51.

1990a   Diachrony Against Synchrony: The Legend of Beruria. *Jerusalem Studies in Jewish Folklore*.

1990b   The Eye in the Torah: Ocular Desire in Midrashic Hermeneutic. *Critical Inquiry* 16:532–50.

1990c   *Intertextuality and the Reading of Midrash*. Bloomington: Indiana University Press.

1990d   The Politics of Biblical Narratology: Reading the Bible Like/As a Woman. *diacritics* 20:31–42.

1991   Literary Fat Rabbis: On the Historical Origins of the Grotesque Body. *Journal of the History of Sexuality* 1:551–84.

1992   "This We Know to Be the Carnal Israel": Circumcision and the Erotic Life of God and Israel. *Critical Inquiry* 18:474–505.

1993a   "Take the Bible for Example: Midrash as Literary Theory." In *The Use and Abuse of Examples*, ed. Alexander Gelley. Stanford: Stanford University Press.

1993b   "Rabbinic Resistance to Male Domination: A Case Study in Talmudic Cultural Poetics." In *Critical Jewish Hermeneutics*, ed. Steven Kepnes. New York: New York University Press.

Brooten, Bernadette

1982   *Women Leaders in the Ancient Synagogue: Inscriptional Evidence and Background Issues*. Brown Judaic Studies, no. 36. Chico, Calif.: Scholars Press.

Brown, Peter

1983   The Saint as Exemplar in Late Antiquity. *Representations* 2:1–25.

1987   "Late Antiquity." In *A History of Private Life*, ed. Philippe Ariès and Georges Duby. Vol. 1, *From Pagan Rome to Byzantium*. Ed. Paul Veyne and trans. Arthur Goldhammer, 235–311. Cambridge: Belknap Press of Harvard University Press.

1988   *The Body and Society: Men, Women and Sexual Renunciation in Early Christianity*. Lectures on the History of Religions, vol. 13. New York: Columbia University Press.

Bruns, Gerald

1987   "Midrash and Allegory." In *The Literary Guide to the Bible*, ed. Robert Alter and Frank Kermode, 625–46. Cambridge: Harvard University Press.

1990   "The Hermeneutics of Midrash." In *The Book and the Text: The Bible and Literary Theory*, ed. Regina Schwartz, 189–213. Oxford: Basil Blackwell.

Bruns, J. Edgar

1973   Philo Christianus: The Debris of a Legend. *Harvard Theological Review* 66:141–45.

Buber, Solomon, ed.

1964   *Midrash Tanhuma*. Jerusalem: Ortsel Press.

Buckley, Thomas, and Alma Gottlieb

1988   "A Critical Appraisal of Theories of Menstrual Symbolism." In *Blood Magic: The Anthropology of Menstruation*, ed. Thomas

Buckley and Alma Gottlieb, 1–50. Berkeley and Los Angeles: University of California Press.

Buckley, Thomas, and Alma Gottlieb, eds.

    1988   *Blood Magic: The Anthropology of Menstruation.* Berkeley and Los Angeles: University of California Press.

Butler, Judith

    1990   *Gender Trouble: Feminism and the Subversion of Identity.* Thinking Gender. London: Routledge.

Bynum, Caroline Walker

    1986   "'. . . And Woman His Humanity': Female Imagery in the Religious Writing of the Later Middle Ages." In *Gender and Religion: On the Complexity of Symbols,* ed. Caroline Walker Bynum, Stevan Harrell, and Paula Richman, 257–89. Boston: Beacon Press.

    1991   "Material Continuity, Personal Survival and the Resurrection of the Body: A Scholastic Discussion in Its Medieval and Modern Contexts." In *Fragmentation and Redemption: Essays on Gender and the Human Body in Medieval Religion,* 239–98, 393–417. New York: Zone Books.

Cantarella, Eva

    1987   *Pandora's Daughters: The Role and Status of Women in Greek and Roman Antiquity.* Trans. Maureen B. Fant. Baltimore: Johns Hopkins University Press.

Caspary, Gerard E.

    1979   *Politics and Exegesis: Origen and the Two Swords.* Berkeley and Los Angeles: University of California Press.

Castelli, Elizabeth

    1986   Virginity and Its Meaning for Women's Sexuality in Early Christianity. *Journal of Feminist Studies in Religion* 2:61–88.

    1991   "'I Will Make Mary Male': Pieties of the Body and Gender Transformation of Christian Women in Late Antiquity." In *Body Guards: The Cultural Politics of Ambiguity,* ed. Julia Epstein and Kristina Straub, 29–49. New York: Routledge.

Chadwick, Henry

    1966   St. Paul and Philo of Alexandria. *Bulletin of the John Rylands Library* 48:286–307.

Chamberlain, Lori

    1991   Consent After Liberalism? A Review Essay of Catharine MacKinnon's *Toward a Feminist Theory of the State* and Carole Pateman's *The Sexual Contract. Genders* 11:111–25.

Chambers, Ross

    1991   *Room for Maneuver: Reading (the) Oppositional (in) Narrative.* Chicago: University of Chicago Press.

Chrysostom, John

    1986   *On Marriage and Family Life.* Trans. Catherine Roth and David Anderson. Crestwood, N.Y.: St. Vladimir's Seminary Press.

Clark, Elizabeth A.

    1986   "Ascetic Renunciation and Feminine Advancement: A Paradox of

Late Ancient Christianity." In *Ascetic Piety and Women's Faith: Essays in Late Ancient Christianity*, 175–208. New York: Edwin Mellen Press.

Clement of Alexandria

1989a   "The Instructor." In *The Fathers of the Second Century*, ed. Alexander Roberts and James Donaldson, 207–98. The Antenicene fathers. Grand Rapids, Mich.: Wm. B. Eerdmans.

1989b   "The Stromata, or Miscellanies." In *The Fathers of the Second Century*, ed. Alexander Roberts and James Donaldson, 299–568. The Ante-nicene fathers. Grand Rapids, Mich.: Wm. B. Eerdmans.

Cohen, Jeremy

1989   *"Be Fertile and Increase, Fill the Earth and Master It": The Ancient and Medieval Career of a Biblical Text*. Ithaca, N.Y.: Cornell University Press.

Cohen, Shaye J. D.

1980   Women in Synagogues in Antiquity. *Conservative Judaism* 34:23–29.

1991   "Menstruants and the Sacred in Judaism and Christianity." In *Women's History and Ancient History*, ed. Sarah B. Pomeroy, 273–99. Chapel Hill: University of North Carolina Press.

Collins, John J.

1985   "A Symbol of Otherness: Circumcision and Salvation in the First Century." In *"To See Ourselves as Others See Us": Christians, Jews, "Others" in Late Antiquity*, ed. Jacob Neusner, Ernest S. Frerichs, and Caroline McCracken-Flesher, 163–86. Scholars Press Studies in the Humanities. Chico, Calif.: Scholars Press.

Conzelmann, Hans

1976   *"1 Corinthians: A Commentary on the First Epistle to the Corinthians."* In *Hermeneia — a Critical and Historical Commentary on the Bible*, trans. James W. Leitch; bibliography and references prepared by James W. Dunkly; ed. George W. S. J. MacRae. Philadelphia: Fortress Press.

Crouzel, Henri

1989   *Origen: The Life and Thought of the First Great Theologian*. Trans. A. S. Worrall. Edinburgh: T & T Clark.

Daube, David

1973   *The New Testament and Rabbinic Judaism*. New York: Arno Press.

1977   *The Duty of Procreation*. Edinburgh: Edinburgh University Press.

Davis, Laurie

1991   Beruriah: Exploring Gender in Rabbinic Writings. Unpublished paper, Berkeley.

Dillon, John

1977   *The Middle Platonists: 80 B.C. to A.D. 220*. Ithaca, N.Y.: Cornell University Press.

Dodds, E. R.

1965   *Pagan and Christian in an Age of Anxiety: Some Aspects of Religious*

Experience from Marcus Aurelius to Constantine. Cambridge: Cambridge University Press.

Dreyfus, Hubert, and Paul Rabinow

1983   *Michel Foucault: Beyond Structuralism and Hermeneutics*. Chicago: University of Chicago Press.

duBois, Page

1988   *Sowing the Body: Psychoanalysis and Ancient Representations of Women*. Women in Culture and Society. Chicago: University of Chicago Press.

Dunn, James D. G.

1990   *Jesus, Paul and the Law: Studies in Mark and Galatians*. Louisville, Ky.: Westminster/John Knox Press.

1991   "The Theology of Galatians: The Issue of Covenantal Nomism." In *Pauline Theology*, ed. Jouette M. Bassler. Vol. 1, 125–46. Minneapolis: Fortress Press.

Dworkin, Andrea

1974   *Woman Hating*. New York: E. P. Dutton.

Eilberg-Schwartz, Howard

1989   Re-organizing the Body: The Demotion of the Penis in the Emergence of Judaism. Paper presented at American Ethnological Society, New Orleans.

1990a   Damned If You Do and Damned If You Don't: Rabbinic Ambivalence Toward Sex and the Body. Paper presented at Center for Hermeneutical Studies Colloquium 61, Berkeley.

1990b   *The Savage in Judaism: An Anthropology of Israelite Religion and Ancient Judaism*. Bloomington: Indiana University Press.

1991   The Nakedness of a Woman's Voice, the Pleasure in a Man's Mouth: An Oral History of Ancient Judaism. Paper presented at Annenberg Research Institute's Colloquium, "Women in Religion and Society," Philadelphia.

Epstein, Jacob Nahum Halevy

1964   *Introduction to the Text of the Mishna*. Jerusalem: Magnes Press.

Fineman, Joel

1989   "The History of the Anecdote: Fiction and Fiction." In *The New Historicism*, ed. H. Aram Veeser, 49–76. New York: Routledge.

Finkelstein, Louis

1964 [1936]   *Akiba: Scholar, Saint and Martyr*. New York: Macmillan [Atheneum].

Fiorenza, Elizabeth Schüssler

1983   *In Memory of Her: A Feminist Theological Reconstruction of Christian Origins*. New York: Crossroad.

Ford, David Carlton

1989   Misogynist or Advocate? St. John Chrysostom and His Views on Women. Ph.D. diss., Drew University.

Foucault, Michel

1980   *The History of Sexuality*. Vol. 1, An Introduction. Trans. Robert Hurley. New York: Random House, Vintage.

1983   Afterword. In *Michel Foucault: Beyond Structuralism and Hermeneutics*, ed. Hubert Dreyfus and Paul Rabinow. Chicago: University of Chicago Press.

1986a   *The History of Sexuality*. Vol. 3, *The Care of the Self*. Trans. Robert Hurley. New York: Random House, Vintage.

1986b   *The History of Sexuality*. Vol. 2, *The Use of Pleasure*. Trans. Robert Hurley. New York: Random House, Vintage.

Fox, Robin Lane

1987   *Pagans and Christians*. New York: Alfred A. Knopf.

Fraade, Steven D.

1986   "Ascetical Aspects of Ancient Judaism." In *Jewish Spirituality*, ed. Arthur Green. World Spirituality: An Encyclopedic History of the Religious Quest. New York: Crossroad.

1991   *From Tradition to Commentary: Torah and Its Interpretation in the Midrash Sifre to Deuteronomy*. Judaica: Hermeneutics, Mysticism, and Religion. Albany: State University of New York Press.

Fränkel, Yonah

1981   *Readings in the Spiritual World of the Stories of the Aggada*. Tel-Aviv: United Kibbutz Press.

Frazer, R. M., trans. and ed.

1983   *The Poems of Hesiod*. Norman: University of Oklahoma Press.

Friedman, Mordechai A.

1990   Tamar, A Symbol of Life: The "Killer Wife" Superstition in the Bible and Jewish Tradition. *AJS Review* 15:23–62.

Friedman, Shamma

1985   "Literary Development and Historicity in the Aggadic Narrative of the Babylonian Talmud: A Study Based Upon B.M. 83b–86a." In *Community and Culture: Essays in Jewish Studies in Honor of the 90th Anniversary of Gratz College*, ed. Nahum W. Waldman., 67–80. Philadelphia: Gratz College.

1989   "Towards the Historical Aggada of the Babylonian Talmud." In *The Saul Lieberman Memorial Volume*, ed. Shamma Friedman, 4–14. Jerusalem: The Jewish Theological Seminary. Preprint.

Friedman, Simha

1983   "The Study of Torah for Contemporary Women." In *Women in the Sources of Judaism* (in Hebrew), 53–67. Jerusalem: n.p.

Frontisi-Ducroux, Françoise, and François Lissarrague

1990   "From Ambiguity to Ambivalence: A Dionysiac Excursion Through the 'Anakreontic' Vases." In *Before Sexuality: The Construction of Erotic Experience in the Ancient Greek World*, ed. David M. Halperin, John J. Winkler, and Froma Zeitlin, 211–56. Princeton: Princeton University Press.

Fuss, Diana

1989   *Essentially Speaking: Feminism, Nature & Difference*. New York: Routledge.

Gafni, Isaiah M.

1986/7   "'Scepter and Staff': Concerning New Forms of Leadership in the

Period of the Talmud in the Land of Israel and Babylonia." In *Priesthood and Kingdom: The Relations of Religion and State in Judaism and the Gentiles*, ed. I. Gafni and G. Motzkin, 84–91. Jerusalem: Zalman Shazar Center.

1989   "The Institution of Marriage in Rabbinic Times." In *The Jewish Family: Metaphor and Memory*, ed. David Kraemer, 13–30. Oxford: Oxford University Press.

Gager, John

1982   Body-symbolism and Social Reality: Resurrection, Incarnation, and Asceticism in Early Christianity. *Religion* 12:345–64.

1983   *The Origins of Anti-Semitism*. New York: Oxford University Press.

Gammie, J. G.

1974   Spatial and Ethical Dualism in Jewish Wisdom and Apocalyptic Literature. *Journal of Biblical Literature* 93:365–85.

Gardella, Peter

1985   *Innocent Ecstasy: How Christianity Gave America an Ethic of Sexual Pleasure*. Oxford: Oxford University Press.

Gaston, Lloyd

1987   *Paul and the Torah*. Vancouver: University of British Columbia Press.

Gleason, Maud

1990   "The Semiotics of Gender." In *Before Sexuality: The Construction of Erotic Experience in the Ancient Greek World*, ed. David M. Halperin, John J. Winkler, and Froma Zeitlin, 389–415. Princeton: Princeton University Press.

Goldin, Judah, trans.

1955   *The Fathers According to Rabbi Nathan*. Yale Judaica Series, vol. 10. New Haven: Yale University Press.

Goodblatt, David

1975   The Beruriah Traditions. *Journal of Jewish Studies* 26:68–86.

Goshen-Gottstein, Alon

1991   The Body as Image of God in Rabbinic Literature. Paper presented at People of the Body/People of the Book, Berkeley.

Gottlieb, Alma

1989   Rethinking Female Pollution: The Beng of Côte D'Ivoire. *Dialectical Anthropology* 14:65–81.

Green, William Scott

1978   "What's in a Name? The Problematic of Rabbinic Biography." In vol. 1 of *Approaches to Ancient Judaism: Theory and Practice*, 77–96. Brown Judaic Studies, no. 1. Missoula, Mont.: Scholars Press.

Greenblatt, Stephen J.

1990   "Towards a Poetics of Culture." In *Learning to Curse: Essays in Early Modern Culture*, 146–60. New York: Routledge.

Griffin, M. T.

1976   *Seneca: A Philosopher in Politics*. Oxford: Clarendon.

Hadarshan, Shim'on

1960   *Numbers Rabbah*. Tel-Aviv: Moriah.

Hadas, Moses, ed. and trans.

    1953   *Three Greek Romances*. Garden City, N.Y.: Doubleday.

Haeri, Shahla

    1989   *Law of Desire: Temporary Marriage in Shi'i Iran*. Contemporary Issues in the Middle East. Syracuse: Syracuse University Press.

Handelman, Susan

    1982   *The Slayers of Moses: The Emergence of Rabbinic Interpretation in Modern Literary Theory*. Albany: State University of New York Press.

Hanson, Ann Ellis

    1990   "The Medical Writers' Woman." In *Before Sexuality: The Construction of Erotic Experience in the Ancient Greek World*, ed. David M. Halperin, John J. Winkler, and Froma Zeitlin, 309–38. Princeton: Princeton University Press.

Harrison, Verna E. F.

    1990a   Allegory and Asceticism in Gregory of Nyssa. *Semeia* 57:113–30.

    1990b   Male and Female in Cappadocian Theology. *Journal of Theological Studies* 41:441–71.

    Forthcoming   A Gender Reversal in Gregory of Nyssa's First Homily on The Song of Songs. Paper presented at Eleventh International Conference on Patristic Studies, Oxford, 19–24 August, 1991. *Studia Patristica*.

Heath, Stephen

    1987   "Male Feminism." In *Men in Feminism*, ed. Alice Jardine and Paul Smith, 1–32. New York: Methuen.

Hecht, R.

    1984   "The Exegetical Contexts of Philo's Interpretation of Circumcision." In *Nourished with Peace: Studies in Hellenistic Judaism in Memory of Samuel Sandmel*, ed. F. Greenspan, E. Hilgert, and Burton Mack, 51–79. Chico, Calif.: Scholars Press.

Heinemann, Joseph

    1971   The Proem in the Aggadic Midrashim: A Form-critical Study. *Scripta hierosolymita* 22:100–122. Jerusalem: Magnes Press.

Higgins, Jean M.

    1976   The Myth of Eve: The Temptress. *Journal of the American Academy of Religion* 44:639–47.

Hirshman, Marc

    1992   Polemic Literary Units in the Classical Midrashim and Justin Martyr's *Dialogue with Trypho*. *Jewish Quarterly Review*, forthcoming.

Hodge, Robert

    1990   *Literature as Discourse: Textual Strategies in English and History*. Baltimore: Johns Hopkins University Press.

Hoshen, Dalia

    1990   The Fire-Symbol in the Literature of the Sages. Diss., Bar-Ilan University.

Huet, Marie-Helen
  1983   Living Images: Monstrosity and Representation. *Representations*
              4:73–87.
Idel, Moshe
  1989   "Sexual Metaphors and Praxis in the Kabbalah." In *The Jewish
              Family: Metaphor and Memory*, ed. David Kraemer, 197–224.
              Oxford: Oxford University Press.
  1990   *Golem: Jewish Magical and Mystical Traditions on the Artificial
              Anthropoid*. Judaica: Hermeneutics, Mysticism, and Religion.
              Albany: State University of New York Press.
Jaeger, Werner
  1961   *Early Christianity and Greek Paideia*. Cambridge: Belknap Press of
              Harvard University Press.
Jardine, Alice, and Paul Smith, eds.
  1987   *Men in Feminism*. New York: Routledge.
Jones, Kathleen B.
  1990   Citizenship in a Woman-friendly Polity. *Signs* 15:781–812.
Justin Martyr
  1956   "Dialogue with Trypho a Jew." In *The Ante-nicene Fathers*, trans.
              and ed. Alexander Roberts and James Donaldson. Grand Rapids,
              Mich.: Wm. B. Eerdmans.
Kalonymos, Yehuda ben
  1963   *The Genealogy of the Tannaim and Amoraim*. Ed. Y. L. Fischman.
              Jerusalem: Mossad Harav Kook.
Kee, Howard Clark, trans.
  1983   "Testaments of the Twelve Patriarchs, the Sons of Jacob the
              Patriarch." In *The Old Testament Pseudepigrapha and the New Tes-
              tament*. Vol. 1, *Apocalyptic Literature and Testaments*, ed. James H.
              Charlesworth. Cambridge, U.K.: Cambridge University Press.
King, Karen L.
  1988   "Sophia and Christ in the *Apocryphon of John*." In *Images of the
              Feminine in Gnosticism*, ed. Karen L. King, 158–76. Philadelphia:
              Fortress Press.
Kitch, Sally L.
  1989   *Chaste Liberation: Celibacy and Female Cultural Status*. Urbana:
              University of Illinois Press.
Klein-Braslavy, Sarah
  1986   *Maimonides' Interpretation of the Adam Stories in Genesis: A Study
              in Maimonides' Anthropology*. Jerusalem: Magnes Press.
Knight, Chris
  1988   "Menstrual Synchrony and the Australian Rainbow Snake." In
              Blood Magic: The Anthropology of Menstruation, ed. Thomas
              Buckley and Alma Gottlieb, 232–55. Berkeley and Los Angeles:
              University of California Press.
Kraemer, David
  1990   *The Mind of the Talmud: An Intellectual History of the Bavli*. Oxford:
              Oxford University Press.

Kraemer, Ross
  1989   Monastic Jewish Women in Greco-Roman Egypt: Philo Judaeus on
          the Therapeutrides. *Signs* 14:342–70.
  1992   *Her Share of the Blessings: Women's Religion Among Pagans, Jews
          and Christians in the Greco-Roman World.* Oxford: Oxford
          University Press.
Kugel, James
  1981   *The Idea of Biblical Poetry.* New Haven: Yale University Press.
Lachs, Samuel Tobias
  1974   The Pandora-Eve Motif in Rabbinic Literature. *Harvard Theological
          Review* 67:341–45.
Leaney, A. R. C.
  1966   *The Rule of Qumran and Its Meaning: Introduction, Translation and
          Commentary.* The New Testament Library. London: SCM Press.
Lichtenstein, Jacqueline
  1987   Making up Representation: The Risks of Femininity. *Representations*
          20:77–88.
Lightfoot, J. B., and J. R. Harmer, trans.
  1956 [London: 1893]   *The Apostolic Fathers.* 2d ed. Rev. Michael W.
          Holmes. Grand Rapids, Mich.: Baker Book House.
Lissarrague, François
  1990   "The Sexual Life of Satyrs." In *Before Sexuality: The Construction
          of Erotic Experience in the Ancient Greek World,* ed. David M.
          Halperin, John J. Winkler, and Froma Zeitlin, 53–81. Princeton:
          Princeton University Press.
Lloyd, G. E. R.
  1983   *Science, Folklore and Ideology: Studies in the Life Sciences in Ancient
          Greece.* Cambridge, U.K.: Cambridge University Press.
Lloyd, Genevieve
  1984   *The Man of Reason: "male" and "female" in Western Philosophy.*
          Minneapolis: University of Minnesota Press.
Loraux, Nicole
  1981   "Sur la race des femmes et quelques-unes de ses tribus." In *Les
          enfants d'athena: idées athéniennes sur la citoyenneté et la division des
          sexes,* 75–117. Paris: François Maspero.
  1990   "Herakles: The Super-male and the Feminine." In *Before Sexuality:
          The Construction of Erotic Experience in the Ancient Greek World,*
          ed. David M. Halperin, John J. Winkler, and Froma Zeitlin, 21–52.
          Princeton: Princeton University Press.
McArthur, Harvey
  1987   Celibacy in Judaism at the Time of Christian Beginnings. *Andrews
          University Seminary Studies* 25:163–81.
Macdonald, Dennis Ronald
  1987   *There is No Male and Female: The Fate of a Dominical Saying in Paul
          and Gnosticism.* Harvard Dissertations in Religion. Philadelphia:
          Fortress Press.
  1988   "Corinthian Veils and Gnostic Androgynes." In *Images of the*

Feminine in Gnosticism, ed. Karen L. King, 276–92. Philadelphia:
Fortress Press.

McEleney, Neil J., C.S.P.

1974   Conversion, Circumcision and the Law. *New Testament Studies*
20:319–41.

Macherey, Pierre

1978   *A Theory of Literary Production.* Trans. Geoffrey Wall. London:
Routledge and Kegan Paul.

Mack, Burton

1984   Philo Judaeus and Exegetical Traditions in Alexandria. In vol. 2 of
*Aufstieg und Niedergang der Römischen Welt: Geschichte und Kultur
Roms in Spiegel der neueren Forschung,* 227–71. Berlin: W. de Gruyter.

MacLennan, Robert S.

1990   *Early Christian Texts on Jews and Judaism.* Brown Judaic Studies.
Atlanta: Scholars Press.

McNamara, Jo Ann

1976   Sexual Equality and the Cult of Virginity in Early Christian
Thought. *Feminist Studies* 3.

Maimonides, Moses

1963   *The Guide of the Perplexed.* Trans. Shlomo Pines. Chicago:
University of Chicago Press.

Mandelbaum, Bernard, ed.

1962   *Pesikta de Rav Kahana.* New York: The Jewish Theological
Seminary of America.

Mauss, Marcel

1979 [1950]   "Body Techniques." In *Sociology and Psychology: Essays,*
trans. Ben Brewster, 95–123. London: Routledge & Kegan Paul.

Meeks, Wayne, ed.

1972   *The Writings of St. Paul.* Norton Critical Editions. New York:
Norton.

Meeks, Wayne A.

1973   The Image of the Androgyne: Some Uses of a Symbol in Earliest
Christianity. *Journal of the History of Religions* 13:165–208.

1983   *The First Urban Christians: The Social World of the Apostle Paul.*
New Haven: Yale University Press.

Meir, Ofra

1988   "Vinegar, Son of Wine": Between Tradition and Innovation. *Leaves
for Literary Research* 4:9–18.

Meyer, Michael W.

1985   Making Mary Male: The Categories "male" and "female" in the
Gospel of Thomas. *New Testament Studies* 31:554–70.

Meyers, Carol

1988   *Discovering Eve: Ancient Israelite Women in Context.* New York:
Oxford University Press.

Milgrom, Jo

1988   "Some Second Thoughts About Adam's First Wife." In *Genesis 1–3 in the History of Exegesis: Intrigue in the Garden*, ed. Gregory Allen Robbins, 225–53. Studies in Women and Religion. Lewiston, N.Y.: Edwin Mellon Press.

Moi, Toril
    1990   *Simone de Beauvoir: The Making of an Intellectual Woman*. *Yale Journal of Criticism* 4: 1–24.

Mopsik, Charles
    1989   "The Body of Engenderment in the Hebrew Bible, the Rabbinic Tradition and the Kabbalah." In vol. 1 of *Fragments for a History of the Human Body*, ed. Michel Feher with Ramona Naddaff and Nadia Tazi, 48–73. New York: Zone Books.

Neusner, Jacob
    1988   *The Incarnation of God: The Character of Divinity in Formative Judaism*. Philadelphia: Fortress Press.
    1990   *The Canonical History of Ideas: The Place of the So-called Tannaite Midrashim*. Southern Florida Studies in the History of Judaism. Atlanta: Scholars Press.

Neusner, Jacob, and Ernest S. Frerichs, eds.
    1985   *"To See Ourselves as Others See Us": Christians, Jews, "Others" in Late Antiquity*. Scholars Press Studies in the Humanities. Chico, Calif.: Scholars Press.

Origen
    1957   *Origen, The Song of Songs: Commentary and Homilies*. Trans. R. P. Lawson. Westminster, Md.: Paulist Press.

Ortner, Sherry B.
    1973   On Key Symbols. *The American Anthropologist* 75: 1338–42.
    1974   "Is Female to Male as Nature Is to Culture?" In *Women, Culture & Society*, ed. Michelle Zimbalist Rosaldo and Louise Lamphere, 67–87. Stanford: Stanford University Press.

Ozick, Cynthia
    1979   Women—Notes Towards Finding the Right Question. *Forum* 35.

Pagels, Elaine
    1988   *Adam, Eve and the Serpent*. New York: Random House.

Paglia, Camille
    1990   *Sexual Personae: Art and Decadence from Nefertiti to Emily Dickinson*. New Haven: Yale University Press.

Panofsky, Erwin, and Dora Panofsky
    1956   *Pandora's Box: The Changing Aspects of a Mythical Symbol*. Bollingen Series. New York: Pantheon Books.

Pardes, Ilana
    1989   Beyond Genesis 3. *Hebrew University Studies in Literature and the Arts* 17: 161–87.

Pelikan, Jaroslav
    1971   *The Christian Tradition: A History of the Development of Doctrine*. Vol. 1, *The Emergence of the Catholic Tradition (100–600)*. Chicago: University of Chicago Press.

Philo
    1929a   "Legum Allegoria." In vol. 1 of *Loeb Classics Philo*. London: Heinemann.
    1929b   "On the Creation." In vol. 1 of *Loeb Classics Philo*. London: Heinemann.
    1932   "The Migration of Abraham." In vol. 4 of *Loeb Classics Philo*. London: Heinemann.
    1937   "The Special Laws." In vol. 7 of *Loeb Classics Philo*. London: Heinemann.
    1953   "Questions in Genesis." In vol. 1 supplement of *Loeb Classics Philo*. London: Heinemann.
    1981   "The Giants." In *Philo of Alexandria: The Contemplative Life, the Giants, and Selections*, ed. and trans. David Winston, 59–72. The Classics of Western Spirituality. New York: Paulist Press.

Plaskow, Judith
    1990   *Standing Again at Sinai: Judaism from a Feminist Perspective*. New York: Harper & Row.

Porter, F. C.
    1901   "The Yeçer Hara: A Study in the Jewish Doctrine of Sin." In *Biblical and Semitic Studies: Yale Historical and Critical Contributions to Biblical Science*, 93–156. Yale Bicentennial Publications. New York: Charles Scribner's Sons.

Räisänen, Heikki
    1980   "Legalism and Salvation by the Law. Paul's Portrayal of the Jewish Religion as a Historical and Theological Problem." In *The Pauline Literature and Theology*, ed. Sigfred Pedersen, 63–84. Teologiske Studier. Århus: Forlaget Aros.

Rapoport-Alpert, Ada
    1988   "On Women in Hasidism." In *Jewish History: Essays in Honour of Chimen Abramsky*, ed. Ada Rapoport-Alpert and Steven J. Zipperstein, 495–525. London: P. Halban.

Robinson, John A. T.
    1952   *The Body: A Study in Pauline Theology*. Studies in Bible Theology, no. 5. Philadelphia: SCM Press.

Rosen, Elisheva
    1990   Innovation and Its Reception: The Grotesque in Aesthetic Thought. *Sub-Stance* 19:125–36.

Rosenzweig, Franz
    1923   Apologetische Denkung. *Der Jude* 7:457–64.

Rubin, Nissan
    1989   "The Sages' Conception of the Body and Soul." In *Essays in the Social Scientific Study of Judaism and Jewish Society*, ed. Simcha Fishbane and Jack N. Lightstone, 47–103. New York: Ktav.

Ruether, Rosemary
    1974   *Faith and Fratricide: The Theological Roots of Anti-Semitism*. New York: Seabury Press.

Said, Edward W.

    1979   *Orientalism*. New York: Vintage Books.

Sanders, E. P.

    1977   *Paul and Palestinian Judaism: A Comparison of Patterns of Religion*. Philadelphia: Fortress Press.

    1983   *Paul, the Law and the Jewish People*. Philadelphia: Fortress Press.

Satran, David

    1989   Fingernails and Hair: Anatomy and Exegesis in Tertullian. *Journal of Theological Studies* 40:116–20.

Sawicki, Jana

    1991   *Disciplining Foucault: Feminism, Power and the Body*. Thinking Gender. New York: Routledge.

Schechter, Solomon, ed.

    1967 [Vienna, 1887]   *Aboth de Rabbi Nathan*. New York: Philipp Feldheim.

Schwarzbaum, Haim

    1983   "International Folklore Motifs in Joseph Ibn Zabara's 'Sepher Sha'ashu'im'.'" In vol. 7 of *Folklore Research Center Studies*. Jerusalem: Magnes Press.

Séchan, L.

    1929   Pandora, l'Eve grecque. *Bulletin de l'Association Guillaume Budé*, 3–26.

Sedgwick, Eve Kosofsky

    1985   *Between Men: English Literature and Male Homosocial Desire*. New York: Columbia University Press.

Segal, Alan F.

    1990   *Paul the Convert: The Apostolate and Apostasy of Saul the Pharisee*. New Haven: Yale University Press.

Shell, Marc

    1985   The Family Pet. *Representations* 15:121–51.

    1991   Marranos (Pigs); or, From Coexistence to Toleration. *Critical Inquiry* 17:306–36.

Shenhar, Aliza

    1976   "The Figure of Rabbi Meir and Its Literary Characterization in the Legends." In *Studies in Judaism*, ed. Jacob Ba'at et al., 259–66. Haifa: Haifa University Press.

Sissa, Giulia

    1990   *Greek Virginity*. Trans. Arthur Goldhammer. Cambridge: Harvard University Press.

Skehan, Patrich W., trans. and ed.

    1987   *The Wisdom of Ben Sira*. New York: Doubleday.

Sly, Dorothy

    1990   *Philo's Perception of Women*. Brown Judaic Series. Atlanta: Scholars Press.

Spidlík, Tomás, S. J.

    1986   *The Spirituality of the Christian East: A Systematic Handbook*. Trans. Anthony P. Gythiel. Cistercian Study Series, no. 79. Kalamazoo: Cistercian Publications.

Steinsaltz, Adin
    1988   *The Strife of the Spirit*. Northvale, N.J.: J. Aronson.
Stern, David
    1985   "Midrash and the Language of Exegesis." In *Midrash and Literature*,
             ed. Sanford Budick and Geoffrey Hartman, 105–27. New Haven:
             Yale University Press.
    1988   Midrash and Indeterminacy. *Critical Inquiry* 15:132–62.
Stiegman, Emero
    1977   "Rabbinic Anthropology." In vol. 19 of *Aufstieg und Niedergang der
             rämischen Welt*, ed. H. Temporini and W. Haase, 488–579. Berlin:
             Walter de Gruyter.
Swinburne, Richard
    1986   *The Evolution of the Soul*. Oxford: Oxford University Press,
             Clarendon.
Tertullian
    1989a   "The Chaplet, or de Corona." In *Fathers of the Third Century*, ed.
             Alexander Roberts and James Donaldson, 92–102. The Ante-
             nicene Fathers, vol. 3. Grand Rapids, Mich.: Wm. B. Eerdmans.
    1989b   "On the Apparel of Women." In *Fathers of the Third Century*,
             14–26. The Ante-nicene Fathers, vol. 4. Grand Rapids, Mich.:
             Wm. B. Eerdmans.
    1989c   "To His Wife." In *Fathers of the Third Century*, 39–49. The Ante-
             nicene Fathers, vol. 4. Grand Rapids, Mich.: Wm. B. Eerdmans.
Theodor, Jehuda, and Hanoch Albeck, eds.
    1965   *Genesis Rabbah*. Jerusalem: Wahrmann.
Thomas, Brook
    1991   *The New Historicism and Other Old Fashioned Topics*. Princeton:
             Princeton University Press.
Tobin, Thomas H., S.J.
    1983   *The Creation of Man: Philo and the History of Interpretation*. The
             Catholic Biblical Quarterly Monograph Series. Washington: The
             Catholic Biblical Association of America.
Torjesen, Karen Jo
    1986   *Hermeneutical Procedure and Theological Method in Origen's
             Exegesis*. Patristische texte und studien. Berlin: Walter de Gruyter.
Tov, Emanuel
    1984   The Rabbinic Tradition Concerning the "Alterations" Inserted into
             the Greek Pentateuch and Their Relation to the Original Text of
             the LXX. *Journal for the Study of Judaism in the Persian, Hellenistic
             and Roman Periods* 15:65–89.
Traub, Valerie
    1989   Prince Hal's Falstaff: Positioning Psychoanalysis and the Female
             Reproductive Body. *Shakespeare Quarterly* 40:456–75.
Trible, Phyllis
    1978   *God and the Rhetoric of Sexuality*. Overtures to Biblical Theology.
             Philadelphia: Fortress Press.

Urbach, Ephraim E.
>
> 1971   The Homiletical Interpretations of the Sages and the Exposition of Origen on Canticles, and the Jewish-Christian Disputation. *Scripta hiersolymitana* 22:247–75.
>
> 1975   *The Sages: Their Concepts and Beliefs.* Trans. Israel Abrahams. Jerusalem: Magnes Press.

Vernant, Jean-Pierre

> 1990   "The Myth of Prometheus in Hesiod." In *Myth and Society in Ancient Greece*, trans. Janet Lloyd, 183–202. New York: Zone Books.
>
> 1991   "Psuche: Simulacrum of the Body or Image of the Divine?" In *Mortals and Immortals: Collected Essays*, ed. and trans. Froma I. Zeitlin, 186–92. Princeton: Princeton University Press.

Veyne, Paul

> 1987   "The Roman Empire." In *A History of Private Life*, ed. Philippe Arias and Georges Duby, 9–234. Vol. 1, *From Pagan Rome to Byzantium*. Ed. Paul Veyne. Trans. Arthur Goldhammer. Cambridge: Belknap Press of Harvard University Press.

von Kellenbach, Katharina

> 1990   *Anti-Judaism in Christian-rooted Feminist Writings: An Analysis of Major U.S. American and West German Feminist Theologians.* Diss., Temple University.

Waldenberg, Eliezer

> 1985?   *The Responsa, Tzitz Eliezer.* Jerusalem.

Warner, Marina

> 1976   *Alone of All Her Sex: The Myth and Cult of the Virgin Mary.* New York: Knopf.

Wegner, Judith Romney

> 1988   *Chattel or Person? The Status of Women in the Mishnah.* New York: Oxford University Press.
>
> 1991   "Philo's Portrayal of Women—Hebraic or Hellenic?" In *"Women Like This": New Perspectives on Jewish Women in the Greco-Roman World*, ed. Amy-Jill Levine, 41–66. Society of Biblical Literature: Early Judaism and Its Literature. Atlanta: Scholars Press.

Weller, Shulamith

> 1989   The Collection of Stories in Ketubbot 62b–63a. In *Tura: Studies in Jewish Thought* (in Hebrew), ed. Meir Ayali, 95–103. Tel Aviv: Hakkibbutz Hameuhad Publishing House.

Whitman, Jon

> 1991   From the Textual to the Temporal: Early Christian "Allegory" and Early Romantic "Symbol." *New Literary History* 22:161–76.

Williamson, Ronald

> 1970   *Philo and the Epistle to the Hebrews.* ALGH, vol. 4. Leiden: Brill.
>
> 1989   *Jews in the Hellenistic World: Philo.* Cambridge commentaries on writings of the Jewish & Christian world 200 BC to AD 200. Cambridge: Cambridge University Press.

Wilson, Katherina M., and Elizabeth M. Makowski

1990   *Wykked Wyves and the Woes of Marriage: Misogamous Literature from Juvenal to Chaucer*. State University of New York Series in Medieval Studies. Albany: State University of New York Press.

Winkler, John

1989   *The Constraints of Desire: The Anthropology of Sex and Gender in Ancient Greece*. London: Routledge.

Winston, David, ed. and trans.

1981   *Philo of Alexandria: The Contemplative Life, the Giants, and Selections*. The Classics of Western Spirituality. New York: Paulist Press.

1988   "Philo and the Contemplative Life." In vol. 13 of *Jewish Spirituality from the Bible Through the Middle Ages*, ed. Arthur Green, 198–231. World Spirituality: An Encyclopedic History of the Religious Quest. New York: Crossroad.

Wire, Antoinette Clark

1990   *The Corinthian Women Prophets: A Reconstruction Through Paul's Rhetoric*. Minneapolis: Fortress Press.

Wittig, Monique

1980   The Straight Mind. *Feminist Issues* 1:103–11.

1992   *The Straight Mind and Other Essays*. Boston: Beacon Press.

Wolfson, Elliot R.

1987a   Circumcision and the Divine Name: A Study in the Transmission of Esoteric Doctrine. *Jewish Quarterly Review* 78:77–112.

1987b   Circumcision, Vision of God, and Textual Interpretation: From Midrashic Trope to Mystical Symbol. *History of Religions* 27:189–215.

Wolfson, Harry Austryn

1947   *Philo: Foundations of Religious Philosophy in Judaism, Christianity and Islam*. Structure and Growth of Philosophic Systems from Plato to Spinoza. Cambridge: Harvard University Press.

Wright, William, ed.

1869   *The Homilies of Aphraates, the Persian Sage*. Vol. 1, *The Syriac Texts*. London.

Yassif, Eli

1984   *The Tales of Ben Sira in the Middle-ages: A Critical Text and Literary Studies*. Jerusalem: Magnes Press.

1990   The Cycle of Tales in Rabbinic Literature. *Jerusalem Studies in Hebrew Literature* 12:103–47.

Zeitlin, Froma

1990   The Origin of Woman and Woman as the Origin: The Case of Pandora. Unpublished paper.

General Index

Aaron, 159–60, 161, 164

Abbaye, Rabbi, 65

Adam: in biblical creation stories, 37–38; chronological priority of, 78–79; in Lilith myths, 95–96; Palestinian interpretation of, 42–44; and Pandora story, 86–87. *See also* Creation stories

Ada the son of Ahva, Rav, 146, 147

Adler, Rachel, 184–88

Adornment, female, 101–5

Aggada (narrative), 11, 15–16

Aggadic Midrashim, 24

Aha, Rabbi, 88–89

Akiva, Rabbi: on feminine adornment, 100–101; historical romance of, 16, 136–38, 150, 153–55; interpreting scripture, 134–35; on marriage, 157, 158

Allegorical reading practice, 8–9

Alpha-Beta d'ben Sirah, 95

American culture, 73–74

Anal intercourse, 110n.1, 112–13, 119. *See also* Sexual practices

Androcentrism: of rabbinic Judaism, 94, 100–101, 104–6, 168, 240, 244–45

Androgyne myth, 36–39, 40, 42–44, 57. *See also* Creation stories

Angels, Ministering, 110, 111–12, 121

Aphrahat, 7, 139–40n

Asceticism, 34–35

Aschkenasy, Nehama, 87–88n, 93n

Augustine, 1, 8, 43n

Avtalyon, Rabbi, 210

Babylonian exile, 61–62

Babylonian Judaism: Ben-Azzai nullified by, 174–77; Beruria legend of, 183–84, 188–89, 190–92; on early marriage, 138–41, 145, 165–66; female commandments of, 91–93; on male sexuality, 140–41; on marital sex, 48–49, 53, 125–28, 142–44; and Palestinian Judaism, 48–49, 56–57, 139–42, 144, 146, 179–80, 195; on Rabbis' marital absence, 145, 146–49, 156–58, 159; on Torah-study, 138–39, 142, 143–44, 155–56, 169–70, 172, 174–79, 180–81, 194–95. *See also* Hellenistic Judaism; Palestinian Judaism; Rabbinic Judaism

Bakhtin, Mikhail, 197, 198, 201–2, 209–10

Bal, Mieke, 119n, 228–29, 230

Baptism, 40

Bar-Ilan, 196n

Beauvoir, Simone de, 237

Ben-Azzai, Rabbi: contradicted by Palestinian Talmud, 172–73, 174; on female Torah-study, 170–71, 172–73; ideological conflict of, 51, 134–35, 154; nullified by Babylonian Talmud, 174–77

Beruria legend: Babylonian view of, 183–84, 189, 190–92; cultural ambivalence of, 186–87, 193; and female Torah-study, 195–96; Palestinian view of, 182–83

Biale, David, 48, 121n.14, 136n.4, 163

Bialik, Haim Nahman, 96n

Biographical narratives (aggada), 11, 15–16

Bloch, R. Howard, 79n.5, 80n, 94, 208n.14

Body: in creation stories, 17–18, 36–38; of feminized male, 215–18; grotesque, 197–98, 201–4, 205–6, 208–9, 217; as human essence, 5, 6, 34, 231; marking cultural difference, 1–4, 5–7; platonic conception of, 9, 31–32, 231–33; woman as, 58–60, 78–79, 81–82, 237–38. *See also* Human being

The Body and Society: Men, Women and Sexual Renunciation in Early Christianity (Brown), 25, 168–69

Borgen, Peder, 232n.4

Brooten, Bernadette, 193–94

Brown, Peter, 2–3, 25, 53, 168–69, 176, 177n

Bruns, Gerald, 27

Index of Primary Jewish Texts